Voices on the River

The Fesler-Lampert Minnesota Heritage Book Series

This series is published with the generous assistance of the John K. and Elsie Lampert Fesler Fund and David R. and Elizabeth P. Fesler. Its mission is to republish significant out-of-print books that contribute to our understanding and appreciation of Minnesota and the Upper Midwest.

The series features works by the following authors:

Clifford and Isabel Ahlgren
J. Arnold Bolz
Walter Havighurst
Helen Hoover
Florence Page Jaques
Evan Jones
Frank A. King
Meridel Le Sueur
George Byron Merrick
Grace Lee Nute
Sigurd F. Olson
Charles Edward Russell
Calvin Rutstrum
Timothy Severin
Robert Treuer

Voices on the River

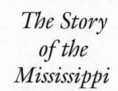

*The Story
of the
Mississippi
Waterways*

WALTER
HAVIGHURST

University of Minnesota Press
Minneapolis

To Marion, once more

Originally published in hardcover by the Macmillan Company, 1964
Republished by arrangement with Scribner,
an imprint of Simon & Schuster, Inc.

First University of Minnesota Press edition, 2003

Published by the University of Minnesota Press
111 Third Avenue South, Suite 290
Minneapolis, MN 55401-2520
http://www.upress.umn.edu

ISBN 0-8166-4177-3

A Cataloging-in-Publication record for this book is available from
the Library of Congress.

Printed in the United States of America on acid-free paper

The University of Minnesota is an equal-opportunity educator and employer.

12 11 10 09 08 07 06 05 04 03   10 9 8 7 6 5 4 3 2 1

Table of Contents

Illustrations

1

Prologue:
Blow for a Landmark

THE OLDEST SOUNDS were wind and water, but history came to the rivers with the murmured Angelus of the missionary explorers. Soon there were other voices, the steersman's cry, the oaths of the oarsmen, the halloo of travelers in a far country. Through morning mist echoed the boatman's horn, the lonely call of the keelboats—"all the way to Shawneetown, a long time ago." Steam came to the rivers and above the splash of paddle buckets rose the clear high music of the steamboat bell. The bells grew larger, five hundred, eight hundred, fifteen hundred pounds, with quarts of silver dollars melted in the metal. By 1840 bells rang on all the rivers, the landing bell rousing the roustabouts on the levee, the departure bell fading in the rush and rumble of the paddle wheels.

Steamboat bells outlived men and their perishable craft. They were dug from the mud, removed from charred decks, salvaged from old hulks on the riverside. Most of them served other packets—an old voice on a new vessel—but some became school bells and church bells away from the clamorous river landings. After the *Saluda* blew up near Lexington, Missouri, in 1852, killing a long list of praying Mormons, her bell rang people to church in inland Savannah. The roof bell of the *Rob't E. Lee* (No. 2), wrecked at Yucatan Point on the lower Mississippi in 1882, was hung in the belfry of the Grand Gulf Methodist Church. In the same year the *Red Cloud* was snagged in Red Cloud Bend far up the Missouri; the old packet lies under the waters of the Fort Peck Reservoir, but her bell rings from the steeple of the Episcopal

Church in Bismarck, North Dakota. When Dan Rice's circus boat *Damsel* snagged and burned near Decatur, Nebraska, river dwellers saved the trick horse Excelsior, and in gratitude Rice gave the *Damsel's* roof bell to the village church. The big bell of the cotton packet *America* hangs silent over the grave of Captain LeVerrier Cooley in New Orleans.

When Captain "Dickie" Hiernaux built the *Leona* at Pittsburgh in 1928, he included in his new steamer parts from five famous vessels of the past: the roof bell from the *Boaz*, whistle from the third *Kate Adams*, steering rigging from the *Resolute*, steering bars from the *Kittanning*, and hog chain braces from the *J. C. Risher*. Up and down the river the *Leona* trailed a cloud of history.

Today a rich-toned bell with many echoes rings from the only remaining passenger boat on the Mississippi system. First cast for the Anchor Line's side-wheeler *City of St. Louis*, in 1883, the bell went to the stately *Queen City* in 1897. After forty-three years on that charmed packet, it passed to the towboat *John W. Hubbard*. In 1948 it was mounted on the hurricane roof of the *Delta Queen* where it rings arrivals in Cincinnati, Pittsburgh, St. Paul, New Orleans and a hundred landings in between.

In the 1840's the packet *Revenue*, built by Captain William H. Fulton, steamed away from Pittsburgh with a white plume jetting from her whistle valve. Captain Fulton, it is said, had heard a steam whistle on the roof of a factory in Philadelphia. When he tried it on his packet, a new voice reached the rivers. The steamers came with windy shouts of arrival, they left with short crisp toots and sent back mournful calls, fading with distance. Like steamboat bells the whistles grew larger and more melodious, each one sounding its own pitch and resonance. Rivermen knew boats by their whistles; boys at the landings named approaching packets before they came around the bend; when the punctual *Two States* tooted for Scuffletown, Kentucky, farmer Barnett's mule stopped in the furrow and waited for the feed bag. The racer *Natchez* zoomed, they said, like an enormous bumble bee. The third *Kate Adams* had a deep bass voice like a million bullfrogs; on summer nights it carried thirty miles over the slumberous Yazoo delta. Bass and treble blended in the organ voice of the big *Eclipse*. From the chime whistle of the *St. Lawrence* came plangent chords and melodious diphthongs. Along the big river below Greenville, Will Percy heard the whistles in his boyhood; they echoed in his memory for forty years. "There is no sound in the world," he wrote "so filled with mystery and longing and unease as the sound at night of a river boat blowing for the landing—one long, two shorts, one long, two shorts. . . . The sound of the river boats hangs inside your heart like a star."

For sixty years the rivers echoed with steam whistles. They called through silver fog at daybreak and under the stars at night. With a pull of the brass ring above the pilot wheel, a captain signaled to his crew, to passing vessels, to people on the bank. Around the bend sounded the "begging whistle," asking for freight and passengers. At Natchez, Cairo and Shawneetown, steamers blew for catfish from the peddling skiffs; at Mile 255 on the Missouri (the charts read Campbellstown but boatmen called it Buttermilk Landing), they blew for buttermilk; at the Falls of the Ohio and the upper Mississippi rapids, they blew for the locks to open.

A persistent tale tells of the side-wheeler *Eugene*, more than a century ago, whose crew stole a melodious whistle from an Italian freighter at New Orleans. At Plum Point shoals soon afterward, the *Eugene* stumbled over the wrecked *Eliza* and went down. The Italian whistle was salvaged, taken up to Evansville and installed on the *Hettie Gilmore*. It was transferred to the new *Tarascon* in 1863. At New Orleans, after the Mississippi blockade was broken, the *Tarascon* blew a triumphant blast which was joyfully recognized by an Italian captain down the levee. To get his whistle back the captain appealed to port officials, but an arbitrating French consul ruled that the *Tarascon*'s possession was legal since her whistle had been acquired from the wrecked *Eugene*. From the *Tarascon* the disputed whistle went to the *James Guthrie*, and from her to the *Tell City*. Finally it passed to the *Nashville* which was rebuilt in 1922 as the *Southland*. On a December day ten years later, the *Southland* was wrecked and burned on the Kentucky shore and the storied whistle was lost.

Now the steamboats are gone, and the music with them. On the diesel towboats electricity has brought back the boatman's voice. The intercom voice box connects the pilothouse with all parts of a pusher and its long string of barges. The radio telephone talks to other craft on the river, to lockmasters at the dams, to company officers as distant as Pittsburgh, St. Paul and New Orleans. But whistles still blow—the flat blaring air horns of the diesels.

3

They blow for locks and landings. They blow for passing tows in the channel. They blow for a house on a hillside where a woman waves a dishcloth from the doorway. They blow for fishermen on a ledge, for a farmer plowing a highland field, for an old man in a shanty on the shore. They blow for houses in a hollow or graves on a hill.

On the Ohio at North Bend steamboatmen steered by the white shaft that marks the grave of William Henry Harrison; they saluted Old Tippecanoe with a soft hoarse whistle as they passed the point where he lies. Up the Mississippi under the bluffs of Wisconsin, they blew for an unnamed captain who legend said was buried standing up, his eyes on the channel. Under a hill that overlooks thirty miles of the Missouri, they blew for Chief Blackbird, buried in a mound on a standing horse, walled in sod and soil, facing the river. Far up the Missouri they blew for Captain Grant Marsh in his windswept grave on Wagonwheel Bluff.

The past stays green beside the rivers. At the Falls of the Ohio, where Louisville was planted, George Rogers Clark took his flatboats through swirling water on his way to Kaskaskia and the winning of the West. Young Sam Clemens watched the river from a silent hill above frontier Hannibal, and Lafcadio Hearn watched it from the ringing levee at New Orleans. Once at Galena fleets of steamboats loaded lead; log rafts were assembled at Read's Landing; at Cairo men envisioned a great city that never grew. At St. Louis the fur brigades loaded their keelboats with trade goods and pulled away for Indian country. Men die and the river rolls on. In Bellefontaine Cemetery on a St. Louis hilltop, the journeys ended for men from all the rivers between the Allegheny ridges and the Rocky Mountains.

The long Bellefontaine Bluff above the Chain of Rocks in the Mississippi channel was once an Indian camp, with a trail climbing from the river. In time it became the Hempstead Farm on the old military road to Fort Bellefontaine. In 1849, while steamboats churned up to Independence and St. Joe, where fifty thousand Argonauts outfitted for the California Trail, Bellefontaine became a cemetery, the dead being moved from busy St. Louis to this leafy hill. The graveyard grew, spreading over the Hempstead acres and the La Baume and O'Fallon farms as well. Eighteen-fifty was a plague year in St. Louis, with the city decimated by cholera. The graves turned green in April, and on summer days white clouds drifted over. Steamboats whistled under the hill.

4

There is no commerce now through the Chain of Rocks; the towboats pass two miles eastward, through the long straight cut of the canal. But the wind brings the diesel horns to Bellefontaine where the rivermen are gathered: William Clark who went up unknown rivers toward the coast of Oregon, Manuel Lisa who brought bales of beaver skins from the Yellowstone, Stephen Watts Kearny who commanded army posts on frontier rivers, Henry Miller Shreve who pulled snags out of two thousand miles of channel, James B. Eads who opened the choked Mississippi delta, Sol Smith who moored a showboat to a hundred landings, Captain Isaiah Sellers whose river column in a New Orleans newspaper evoked the first writing by a young pilot who would sign himself Mark Twain. The lives that led to that bluff would make a history of the river system.

Bellefontaine's winding Meadow Lane leads to a granite obelisk, overlooking the Mississippi, marked with the name of William Clark. From Virginia he had followed his older brother to the Ohio valley. With Meriwether Lewis he fought under Anthony Wayne; eight years later the two Virginians were on the way to the Pacific. Captain Clark was a burly man with humorous blue eyes and a shock of fiery hair; Red Head the Indians called him. On the Journey west he needed all his stoical endurance. Up the Missouri the expedition toiled in their long keelboats, accompanied by two open pirogues. Each craft carried sails, poles and towlines. Two horses stamped in the lead boat, along with Clark's big black dog Scannon and his huge Negro servant York whose black skin and rolling eyes would fascinate the Indians. There was wind enough for sails, but the river channel was snarled with snags and sandbars; with oars and poles they crept up the long Missouri. One night the sandbank they were camped on crumbled and the weary boatmen jumped for their boats. They got away just as their mooring collapsed into the river.

After three months of backbreaking labor, they reached the mouth of the Platte, where two men deserted. Two weeks later at Council Bluffs they held the first United States parley with the plains Indians. There were presents for the tribesmen and medals for the chiefs; in return the Indian women heaped a pirogue with watermelons. They toiled on to the Sioux country and wintered with the Mandans, 1609 miles up the Missouri. There they hunted, scouted, learned Indian arts and language, and collected specimens to send down the river. In bitter weather, crouching beside the fire, Clark limbered his hands with bear's

5

grease. He drew scale maps of the country and sketched birds, fish, plants and animals for his journal. It was a country as strange almost as the moon.

With spring they put their boats in the water and wrestled with the current. In Sioux camps they passed out mirrors, bells, kettles, knives, needles, and colored beads. They met warriors in deerskin leggings fringed with the scalps of their enemies. They saw herds of antelope (which they called "goats") skimming across the prairie and masses of buffalo shadowing the plain. They followed huge tracks and faced grizzly bears that reared up eight feet tall. At night wolves quavered from the buttes and dawn brought the roar of mating buffalo.

At last they saw the Rocky Mountains like a cloud bank across the sky. On a homesick day Clark named the Judith River for his sweetheart in Virginia. They went on, laboring at oars and poles or wading icy water and hauling the boats behind them, to the three forks of the Missouri which they named Jefferson, Madison and Gallatin. Wrote Clark, "The confluence of those rivers is 2848 miles from the mouth of the Missouri, by the meanders of that river." They followed the westward-leading Jefferson as far as it could float them, then beached their boats and crossed the Continental Divide on horses obtained from the Shoshones. On the western slope they built pirogues and descended the Columbia. Twenty years later a fantastic story, mocking their peril and hardship, told of a portage where steamboats could be trundled over the Rocky Mountains.

The expedition had planned to return by sea in one of Astor's cargo ships from Oregon, but they found no vessel at the mouth of the Columbia. On the return journey the captains separated, exploring new mountain passes. Clark descended the swift Yellowstone and met Lewis on the Missouri. When they reached St. Louis on September 23, 1806, they had been given up for dead. Wrote Clark to his brother, "We arrived at this place at 12 o'clock today from the Pacific Ocean."

Meriwether Lewis, appointed Governor of Louisiana Territory, lived but three more years. In 1809, he died, probably by suicide, in a settler's cabin in Tennessee while on his way to Washington. Clark lived for another thirty years. As Superintendent of Indian Affairs and as Governor of Missouri Territory, he controlled the Missouri River trade, in which his O'Fallon nephews grew wealthy. John O'Fallon, wounded in the Battle of Tippecanoe, had gone to St. Louis for recuperation, and there he entered the service of his uncle. As an Indian trader and army contractor O'Fallon came and went on the rivers—up the Illinois with a band of Indian's en route to visit the President in Washington, to Pittsburgh in keelboats with $20,000 worth of deerskins, to Prairie du Chien and the Missouri posts with cargoes of merchandise and whiskey. In St. Louis he organized the first Sunday School west of the Mississippi. With a fortune made from the Indians' appetite for ardent spirits, he endowed the city. The O'Fallon farm became a part of Bellefontaine Cemetery in the 1850's. Now Colonel John O'Fallon lies under a gray granite monument above the river where his boats labored upstream with trade goods and came down piled with peltry.

On the central ridge of Bellefontaine Cemetery, under a shaft of red granite lies the grave of Thomas Hart Benton. He and Clark had talked of the rivers, tracing them on the map and foreseeing a huge inland network of navigation. "Many years ago," said Senator Benton late in his life, "Governor Clark and myself undertook to calculate the extent of boatable water in the valley of the Mississippi; we made it about fifty thousand miles! of which thirty thousand were computed to unite above St. Louis and twenty thousand below." At that time flatboats came down scores of rivers on the spring rise, but to make their fifty thousand miles the two Missourians calculated the freshet in many more. As they bent over maps in the candlelight, the room filled with the music of savage names—Monongahela, Kanawha, Muskingum, Scioto, Miami, Licking, Wabash, Tennessee, St. Croix, Chippewa, Maquoketa, Wapsipinicon, Sangamon, Kaskaskia, Yellowstone, Sioux, Cheyenne, Osage, Ouachita, Atchafalaya, Tallahatchie, Yazoo. "Of course," said Senator Benton, "we counted all the infant streams on which a flat, a keel, or a bateau could be floated; for every tributary of the humblest boatable character helps to swell not only the volume of the central waters but its commerce upon them."

Now the Missouri carries grain, fertilizer, barbed wire, burlap, cement —more than two million tons of cargo annually—but its first trade was furs. When the white man came to the New World there were some ten million beaver in North America. Not a prolific animal, and easily captured in their pond villages, they were already depleted east of the Mississippi when Lewis and Clark went up the Missouri. Manuel Lisa soon followed them to the virgin beaver streams of the far Northwest.

7

A man of courage, zest, hardihood, shrewdness and resolution, Lisa left his name on a vast and remote country. He was an enigma to rival traders, a comrade to his boatmen—he toiled, starved, feasted, drank and sang with them—and a great white chief to the Indians. The urn-capped shaft on his grave at Bellefontaine gives his birth year as 1772 and his birthplace as New Orleans, though he was probably born in the West Indies where his father served the Spanish government. Lisa lived until 1820, forty-eight years which took him to the far reaches of the river system. During his last thirteen years he made thirteen journeys up the Missouri—26,000 miles on that river—toiling up and swirling down its muddy current. In good years pelts overflowed his stone warehouse at Chestnut Street on the St. Louis levee; they were piled horse-high in stinking "fur rows" in the hot June sun. He had not enough names to give his posts: Fort Lisa marked the mouth of the Platte, Fort Manuel drew the trade of the Arikara Sioux three hundred miles upstream, and remote Manuel's Fort, the outpost, lay under the mountains where the Big Horn River joined the Yellowstone.

During the War of 1812, as subagent to the Indians of the upper Missouri, Lisa kept the tribes on the American side. His salary, $548 a year, he spent twice over on tobacco and other presents for them. Up the river he carried anvils, forges, traps, guns, knives, and the seeds of pumpkins, squash, beans and turnips. In 1815 he brought down from the high plains forty-three blanketed chiefs and headmen. (Indians from far up the Missouri would be familiar in St. Louis for half a century; Buffalo Bill's Wild West Show wintered there in the 1880's.) In the governor's office they signed treaties of friendship and accepted gifts for themselves and their people. Lisa visited his wife in St. Louis and returned with the tribal delegation to the upper river.

At Fort Lisa, Manual had a handsome Omaha wife. When his white wife died in 1817, he brought his half-Indian daughter Rosalie, two years old, to be educated in St. Louis. A year later he married a widow, Mary Hempstead Keeney, though Lisa spoke little English and Mary Keeney knew neither Spanish nor French. They laughed together at their misunderstandings and sometimes used the boatmen as interpreters. In 1819 Lisa took his new wife up the river, sending word that his squaw Mitain must be kept away from the post. With Mrs. Lisa went a friend from St. Louis. Indians came for miles to see these first white women to ascend the Missouri. Their presence at Fort Lisa was a sign: the never-

never land was changing. Already the steamboat *Pike* had arrived in St. Louis from Louisville, and steamboats would soon be puffing up the Missouri. Said the *Missouri Gazette* in 1819: "The time is fast approaching when a journey to the Pacific will become as familiar, and indeed more so, than it was fifteen or twenty years ago to Kentucky or Ohio."

Lisa belonged to the time that was passing, and this was his last journey. Still resolute and hardy—"I go a great distance while some are considering whether they will start today or tomorrow"—he died in St. Louis of a sudden illness in the summer of 1820. Up the Missouri his three posts would vanish without a trace, but at St. Louis he left a landmark, his stone depot at the foot of Chestnut Street. It stood until 1959 when wreckers razed the riverfront to make room for the Jefferson Memorial Park. Lisa was buried above the river in the family graveyard on the Hempstead Farm which thirty years later became a part of Bellefontaine Cemetery. He was the first of the rivermen to come home to the hill.

On a hot summer day in 1829 a twin-hulled boat was snorting and creaking in the timber-strewn Plum Point channel fifty miles above Memphis. It was Henry M. Shreve's first snag boat *Heliopolis* beginning its Herculean labors. Captain Shreve was a brooding man of long silences and sudden energies. He built the first shallow-draft steamboats, craft that floated on the water instead of cutting through it. With his snag boats he cleared hundreds of Mississippi crossings, and from the Red River he removed a solid raft of brush and driftwood more than a hundred miles long. His strenuous life led to a quiet place above the river at Bellefontaine. The granite gravestone, between a pin oak and a buckeye tree, is half erased by time, but his name is written, for as long as the river flows, in the open channel of the Mississippi.

On the shady ridges above a leafy hollow stand the gravestones of two men who roamed the rivers in the restless 1830's not with merchandise but with entertainment. Sol Smith and Noah Ludlow unloaded scenery and costumes at a hundred landings, bringing stage comedy and drama to the river towns. Ludlow built the St. Louis Theater in 1835. A great comedian, Smith was also, at times, a printer, editor, lawyer and preacher. In 1847 he bought the Chapman family's *Floating Palace*, the first steam showboat. When his boat collided with a steamer between Louisville and Cincinnati, Old Sol and his company got ashore and watched their *Floating Palace* sink. It was a painful memory in a

9

rollicking life; Smith never mentioned the showboat in his *Memoirs*. His tomb in Bellefontaine Cemetery reads:

> All the world's a stage
> And all the men and women merely players.
>   Exit Sol

On Wildrose Avenue a boatman's voice would carry from Shreve's grave to the monument of Stephen Watts Kearny who spent his life beyond the settlements in frontier country. As a young lieutenant, in 1819 he went by keelboat to Fort Missouri, the site of present Omaha, and the next year he was far up the Mississippi at Camp Cold Water which would soon become Fort St. Anthony. In 1824 he ascended the Missouri to Council Bluffs in a keelboat propelled by machinery—two rows of men pulled crossbars which turned a waterwheel. They made smooth slow progress, two and a half miles an hour, passing keelboats dragged by men wading in bramble, brush and mire. A year later Kearny went with General Henry Atkinson's expedition to the mouth of the Yellowstone.

In 1828 Captain Kearny was back on the upper Mississippi, taking command of Fort Crawford at Prairie du Chien. Here he sat in officers' mess with Zachary Taylor and Jefferson Davis, and with a studious army surgeon who was then making medical history.

After the War of 1812 Dr. William Beaumont had been sent west from Vermont to duty on the frontier. At Michilimackinac, between the silver fogs of Lake Michigan and the blue leagues of Lake Huron, he seemed cut off from the world. He treated an occasional knife wound or powder burn; then he watched schooners beating through the strait and wondered when the *Walk-in-the-Water*, the Lakes' first steamship, would again find its way to that remote place. Below the fort Indians and traders lounged in the store of the American Fur Company, whittling tent stakes and cleaning their muskets. One June day a gun went off and a man raced up the steep fort trail to summon the surgeon. Dr. Beaumont found a young half-breed, Alexis St. Martin, with the wall of his stomach blown open. The surgeon gave him half an hour to live, but St. Martin had a woodsman's hardiness. He was alive and alert next morning, and the surgeon took him to his cottage at the fort. St. Martin grew strong and active, though his wound did not close. Peering into the man's stomach Dr. Beaumont realized that he had a gastric laboratory. So he began experiments, suspending food on a fishline and watching the stomach's reaction, spooning up gastric juice to study digestion outside the body. In time a flap grew over the wound which still did not close. After three years young St. Martin ran away.

In 1828 Dr. Beaumont was transferred to Fort Crawford at the mouth of the Wisconsin. It was a busy post. Keelboats brought trinkets, traps and whiskey up the Mississippi; canoe caravans came down the northern rivers with bundled peltry. Dr. Beaumont sent messages to Montreal and there located St. Martin who now had a wife and children. At the surgeon's expense St. Martin brought his family to Prairie du Chien, and Beaumont was delighted to find the stomach wall still open. He lifted the flap and resumed his studies. For two years he made daily observations, compiling the data for his *Experiments and Observations on the Gastric Juice and the Physiology of Digestion*. In 1831 St. Martin, with four children now, returned to Canada. He lived to the age of eighty-three and had twenty children.

From the upper Mississippi, William Beaumont was sent to Jefferson Barracks, just below St. Louis, and then to the St. Louis Arsenal. While General Kearny campaigned in California and Mexico, Beaumont fought cholera and yellow fever in St. Louis. The messmates' paths had parted, but they came together again above the Mississippi. Their graves are within speaking distance on the ridge of Bellefontaine.

In 1874 James B. Eads threw his three great spans across the Mississippi at St. Louis; four years later, at the delta mouth twelve hundred miles away, he opened the river to the ocean commerce. Both the bridge and the jetties resist time, while at the leafy corner of Memory and Autumn lanes his Bellefontaine monument wears away. On autumn nights wind shakes the trees and brings the sound of traffic from the river where he began as a steamboat clerk, aged fourteen. He explored the channel floor in his bell boats and salvaged sunken cargo. He built ironclad gunboats to break the war blockade in 1863. The river moved him to grandiloquent language—"This giant stream, with its head shrouded in Arctic snows, embracing half a continent in the hundred thousand miles of its immense network, and coursing its majestic way to the Southern Gulf." It flowed through his whole life.

From Meadow Avenue the Bellefontaine hillside rises steeply to the grave of Commodore John McCune, director of the Keokuk Packet Company in the 1850's. He was aboard the *Di Vernon* in 1853 when she raced the rival company's *West Newton* from Galena to St. Paul. Near his grave is that of Captain Thomas H. Griffith, a founder of the

Northern Line which daily raced the Keokuk packets up the river. After a few seasons of this competition, the two lines combined, with Captain McCune as president. On the next cemetery ridge a shaft of white marble bears the name of McCune's partner, Samuel Gaty, the first maker of steamboat machinery in the West. In 1854, Sam Gaty won $40,000 in the Havana lottery and used it to build the steamer *St. Mary* which he sold to Captain Joseph La Barge. At the base of Gaty's memorial, relief carvings symbolize the four seasons: his engines churned the paddle wheels through rain and sunshine, frost and snow.

As pantry boy, steward, mate and captain, George C. Wolff had a long life on the river. Thousands of times he steamed past Bellefontaine Bluff in the vessels of the Illinois Packet Company. A devout Baptist when he was ashore, he had a shrewd eye for the profits from old bourbon and rock and rye in the river trade; in partnership with a St. Louis liquor dealer, he ran thirty bars on Mississippi steamboats. He had a much longer and more prosperous life than the steamer named for him by the Illinois Packet Company. Just two years afloat, that craft survived an explosion at Helena, Arkansas, and was sunk by a Missouri River snag at Bowling Green Bend in 1874. When he died nine years later, a silhouette of the *George C. Wolff* was carved on his monument at Bellefontaine.

In the heart of the burial ground on a little knoll shaded by three sweet gum trees, a gravestone marked I. SELLERS shows a bearded figure, in weather coat and mariner's cap, grasping the upper spokes of a tall pilot wheel. This was the man Mark Twain called "the patriarch of his craft," an Old Testament character from the river's legendary years.

Captain Isaiah Sellers first shipped on the steamer *Rambler* in 1825, then on the *President* and the *Jubilee*, all in the lower Mississippi trade. He carried slaves, cotton, sugar, lard, bacon, mules, army men, immigrants, merchants and missionaries. In 1836 at Pittsburgh he took out the spanking new *Prairie*, the first stateroom boat to call at the St. Louis levee. On the famous *J. M. White* (No. 2) in 1844, he ran from New Orleans to St. Louis in 94 hours and 9 minutes, a record that held till 1870 when the *Rob't E. Lee* raced up the river against the *Natchez*. In 1857 Captain Sellers introduced the whistle signal for passing steamers, one blow to port and two to starboard, a code now in the second century of use. He died on the river, succumbing to pneumonia near Memphis;

legend says that flags hung at half-staff on the St. Louis levee when his body came home. He was buried in February, 1864, at Bellefontaine.

In thirty-five years Captain Sellers made 460 round trips between St. Louis and New Orleans, which figures up to more than a million miles. He had a memory precise and vivid; twelve hundred miles of river channel, past and present, unrolled in his pilothouse talk. He told of islands disappeared, of wrecks forgotten, of banks caved in and channels carved, of towns born and buried in his years on the river. A severely humorless man, he designed his own gravestone years before his death, showing himself as stiff and important as in real life.

For the *St. Louis Gazette* and the New Orleans *True Delta* this patriarch of pilots wrote river reports, discoursing on high and low water, on chutes and bars and islands in the changing channel. With omniscient memory and oracular prophecy, he lorded it over his younger colleagues, until a fledgling pilot named Sam Clemens wrote a burlesque of the Sellers column. Appearing under the harmless heading "River Intelligence" in the New Orleans *Daily Crescent* in 1859, it told how Sergeant Fathom came down the river in the old *Jubilee* with a Chinese captain and a Choctaw crew in the record high water of 1763. "There was no malice in my rubbish," wrote Sam Clemens twenty-five years later, "but it laughed at the captain." And it silenced him. He never printed another paragraph.

Four years later, when he was a newspaper reporter at Virginia City, Nevada, Sam Clemens signed "Mark Twain" to his grotesque story, *Jim Smiley and His Jumping Frog*, saying that this pseudonym had formerly been used by Captain Sellers for his river reports. This was another of Sam Clemens' inventions. Late in his life Mark Twain commented on his strange literary fortunes: nothing he ever wrote as the truth was believed, and nothing he wrote in jest was doubted. Whether the identifying of Captain Sellers with "Mark Twain" was jest or a mistaken memory, it started a report that is still current. But Captain Sellers never used a pseudonym, and Sam Clemens himself was the first "Mark Twain." Far from the river that mellow term—the leadsman's cry for a sounding of two fathoms—began its immortality. It would come back to the Mississippi, from the mining camps of the Sierras and the lecture halls of San Francisco, in the books that drew upon Sam Clemens' memories, as boy and man, of the everlasting river.

Under the graves on the hill, where now the night wind brings the sounds of towboats in the Chain of Rocks Canal, the river carried its changing trade. Four thousand steamboats were launched in the Western rivers between 1811 and 1900. They whistled under the bluffs of Wisconsin, in the bottom timber of Illinois, up the hill-framed Tennessee, over the gaunt Dakota plains, up the dense Ouachita and the slumbering Yazoo. They came to their ends in fire and ice, on snags, shoals and sandbars. They are all gone now. Hundreds of steamboats lie on the Mississippi bottom in the "graveyard stretch" between the mouth of the Missouri and the mouth of the Ohio. Some lie in the Chain of Rocks, under the graves of the rivermen on the Bellefontaine hill.

I

~~~

Mississippi Sunrise

Judge now whether another such river can be found on the globe . . . which combines so many wonders with such great utility . . . and to which futurity promises such brilliant destinies.

GIACOMO CONSTANTINE BELTRAMI

2

Great River

*The Mississippi . . . was to the great portion of
the American people, as it was to us, the ultima
Thule—a limit almost to the range of thought.*

TIMOTHY FLINT

THE UPPER MISSISSIPPI is many thousands of years older than the lower
river. It is bedded and framed in rock, an ancient channel which ends
abruptly a hundred miles below St. Louis. In a time long past an ocean
gulf reached northward, between the Ozark Mountains and the highlands of Tennessee, narrowing to the river mouth near present Cape
Girardeau. Here, in a grandeur that no eyes ever saw, the primordial
Mississippi plunged 285 feet from its rock ledge to sea level. And here
began the ancient delta, by which the silt-laden river extended its
course through land of its own making. During the past century of
recorded surveys, the Mississippi has deposited one-third of a mile of
new land in the Gulf of Mexico. In past aeons it made the whole lower
valley, from Cape Girardeau to the Gulf, through which the present
river winds twelve hundred miles to tidewater.

Five times in the patient past, the basin of the upper Mississippi was
buried in ice, the prodigious glacier, ten thousand feet deep, creeping
over the present states from Ohio to Iowa and the Dakotas. During the
melting of the Illinoian glacier, before eastward drainage began through
the Great Lakes, the Mississippi was vaster than any river known to
man. Its massive burden of sediment formed the huge alluvial valley.

Though the glaciers are long gone, their lower outline can be seen in
the broad *U* formed by the Ohio and Missouri rivers; these streams,
much younger than the upper Mississippi, carried the glacial runoff into
the central valley. The last great glacier pushed the mouth of the Ohio
southward from its earlier channel through the Cache River Sag in
southern Illinois. At the same time the Missouri River, fed by the rotting

ice, picked its way at the western edge of the glacier, receiving from the west the streams—now called Kansas, Platte, Niobrara, White, Cheyenne and Grand—that were blocked by the ice mass.

The upper Mississippi followed its ancient bluff-walled course as far as Clinton, Iowa. From there the present river has a new channel, east of the original course, cut by the rush of glacier water through the Upper Rapids past Rock Island and the Lower Rapids near Keokuk. The Illinois River, carrying an overflow from the Great Lakes, cut a majestic valley; now towboat men on the Illinois Waterway and motorists on State Highway 29 see across rich bottoms the old banks of the noble river. Diminished streams within the bold channels of prehistoric rivers are seen today on the Wabash, the Miami, and other northern tributaries of the Ohio.

From Clinton, Iowa, the preglacial Mississippi took a southerly course beyond a dividing ridge which lifted into the Ozarks; it united with the ancient Ohio at a point near Helena, Arkansas, two hundred miles south of their present junction. Then as now these two rivers were reluctant to mingle, the clear gray of the Ohio flowing for miles beside the brown Mississippi current before the waters merged. In glacial times the upper Mississippi broke through the barrier ridge and found its present southerly course which joins the Ohio at Cairo. Said Henry Thoreau after studying a Massachusetts stream near Concord: "Thus in the course of ages the rivers wriggle in their beds, till it feels comfortable under them. Time is cheap and rather insignificant."

Rivers are more alive than any other of earth's features, except for the briefly violent volcano. A river is always carving its channel and always depositing sediment along the way. The ancient Mississippi carved a rock trough two hundred to six hundred feet deep and one to seven miles wide. Now, after the melting of successive ice sheets, the trough has filled with sand and gravel—which the engineers dredge up for levees, dikes and dams—through which our diminished river flows. Unable to fill its spacious bed, it turns from one side to another, undercutting banks and bluffs and picking up new sediment to drop somewhere else. Below Cairo the alluvial Mississippi had built a broad soft ridge through which the current folds and loops and bends. Said Zadok Cramer a century and a half ago, "The Ohio enters the Mississippi in a southeast direction but the latter turns immediately to the southwest and thence it moves majestically to all points of the compass." This sinuous stream, constantly releasing the silt from distant valleys, is higher than the flood plain beyond the levee borders; flood water, fifty miles across, can inundate whole counties on either side. On the east bank are occasional bluffs, once capes and headlands on the ocean gulf. These Chickasaw bluffs, long occupied by Indian camps, are now the site of Memphis, Vicksburg, Natchez, Baton Rouge—the cities of the lower river.

Like the North American continent its great river system was discovered at distant points, with speculation bridging the vacant spaces. The first white man to see the Mississippi never realized its importance; Hernando de Soto, Spanish governor of Cuba, was looking for gold and rubies. Marching overland from Florida with a herd of squealing hogs, he discovered the Mississippi a few miles south of present Memphis. "The stream was swift and very deep; the water, always flowing turbidly, brought along from above many trees and much timber, driven onward by its force." On the bank of this river, "larger than the Danube," De Soto built boats and ferried his force—*caballeros*, Negro slaves and swine—across to Arkansas. He was searching for treasure but he found desolation. Floundering through swamps, bayous, oxbows and cane-brakes, he found the Ozark highlands and then turned back down the Red River. In the spring of 1542, exhausted and despairing, he reached the west bank of the Mississippi. He died there of fever, and his weighted body was buried in the river's muddy waters.

A hundred and twenty years later, the imperial-minded La Salle found his way from the St. Lawrence to the headwaters of the Ohio. Perhaps he spent the winter of 1670 in the Ohio valley; possibly he was the first white man to see the beautiful river, descending it to the falls at present Louisville. The records are too vague for certainty.

In the far northern wilderness French traders and missionaries heard from Lake Superior Indians of the "Messipi"; it was a rumored river long before they traced it on their maps. At Green Bay in 1634 the Winnebago chiefs told Jean Nicolet about a great river on the western border of their country. They led him up the Fox River and showed him the portage path to the westward-flowing Wisconsin. Perhaps the far-ranging brothers-in-law Radisson and Groseilliers passed down the Wisconsin and into the Mississippi in 1659; Radisson told of a forked river whose two branches, "the one toward the west, the other toward the south," suggest the Missouri and the Mississippi. But again the records are almost as vague as the unmapped wilderness. The upper Mississippi did not come into clear knowledge until that June day of 1673 when Marquette and Jolliet, with their five paddlers, steered through new currents at the Wisconsin mouth and saw the vast river rolling southward toward an unknown sea. They thought it emptied into the Gulf of California, but when they had descended to the mouth of the Arkansas they knew otherwise. The Mississippi was a *central* river, carrying the waters of the mid-continent to the Gulf of Mexico.

It would be generations before all the reaches of the river were explored, but speculation did not wait upon the toil and danger of the *voyageurs*. Wrote an English geographer in 1720, *The Mississippi springs from several lakes to the westward of Hudson's Bay and bending its course directly south falls through six large channels into the Gulf of Mexico. . . . It is reported 800 leagues long and very probably it may be much longer. The Missouri runs from the northwest, at least 6 or 700 leagues, beginning, as it is commonly believed, from a certain mountain in Cibola, where another river issues forth into the Gulf of California.*

To the majestic, mysterious river the Europeans gave their most exalted names. "River of the Holy Ghost" Spanish explorers called it; "River of Immaculate Conception" the French wrote on their mission maps. Traders seeking political favor named it "Rivière Colbert" for the French minister, and " Rivière Boude ou Frontenac" for the governor of New France. In honor of the French king it was called Rivière St. Louis and Rivière Louisiane. But neither Christian nor political names could supplant the savage Mee-zee-see-bee of the Chippewas. The native names of the rivers, said Walt Whitman, give their true length, breadth and depth. "Mississippi—the word winds with chutes—it rolls a stream three thousand miles long."

Actually for the Indians the great river had as many names as the various tribes and languages between its forest sources and its alluvial mouth. As they passed down the river, European explorers heard it called Messipi, Namosi-sipu, Nilco, Mico, Culatta, Okachitto, Olsimo-chitto, Sassagoula, and Malabanchia. Winding through the northern forests, it was not yet the mighty stream that gathered in the midlands, but it was the greatest river known to the Algonquin tribes and they gave it their venerable name, variously pronounced Michi-sipi, Kitchi-

Zibi, Mis-sipi, but always meaning Old Big Deep Strong River. French explorers journeying *down*stream carried that name with them and gave it to a river that flowed beyond the reach of the Algonquins and their language.

Modern scale maps, showing every mile of the navigable river system, are filed in the district offices of the U. S. Army Engineers. But for the first maps of the Mississippi one must go to archives in Montreal and Paris. When it was a French river in a French empire, the cartographers enlarged and revised the Mississippi with each new exploration. The river of Marquette and Jolliet, of La Salle, Tonty and Hennepin is there, filled in with speculation and surmise where the boatmen had not been, and animated with Indians, buffalo, beaver and unnamed species that the *voyageurs* had described. These maps have fewer statistics and more wonder than the navigation charts.

On the left bank of the Seine in Paris, in the curving rue de l'Université, is the old Ministry of the Marine, a gray stone building enclosing a cobbled courtyard. The Dépôt des Cartes, a balconied room on the second floor, is crammed with folio maps of New France. Seldom brought to the light of the north window, they are the record of discovery, of the patient laborious progress of the explorers. Behind the folios are the thrust of canoe paddles, the swirl of swift water, the sting of black flies and mosquitos, the muddy toil of the portages.

An unsigned, undated map, probably drawn in 1674, accurately outlines the Great Lakes—for the first time—showing the site of Chicago with an inscription: "The largest vessels can come to this place . . . and from this marsh into which they can enter there is only a distance of a thousand paces to the Rivière la Divine [the present Des Plaines] which can lead them to the Rivière Colbert [Mississippi] and thence to the Gulf of Mexico." The Ohio—"which the Sieur de la Salle descended"— is shown converging with the Mississippi in approximately the proper place.

A rude map from the hand of Father Marquette shows, without naming them, the Wisconsin and Illinois rivers—he had discovered one and ascended the other. The Mississippi appears as "Rivière de la Conception," the Missouri as "Pekitanoui," the Ohio as "Ouabouskiaou." This last was the modern Wabash, then supposed to be the same river as the Ohio. This map extends, as did Marquette's voyage, to the mouth of the Arkansas which it does not name.

Later in his life Louis Jolliet was a trained cartographer, but it was an unskilled hand that drew the maps of his explorations in 1673. One of them shows the "Rivière Colbert" flowing from three round lakes in latitude 47 degrees and represents the unnamed Missouri as leading to the Gulf of California. Another map made by the Jesuits in 1673 or 1674 traces the Mississippi from present La Crosse, Wisconsin, to the Gulf of Mexico. It is named "Mitchisipi ou grande Rivière." Colored ink depicts the robed Jesuits instructing savages at various points along the river. Still another Jesuit map makes the first tracing of the upper Mississippi, with a "Saut" indicating the Falls of St. Anthony. Jesuit stations are marked by crosses in the wilderness.

A map drawn by the royal cartographer, Jean Baptiste Louis Franquelin, upon the basis of Jolliet's discoveries is full of error and marvels. It shows the whole length of the Mississippi from the Gulf to a source near the "Mer du Nord" in the vicinity of Hudson's Bay. The Wisconsin is labeled "Miskous" and the Ohio "Oubastikau." The map swarms with animals—among them camels, ostriches and a giraffe. On the upper Mississippi is shown the creature described in Marquette's journal: "We saw on the water a monster with the head of a tiger, a sharp nose like that of a wildcat, with whiskers and straight erect ears; the head was gray and the neck quite black; but we saw no more creatures of this sort."

The greatest of all the maps of New France was drawn by Franquelin in 1684. On its blanket-size parchment is shown the whole sweep of interior America dominated by the "Missisipi ou Rivière Colbert." The river is accurately drawn except for its lower segment which makes a big westward bow—into present Texas and back again—before reaching the Gulf. On this map the Ohio is given three names, two of them having since then become the names of cities which Franquelin could not have envisioned; he called the river "Fleuve St. Louis, ou Chucagoa, ou Casquinampogamou." The name Ohio he gave to a branch that resembles the Allegheny.

For a hundred years French trade usurped the rivers, and *voyageurs* found the way up scores of tributaries. They left a necklace of names in the interior, from St. Croix and St. Ignace in the northern woods to Baton Rouge and Nouvelle Orleans in the lush and languid South. And they left waters still unentered and unmarked on their maps.

Southward from the Ohio led the Tennessee and the Cumberland, explored by Virginians who came over the Blue Ridge in the decade before the American Revolution. The Cumberland was named for an English duke who never saw the cliffs, caves, rock towers and natural bridges of the wild valley. Down the Holston, longest tributary of the Tennessee, came hunters from the Piedmont. In 1770 a couple of them passed the site of Nashville where they heard a roaring like a cataract. Looking for a waterfall, they found a bellowing herd of buffalo at a salt lick.

Exploration of the westward-leading rivers followed the Louisiana Purchase. In the summer of 1806, while Lewis and Clark were returning from Oregon, young Lieutenant Zebulon Pike led an expedition up the Missouri and the Osage into present Kansas. Crossing the buffalo prairies to the Arkansas, they followed that river to the front range of the Rocky Mountains. Pike's report, widely read in the United States and England, was soon published in the French, German and Dutch languages. In 1819 the naturalist Thomas Nuttall poled a skiff up the chocolate-colored Arkansas and made his great tour of discovery, collecting plants, birds and animals all the way from the Ozarks (named from the *Rivière aux Arkansa*) to the springs of the Red River. The next year, 1820, Major Stephen H. Long led a party up the Platte River to the Rocky Mountains, where they climbed Pike's Peak and saw snow water rushing down to the great gorge of the Arkansas on its way to the Mississippi.

Where the Neosho and Verdigris rivers joined the Arkansas, an army post was created in 1824. To Fort Gibson came displaced Indians along with squatters, traders and army men. Up the Arkansas keelboats freighted plows and axes, hogs and horses, seed corn and whiskey. In 1832 came two men with pen and notebook—Washington Irving and the rambling English essayist Charles Latrobe—and soon the world had some vivid impressions of the huge American Southwest. A few years later George Catlin arrived with his sketching pad to add the Osage and Choctaw chiefs to his great Indian Gallery.

The last part of the Mississippi to be explored was its source. The river rises near the geographical center of North America in a dark land of forests, swamps and glacial lakes where a bewildering network of streams find their devious ways together. In 1805, at the beginning of his career, Zebulon Pike went up the Mississippi to seek the river's source. Actually Pike's expedition had three objectives—to make peace between the Sioux and the Chippewas, to assert the rights of American traders on the upper river, and to map the Mississippi headwaters. He left St. Louis with twenty men in a seventy-foot keelboat. For sixty gallons of whiskey and some boxes of knives, hatchets and kettles he bargained for military sites at the mouths of the St. Croix and Minnesota rivers. In midwinter 1806 on snowshoes and sledges he reached Leech Lake, his farthest penetration. The land was locked in ice, and there was no flowing water to lead to the river's beginning. He was still a hundred miles, as the river flows, from the source of the Mississippi.

After the War of 1812 came a new search for the river source. In 1820 Governor Lewis Cass of Michigan led a party north from Detroit. They paddled up Lake Huron, portaged around the Soo, and voyaged along the wild shore of Lake Superior. Passing the site of present Duluth, they ascended the St. Louis River and made the Sandy River portage to the Mississippi which they reached near Leech Lake where Pike had planted the American flag fourteen years before. With their Indian guides and paddlers, they pushed on to a lake which they named for Cass—its Indian name was a jawbreaking "Ga-misquawakogog saigaiigun."

The true source of the Mississippi lay hidden in the northern wilderness until Henry Rowe Schoolcraft set out in 1832. Schoolcraft had been with the Cass expedition and was serving as Indian Agent at Sault Ste. Marie; he was an explorer of rivers and ethnology. In his 1832 party were young Douglass Houghton, surgeon and botanist; the Reverend William T. Boutwell, missionary to the northwestern Indians; and a Chippewa guide named Ozawindeb—"Yellow Head." After crossing pine-fringed Lake Bemidji they turned southward, ascending an east fork of the Mississippi now known both as the Yellowhead and the Schoolcraft river. Two days' hard progress in the narrowing stream brought them to a long portage—"of thirteen pauses"—and at its end they found a clear blue Y-shaped lake hemmed in wooded hills. This was the "Elk Lake"—Omushkös—which the Indians had described to General Cass, the source of the Mississippi. Schoolcraft named it "Itasca," from the Latin words *veritas caput*—"true head." Actually the contour maps now show that Little Elk Lake, five miles above Lake Itasca and 2466 miles from the sea and 1470 feet above it, is the ultimate source of the Mississippi.

Into Lake Itasca ran a shining rivulet that Schoolcraft stepped across. It was the beginning of the river that poured its vast flood,

"Raftsmen Playing Cards" by George C. Bingham
(City Art Museum of St. Louis)

Steamboat wooding at night (Courtesy Historical and
Philosophical Society of Ohio)

View on the Mississippi River at St. Louis, 1836. Steamer *Yellowstone*
bound for the Upper Missouri (Courtesy Smithsonian Institution)

gathered from half the continent, into the Gulf of Mexico. When Charles Latrobe, returning to Europe, sailed out of the river mouth in 1843, the greatness of the Mississippi followed him. "Long after we had lost sight of the land," he wrote, "the turbid waters heaving around us told us that we were still within the domain and influence of the Mississippi. At length we shot over a line clearly defined and distinct— passed from a yellow wave into one of sea-green hue—and bade adieu to the mighty Father of Waters."

See one river, said an ancient Greek, and you have seen them all. It was not so in the great valley of America. Each tributary that found its way to the Mississippi had its own character—the cliffs and forest of the Ohio, the prairies of the Wabash and the Illinois, the abrupt bluffs of the upper Mississippi, the sloughs of the Wisconsin, the pine forests of the Chippewa, the windswept plains and mesas of the Missouri, the bends and bayous of the Arkansas. A European traveler once estimated the volume of the Mississippi as greater than all the rivers of Central Europe combined. It equaled, he said, three Ganges, nine Rhones, twenty-seven Seines, eighty Tibers, and its watershed spanned a country greater than that from Gibralter to the Dardanelles.

"This noble and celebrated stream, the Nile of North America, commands the wonder of the Old World," wrote Zadok Cramer in 1820, "while it attracts the admiration of the New." Twenty years later that admiration inspired the mammoth Mississippi panoramas, the largest paintings in all history. In the 1840's, in a burst of native art, five panoramists pictured the great valley. One of them announcing a painting three miles long was quickly followed by another who boasted of a four-mile canvas. These vast paintings were the work of young men who roamed the rivers, restless and wonder-struck, when the Mississippi was a borderline between wilderness and civilization.

In the summer of 1836 a rangy youth of sixteen was drifting down the Ohio in a flatboat. John Banvard had gone west from New York with no resources and little training, but he dreamed of painting the largest canvas in the world. In his cabin he had a diorama of river life on the Wabash (he had spent a season at bizarre New Harmony) which he planned to show at Shawneetown. Past him came the commerce of the Ohio, steamboats, keelboats, arks and rafts. The river drew dreamers and enterprisers alike.

Banvard paid more attention to the wild landscape than to the river channel. In sight of the old Shawneetown landing, his boat grounded on a bar. Stranded there, the artist went to sleep at nightfall. At daybreak he was still aground but in a different place; a steamer's wash had lifted off his craft at midnight and carried it a dozen miles downstream. He poled away and made an Illinois landing where he showed his horseshoe-shaped painting to some villagers for a bushel of potatoes, a stewing chicken and some eggs.

For five years Banvard traveled the river as a roving artist and peddler, filling his sketchbook with cities, forts, camps, landings, plantations, bluffs, cliffs, points and islands. In a riverfront loft at Louisville he began work on a huge reel of canvas, and at last, in 1846, he announced *Banvard's Panorama of the Mississippi, Painted on Three Miles of Canvas, exhibiting a View of Country 1200 Miles in Length, extending from the Mouth of the Missouri River to the City of New Orleans, being by far the Largest Picture ever executed by Man.* His pamphlet of "Program Notes" included a sketch of "Life on the Mississippi" lifted from the *Recollections* of Timothy Flint along with Morgan Neville's story of Mike Fink, king of the keelboatmen.

After unrolling it in river cities, where boatmen in his audience cheered familiar landmarks, Banvard took his painting east. It reached Boston just in time to help the poet Longfellow ("The river came to me," he noted gratefully, "instead of my going to the river") with his western scenes in *Evangeline:*

> Far down the Beautiful River
> Past the Ohio shore and past the mouth of the Wabash,
> Into the golden stream of the broad and swift Mississippi . . .
> Onward o'er sunken sands, through a wilderness somber with forests
> Day after day they glided a-down the turbulent river.

After Boston came triumphs in New York and Washington, where Congress passed a resolution in praise of the "wonderful and magnificent production." Then Banvard took his show to the Old World. During the Christmas season, 1848, London crowds streamed into Egyptian Hall, in Piccadilly, to see the Mississippi. Charles Dickens watched the unrolling of the painting with more enthusiasm than he had felt for the river itself, five years before, and he compared the momentum of America with the backwardness of Britain. It would be well to have a panorama, three miles long, of England, he wrote, "a moving panorama, not one that stood still or had a disposition to go backwards." After a performance for the Queen at Windsor Castle, Banvard began a tour of the Continent.

Banvard's painting seemed beyond compare, but a bigger one was coming. It was the work of a young carpenter and scene-painter, Henry Lewis, who had been born in England and reared in Boston. In 1836, as a youth of seventeen, he went west to St. Louis. In the summer of 1848 Lewis traveled to St. Paul on the steamer *Senator* to paint the upper Mississippi, which was not represented in Banvard's panorama. Lewis proposed "a gigantic and continuous painting of the Mississippi River from the Falls of St. Anthony to where it empties into the Gulf of Mexico." Under the cliffs of Fort Snelling he built a houseboat-studio on a double keel provided by two long canoes. He named his craft *Minnehaha* and equipped it with two small sails and a pair of heavy oars. He could sketch from the cabin roof in fine weather.

On his way downstream Lewis fought mosquitos, visited white settlements and Indian camps, studied islands, bluffs and headlands. He sketched scores of scenes—the broad expanse of Lake Pepin, the lift of Maiden Rock and Trempealeau Mountain, the spacious Wabasha Prairie, the frescoed Piasan Rock and other landmarks. Careful detail went into his drawings of the river cities. He showed the abrupt Mormon temple on the hill above Nauvoo, the churches of Alton under the wooded bluff, and a mile of steamboats lining the levee at St. Louis. Most of his sketches included rivercraft—rafts, flatboats, steamers—and like a good riverman he always named his steamboats. His scenes showed the *Alec Scott, Illinois, Uncle Sam, Hiram Powers, Grand Turk, Time and Tide, Gen. Washington* and other famous packets.

In Cincinnati in the fall of 1848, Lewis spread out his sketches and began the big painting. A year later his "Great National Work" was ready. After a premier showing in St. Louis, he took his panorama east. Following a Canadian tour from Hamilton to Quebec, he sailed across the Atlantic. Two years of European showings ended in Düsseldorf where he sold his huge canvas to a Dutch planter who took it to Calcutta and Java. By then the Mississippi had gone nearly around the earth.

In Düsseldorf in 1858 Lewis produced *Das illustrirte Mississippithal*— a lithograph portfolio of seventy-eight views of the great valley accompanied by a German text. Soon afterward the publisher failed, but a few copies were sent to America and a few others were sold in Germany. In 1945 a copy from the Russian Imperial Library was auctioned for a thousand dollars. Some twenty copies of the *Mississippithal* are now catalogued in America and Europe.

After long travels Banvard's huge painting came to rest in Watertown, South Dakota, where the artist retired in the 1880's. Into the cellar, lashed up like a ship's canvas, went the dark cliffs and the shining waters, the little landings and the great levees of the Mississippi. A few years later some portions of it were used on the wall of a local building, and there Banvard's wonder was lost to sight under coats of varnish and wallpaper. By then the river that Marquette had discovered "with a joy that I cannot express" was known to all the world.

3

All the Way
to
Shawneetown

THE FIRST WAY to Shawneetown was by water, nine hundred miles from
Pittsburgh, and fleets of flatboats lined the landing in the early years.
Now you go by Illinois 13, through Harrisburg, past Muddy and
Equality, deeper into the summer somnolence of Gallatin County. The
highway keeps to high ground, rising in the approach to the new arched
bridge over the Ohio. But a side road drops down to the wooded river
bottoms and Old Shawneetown.

It is deep South there, crumbling houses of brick and timber, weedy
gardens in the sun. There is no sign of the river except the steep lift of
the levee fringed with locust shoots and ragweed. The front street, which
faced the river before the levee walled it off, has two blocks of faded
brick buildings. Half of them are empty; the rest are mostly taverns
offering "Hot Fish—Our Specialty." On the corner of Main Street and
Washington, serene in the sunlight with a dog sleeping in the columned
shade, is the First State Bank of Illinois, as empty now as a temple in
Sicily. (A money vault housed the gods of the frontier.) Across from it
is a Quonset hut labeled "Old Shawneetown Pecan and Fur Market"
with an old man tilted in a chair in the doorway. A block farther, past
scattered shacks in deep shade and chickens stalking on the porch of a
gutted mansion, a path angles up the levee. It leads to a landmark, a
sagging brick cottage in a tangle of giant ragweed and wild muscadine
under a honey locust tree. A bronze plaque beside the door identifies

The John Marshall Residence
which housed the first bank
in Illinois Territory.

Its boarded windows face the river which brought a restless life to Shawneetown when all was wilderness around it.

The path on the levee is worn through ragweed, foxtail and wild cucumber. On one side lies the old town full of shadows and decay. On the other side, moored to willow roots along the shore, is a line of shantyboats with open porches—Yackle's Fish Market, Durham Fish Market, Clayton's Fish Market, and one offering "Fresh fiddler catfish and Channel Catfish." Beyond the rustling cottonwoods a throbbing barge tow moves up the river.

For forty years this place of shadows was the most important town in Illinois. The first settler came in 1800, building his cabin amid Indian mounds on the riverbank. Settlement gathered there. A ferry brought oxteams and covered wagons from Kentucky. Keelboats and flatboats lined the landing. Men staggered under bales and boxes; they rolled barrels over the sagging gangway; lead, gunpowder, pork, flour and whiskey came ashore. Trappers and traders, squatters and speculators passed through the dusty street. Silt smoked under the hoofs of oxen, mules and horses. Outside a bare slab building on Main Street a line of emigrants waited to sign for tracts of wilderness, in the United States Land Office. Wagons creaked in from the saltworks at Half Moon Lake and Nigger Spring, and barrels of salt were loaded onto keelboats for the upper Ohio and flatboats for the Mississippi. Movers' wagons rolled out of Shawneetown on the road to Kaskaskia. This was the gateway to the Wabash and the Illinois country. Far up the Ohio the boatmen sang:

> Hard upon the beach oar!
> She moves too slow.
> All the way to Shawneetown,
> A long time ago.

The last boat called at Shawneetown in the winter of 1937, when floodwaters lapped at the levee. The town was cut off by drowned lowlands, the inland road lay twelve feet underwater. Telephone lines were down, but word went out on a fisherman's shortwave radio. It brought a towboat to evacuate the settlement. Boatmen had brought life to Shawneetown in the beginning; now they were taking it away. As the rescue boat backed off, the water broke over the levee and poured twenty feet deep into the empty town. It flooded three-fourths of Gallatin County.

30

In 1817 in a Shawneetown tavern, waiting to claim 1440 acres of the Wabash prairie in the land office, the English colonist Morris Birkbeck wrote in his *Notes on a Journey in America,* "As the lava of Mount Etna cannot dislodge this strange being from the cities which have been repeatedly ravished by its eruptions, the Ohio, with its annual over- flowings, is unable to wash away the inhabitants of Shawneetown." Now, 120 years later, with steamboats passing down the Main Street past the columned bank and Rawlings Tavern, it seemed that the life of Shawneetown had ended.

After the flood of 1937 a new Shawneetown was located on high ground three miles from the river. Bald, bare and regular, with low roofs, broad streets and a stilted water tower, it looks like a Kansas town. But while the combined agencies of the Federal and state governments were building the new settlement, some families returned to the river- front. They moved back with their dogs and chickens, their traps and trotlines. There was no river traffic to keep the town alive, but there were catfish in the channel and muskrats in the marshes. After a cen- tury and a half of overflowings, the river has not washed away the inhabitants of Shawneetown.

In 1791 John Pope, gentleman, made a river voyage from Pittsburgh to New Orleans. A literary-minded man, always ready with an allusion, a quotation, or a verse of his own, he kept an observant journal. At New Madrid, a poor town with a proud name, he boarded a Mississippi flatboat named *Smoke House.* Its crew, prophetic of the many nations that would come to the river, consisted of an Irishman, a German, a Virginian, a Kentuckian, a Welshman, and a man born at sea. With these six men Pope lived for four weeks in a reek of wet wool, tobacco smoke, frying pork and catfish.

On the Mississippi John Pope kept watch for hostile Indians and scattered American settlements. Occasionally he saw another boat drift- ing downstream from Kentucky with barreled flour and tobacco. Near the mouth of the Arkansas he found a pirogue manned by a Pennsyl- vanian and a boy, freighting buffalo meat to a remote landing. Below the Yazoo in Spanish territory he noted a shingle-roofed frame house occupied by New Yorkers. Once he hailed a keelboat beating upstream under a dirty square of canvas.

The lower river had more settlement. Through clouds of mosquitos

Pope saw long-oared boats at muddy landings. In the Bayou Pierre country, beyond canebrakes forty feet high, came a district "pretty thickly inhabited by Virginians, Carolinians and Georgians, and some few stragglers from the Eastern states." Though the sunrise gun boomed from Spanish garrisons along the river, Americans were peopling this far country. In New Orleans he found merchants from New York, Philadelphia and Baltimore doing brisk business with imported goods from the United States.

Twelve years later, with the Louisiana Purchase, the Mississippi became an all-American river, and the flatboat fleets appeared. The frontier trade in deerskins and bear oil was soon dwarfed by a commerce of flour, pork, beef, tobacco, corn, butter, hams, meal, lard, beans, hides, hay and barrel staves. It was mostly a downstream traffic, though a few cargoes of cotton, sugar, rum and molasses went laboriously up the river.

The one-way trade required an endless production of rivercraft. At Pittsburgh, Cincinnati, Louisville and lesser places, the hammers clattered and the boats took shape. Or they took many shapes. The flatboat was always a cumbrous craft, but it assumed various forms and sizes. At its crudest it was a scow or "shed," a flat-roofed box on an oblong deck, with shelter for families and room outside for horses, hogs and cattle. Timothy Flint, a Harvard-trained missionary who came West in 1815, was reminded of Noah's aggregation when he saw family boats housing "old and young, servants, cattle, hogs, sheep, fowls and animals of all kinds, bringing to recollection the cargo of the ancient ark, all embarked, and floating down on the same bottom." The Allegheny skiff was a covered cargo carrier with a long steering oar. The Kentucky flat, the commonest freight boat, had a ridged, slightly sloping roof to shed rain; it could carry up to four hundred barrels. A raised deck at the stern covered the crew's living quarters and provided a platform where a man stood at the heavy steering oar. Two masts supported square or schooner sails when the wind was right.

It was a seasonal trade that left the Ohio landings on a crest of water after the autumn rains. All summer, while sandbars ribbed the shrunken stream, mallets and sledges thudded in the boatyards, and in frosty fall weather the new craft were loaded. Between October and May, 1810–11, nearly a thousand flatboats passed Louisville packed with the produce of the Ohio valley. Along with the barreled goods went livestock—fifteen hundred hogs grunting at their feed troughs; two million chickens, ducks and geese cackling and quacking down the river; five hundred horses watching the passing shores. The lesser cargo included two tons of shoe thread, seven tons of country linen, 8500 boxes of cheese, twenty tons of butter and 380 tons of lard. All this merchandise had a ready market in New Orleans, where the boats were sold for lumber and the crews went noisily ashore. After a few days on the town, gawking at the architectural splendors of the Place d'Armes and stalking the balconied streets above the French market, the boatmen shouldered their blanket rolls and headed homeward. Crossing Lake Pontchartrain by schooner, they landed at Covington on the bayou; there they struck the Natchez Trace and began the long walk back to the Ohio.

The Trace, which was also the Old Chickasaw Trail, led north to Natchez and then northeast through the Choctaw and Chickasaw country. It crossed the Tennessee River at the mouth of Bear Creek just below Muscle Shoals, where the Chickasaw chief James Colbert ran a ferry—now Bear Creek is a broad deep arm of Pickwick Lake and the Colbert Hydroelectric Power Station rises above the old crossing place. From there the Trace led through canebrakes and oak barrens to Nashville. Beyond Nashville two rough roads ran over the ridges of Kentucky, one ending at Louisville and a longer one leading to Maysville, originally called Limestone; both terminals were flatboat depots. Except for the approaches to Natchez and Nashville, the Trace was a stump-studded path impassable for wagons.

For thirty years the boatmen made their thousand-mile trek after each voyage down the river. In the 1820's when the steamboats established upstream schedules, the Trace grew up in brush and brambles. It lost its traffic but retained its legends—of Indian ambush, of outlaw bands, and of the hardihood of Kentucky boatmen. Generally the boatmen traveled in parties and spent the night in familiar camping places. Some rode horses, but more of them walked; in races with mounted mail-riders boatmen often outdistanced horses. One, remembered as "Walking Johnson," three times beat the mail from Natchez to Louisville. Another, "Walking Wilson" from Maysville, made thirty-three voyages between 1803 and 1824. Twenty times he walked back from New Orleans, a total of sixteen thousand miles; twelve times he traveled the Trace on horseback; once, on his final trip, he came home by steamboat. In his early years he was never passed by a horse; he was at home in Maysville when his mates rode in.

To bring a loaded flatboat up the river was a task of great difficulty and endless toil. A double crew, using oars, sails, poles and ropes might make the laborious journey from New Orleans to Louisville in a hundred days. By 1808 keelboats were taking over the upstream trade. These craft, longer and narrower than the clumsy arks, built with curved bow and rounded bottom, offered less resistance to the stream. They kept close to shore, away from the booming current and swirling eddies. They carried sails to lighten the toil of men at the setting poles and at the rope cordelles attached to trees and roots on the river bank.

Keelboatmen had their own life and lore, even their own language—full of roaring oaths and exaggeration. They had their own costume—red flannel shirt, tanned leather cap, butternut trousers and faded blue jacket. They tapped barrels of cider and whiskey, cooked their meals in a box of earth on the cargo roof, took turns at the steering oars—the front gauger, the two side broadhorns, the long stern rudder oar. They napped on the deck and jumped up to face the river hazards; the early river was a thicket of planters, sawyers and snags—dead trees lodged in the mud bottom, trees floating in the current, trees lying on shoals—and "wooden islands" of floating timber and debris. Their life held the romance of extremes, blissful indolence and Herculean toil, the solitude of the river and riotous nights ashore, serenity and danger, frolic and death. Timothy Flint never traveled the Ohio without hearing of wrecked flatboats or seeing a red-shirted corpse floating amid driftwood in the current. On every point were broken hulls and wreckage, and no one knew how many men were lost in "this wicked river."

It was a silent river with some noisy places. At Shawneetown, New Madrid, Natchez and New Orleans the boatmen landed planks from the Allegheny forests, cider and cheese from Ohio, flocks of Indiana turkeys and great heaped hills of Indiana hay, Illinois horses, lead and peltry from Missouri. At the landings were scores of boats from diverse places, all lashed together in an island, with fowls cackling, hogs grunting and squealing, fiddles twanging. The boatmen went from one craft to another, yarning, carousing, singing, ganging up to "raise the wind in town." After a few raucous hours ashore, they came roaring back and fell asleep on deck under the stars. At midnight the fleet was silent. In the morning mist they gulped hot coffee and loosed the mooring lines. "Stand to your poles and set off!" The boats scattered down the great river. Soon the solitude was around them.

3 4

Keelboating, the two-way trade, lasted only a decade, from 1808 until Captain Shreve's shallow-draft steamboat *Washington* came successfully up the rivers in 1818. But that decade left the legend of Mike Fink, an embodiment of the early river lore. Like Daniel Boone, Davy Crockett and Paul Bunyan, Mike was less a man than a myth, a folk hero created by the frontier imagination.

One of the few traces of the actual Mike Fink was found by Henry Howe who wandered up and down Ohio in the 1840's making notes and sketches. In the upper river town of Bellaire, Ohio, Howe talked to Captain John Fink, a nephew of the "snapping turtle," who remembered when Mike ran his own keelboat down the river from Wheeling.

Mike Fink had grown up on the Pennsylvania border. He was a young woodsman, darting in and out of the Indian wars; he could bring in the skin of a panther or the scalp of a Mingo. In the 1790's, a stocky youth as solid as a barrel, he first went in to Pittsburgh and saw the rivers alive with canoes, skiffs, galleys, arks and barges. Then he heard the boatman's horn, the long, wild, mellow music echoing under the hills. The spell was on him and he joined a keelboat crew. He was a natural riverman, with a love of roving life and a magnetism for the men around him. He had great strength, great gusto, and great skill. Soon he was known from Pittsburgh to New Orleans; on the Mississippi he was called "the snapping turtle," on the Ohio "the snag." For a dozen years he rode the crest of the keelboat trade, and when steamboats brought civilization to the Mississippi he followed the keelboats to a wilder land. About the year 1815 he went up the Missouri and became a trapper and fur trader. At a trading post on the Yellowstone, he was killed in a fight over an Indian woman. The king of the keelboatmen was buried in an unmarked grave on the windswept plains.

That was in the 1820's, the end of the real Mike Fink with the legendary hero yet to be born. He first appeared in a Cincinnati magazine, *The Western Souvenir*, in 1829. In the same year Morgan Neville, a Cincinnati lawyer and editor, wrote a Mike Fink sketch which was reprinted in Cumming's river guide, *The Western Pilot*, and the legend was launched. Mike was the biggest bragger, the burliest fighter, the teller of the tallest tales, the greatest marksman, the best in a tussle or a frolic, a Hercules with a long oar or a setting pole or with a mountain of barrels to put ashore. The legend spread and grew—in sketches, novels, plays and in fanciful biographies. In 1933, a hundred and ten years after

3 5

his death, the illiterate Mike Fink was a feature subject in the *London Times Literary Supplement*. The keelboat passed but the keelboatman was immortal.

When the steamboat took over the Ohio and Mississippi trade, keelboats plied the lesser rivers. They carried army expeditions and supplies to the upper Mississippi and the Missouri; they freighted cargo to and from new settlements. A bill of lading on a nameless Missouri keelboat in 1822 includes *1 keg powder, 1 brl coffee, 2 sacks salt, 2 bbls sugar, 1 brl whisky, 12 boxes tea, 1 bag rice, 1 keg pepper*—where now the barge tows carry wheat, corn, soybeans, barley, alfalfa pellets, fertilizer, petroleum and chemicals. From the forks of the Arkansas, keelboats freighted peltry down to New Orleans and brought back trade goods and whiskey. A shipyard on the Verdigris launched scores of slender, sturdy keelboats that survived collision with submerged rocks and logs. One keel could carry 40,000 pounds of skins, a stinking load in warm weather and a profitable cargo in New Orleans. In the 1820's keelboats transported troops up the Arkansas to Fort Smith, Fort Towson and Fort Gibson, along with displaced Indians from east of the Mississippi. When the Union Mission was established in Indian Territory, keelboats brought the New York and Connecticut missionaries to their new home three hundred miles beyond the last post office. Ten years later, in the 1830's, keelboats delivered Sam Houston's cargoes for trade with the tribes while he dreamed of the conquest of Texas.

On the big rivers flatboats, with their one-way traffic, flourished during the first golden age of the steamboats. In the age of Jackson, the West was rushing into life; every year brought new towns, new landings, new fleets on the rivers. By 1842 there were 450 steamboats on the Western rivers and ten times that many flatboats riding the current.

Scores of them were family boats, floating shanties with a dog asleep in the doorway and a clothesline flapping on the roof-deck. River families sold fish and turtles, they stopped in likely creeks and bayous to trap mink, otter, raccoons and muskrats; sometimes they stole hogs and chickens from riverside farms. In New Orleans they sold their peltry—coonskins brought 35 cents, mink $1, otter and beaver $1.50— their hogs and fowls, if any, and also their boat. They bought deck passage on steamboats to Cairo or Pittsburgh, at four to six dollars a head. On the upper river they built another shantyboat for the next season's journey.

Hundreds of flatboats were built and manned by Ohio valley farmers who took their produce to Southern markets. Their boats had family names—*Lucy, Eleanor, George, Julian, Polly, Molly, Sally, Betsy, Brother and Sister* from a farm a thousand miles away; or nautical names—*Neptune, Sprightly, Triton, West India Trader, Orleans Packet, Rover, Queen of Kingcraft;* or auspicious names—*Experiment, Hopewell, Liberty, Adventure, Swift Safety, Victory, Resolute, Good Return.* They traveled on high water after the autumn harvest, passing from raw Northern weather to the green shores and balmy air of Louisiana. At New Orleans the commercial year began October 1. By Christmastime the flatboats were arriving. All through the winter months they lined the upper levee—a solid mile of flatboats, three and four deep, ending suddenly in a forest of masts where ships of all nations lay moored along the river crescent. The city's wholesale business was done on the levee with its rich smells, its medley of voices, the rattle of hoofs and the clatter of wagon wheels.

A few of the flatboats would go back up the river, lashed alongside a steamboat. The rest would be broken up. It was a short life for *Brother and Sister* and the *Queen of Kingcraft.* Six months past they were built with a clatter on the Wabash or the Scioto. Now with another clatter they came apart and their lumber was piled on the levee. The planking went into new houses in New Orleans; the warped, waterlogged bottom timbers were sawed up for steamboat fuel. Some flatboats were abandoned on the levee, and the wharfmaster set them adrift. They floated down the delta where the Gulf current carried them eastward; scores of Mississippi scows came ashore on the coast of Florida. Meanwhile the boatmen-farmers boarded northbound steamboats for the journey home. They would be plowing their fields in May.

The rich river life of the age of Jackson included every variety of trade and enterprise. Timothy Flint once traversed a line of eight flatboats at a landing. On one, men were killing hogs; another was selling apples, nuts and cider; a third was doing brisk business as a grogshop. Down the valley went floating foundries, forges, gristmills, tinsmiths, art shows, cabinetmakers, and printing shops. In a country without roads, the river was the great thoroughfare.

3 7

Store boats traveled the rivers until 1860. The proprietors were often Yankees, like Nathan Brown who annually stocked his bins and shelves and floated down the Ohio, selling hardware and yard goods along the way. He stopped at little towns with great names: Aberdeen, Manchester, Portsmouth, Liverpool, London, Rome, Carthage, Ghent, Warsaw, Moscow, Cairo, and at countless unnamed landings. A calico flag from a willow pole designated his dry goods business and some toots on a tin horn drew customers to the riverbank.

A methodic peddler who kept a diary was Jonathan Newman Hamilton of Cincinnati. In his second trading season he left home in early August, 1839, on the boat *Helen,* named for his small daughter, with a stock of clothing, books and kitchenware worth $2014. With him went his son, a Negro servant, a dog and "quite too many rats and mice." The first mishap came as he left the Cincinnati landing; one of his guards was damaged by an "awkward ferry boat" coming across from Covington. He had little trading for three days; but at North Bend, where workmen were cutting stone for lock walls in the Miami and Erie Canal, some German laborers bought $9.20 worth of clothing. While the store boat lingered there, Dr. Benjamin H. Harrison, a son of Old Tippecanoe, came down from the Harrison farm. This Ben Harrison, an uncle of the later President, was overfond of whiskey, and Hamilton noted that he "looked not at all prepossessing." He bought two books at $4.30 without paying—he said he would send the money to Cincinnati. Hamilton did not sell on credit, but he could not refuse General Harrison's son.

At the next stop a drunken Irishman came aboard: no sale. But on the Kentucky side Negro field hands swarmed down to the boat, and Hamilton turned over $28.40 worth of merchandise.

When business was slow the storekeeper went ashore to look for customers. He called from house to house reciting his wares—cloth, clothing, books, pins, needles, thread, flannel, socks, pantaloons and wallpaper. Some villagers came down, looked at his stock but showed no money; they might have bought some whiskey but Jonathan Hamilton was not in that business. Some Negroes brought gunnysacks full of chickens and muskmelons, but Hamilton wanted cash. "Sales today 31 cents." Reluctantly he took in trade—dried apples, onions, feathers, bacon, green apples. The apples he sold to grocers in Madison and Jeffersonville. He found the feather bags weighted with sand. At New

Albany he bought some hardware at auction and peddled it at Evans-ville and Cloverport. Hamilton never sold on Sunday. On that day he read *Bible Dialogues* or went ashore if he could find a church service. He listened to the local preachers with a critical ear.

All the way to Shawneetown, the *Helen* nosed in to the landings. There Hamilton auctioned his remaining stores and paid a steamboat captain twenty dollars to tow him back to Cincinnati where he began putting in stock for his next trip down the river. This was a trade as old as history on the Yangtze and the Nile; for centuries sampans and feluccas have peddled household goods to villages along their shores. But in America it lasted only a generation. Store boats plied the rivers while the West was taking shape; they vanished when railroad trains came clanging into town.

In 1861 war blockaded the rivers, but five years later the flatboats were moving again. Southward the great waterway carried the produce of the midland states. Again the Mississippi was a unifying river, linking North and South, making the nation one. Hundreds of flatboats passed Louisville every month in the winter of 1870. In one of them was William Dudley Devol, an Ohio farmer on the Muskingum three miles above Marietta. He became "Captain Devol" after the crops were in, and he kept a diary of his river journeys from 1867–73.

William Devol belonged to an old river family. One of his ancestors had built the ark that brought the first settlers to Marietta in 1788. Another had built tall-masted brigs that sailed down the rivers and across the Atlantic. A third was the most notorious gambler on the river. In his own time William Devol found that flatboating was a strenuous gamble.

During the summer of 1868 Devol hauled planks from the sawmill, piling them on the riverbank of his 300-acre farm. In September he was building his boat, a floating box 18 feet wide and 90 feet long. It would hold a thousand barrels, five tiers deep with a sixth tier under the ridge-pole. Into the stern cabin, six feet wide, went an iron stove, a hinged plank table, and bed frames resting on apple barrels. While the autumn days shortened and the woods grew bare, the neighbors were barreling potatoes, apples and salt pork. In mid-November they rolled this cargo aboard, along with some boxes of grain and some tubs of apple butter. It was all worth six or seven thousand dollars.

3 9

A week before Thanksgiving, Mrs. Bitha Devol served a big dinner for the flatboat hands. Early that afternoon they waved good-bye and pushed into the stream. On a good current they swung around the bend, passed under Harmon Hill and the streets of Marietta, and entered the broad Ohio. They had a fiddle in the cabin and a fire in the stove. Like an old-time flatboat crew they swung past Parkersburg and Blennerhassett Island in the November dusk. A week later they passed Louisville, one of one thousand seven hundred cargo flats that ran the falls that season with farm produce for the lower Mississippi.

December brought high winds and flurries of snow. Near Shawneetown, where the old flatboat trade was a fading memory, they ran aground on Saline River Island. They got off in a gale of wind and soon took shelter in a cove. For two nights and a day they laid by. While wind blew the last crumpled leaves from the sycamores, they toiled over the barrels in their dim cargo hold, resalting the meat and sorting out spoiled apples.

Ice was running in the Mississippi as they rounded the bend at Cairo, and the wind came cold from the Missouri woods. At Columbus, Kentucky, the ice closed in. With a change of weather they moved on in drift ice to Hickman where they sold a few barrels of apples and potatoes. On a fine morning they pushed off but were soon aground on a sandbar in midstream. After an all-day rain, the current lifted them off; they drifted on toward Memphis. On Christmas Day they took turns at the big steering oar in the rain, then ducked into the cabin that smelled of wet clothes and frying pork. Their apple butter had gone sour. Now they cooked it over, one dishpan after another on the cabin stove, and put it in gallon jars for the retail trade.

The Memphis market was glutted with potatoes and no buyers came through the endless rain. Devol's apples were rotting, and wharfage taxes ran ahead of his sales. From other boatmen he heard that markets were better down the river. After firing a drunken boat hand he went on to Lake Providence, Louisiana, where he unloaded some barrels of pork. "If we sell to the niggers," he wrote, "we do not have to knock the salt from the meat." They moved on to Vicksburg in the rain.

Besides the hazards of navigation, the spoilage of cargo and problems of the marketplace, the boatmen had a contest with local officials. At Lake Providence the wharfmaster demanded "a big bonus," and Devol took his boat below the town limits, trying to sell his goods from a timber-strewn riverbank. At Tulana Landing in Arkansas, the sheriff watched them roll some barrels ashore and then claimed a fifty-dollar license fee. Devol stalled him off until the next day. "That night," he wrote, "we left for points below." (It was like the hasty exits described by George H. Devol in his *Forty Years a Gambler on the Mississippi River*.) At Vicksburg he sold the last of his cargo and took the train for Ohio. He was just three months away.

In Mike Fink's time the rivermen were free as the wind, but the farmer-boatman found letters from his wife and family at every port of call. Mrs. Bitha Devol took a dim view of flatboating. She worried about her husband's health and safety and doubted that the long trip would be profitable. She disapproved of the drunkenness of his boat hands, and she had heard about murders on the Memphis riverfront. "Do be careful," she wrote from her kitchen table. "Don't get out after night alone no time. . . . It makes me shiver to think about it." Devol replied that the lower Mississippi was just as peaceable a place as Ohio as long as a man tended to his own business. His wife reminded him of remedies for coughs and aches and reported that a disease was spreading among their pigs. Devol regretted the sickness of the pigs but assured her that he was in the best of health. He judged that there had been heavy rains at home because of the high water at Vicksburg.

William Devol's last trip in 1872–3 shows times changing on the rivers; he chartered a towboat and took a string of flats downstream. Despite steam power it was a frustrating trip. Trouble began at Louisville, where they were held by low water and an ice-clogged canal. "I write you again from this place for the simple reason that it is impossible for me to get any other place to write from." The week before Christmas his thermometer dipped below zero, and Louisville youngsters skated across the river. The boatmen fed stoves night and day to keep their potatoes from freezing. They had plenty of fuel, for they were lying close under a coal fleet, sixteen acres of barges waiting for open water. The crew had a glum Christmas dinner in their cabin, and a grim dinner on New Year's Day. By that time forty produce boats were wrecked and broken in the ice.

After five weeks the weather turned mild and the ice broke up. "We ought to make Cairo in four days," Devol wrote. Twelve days later they were just halfway. Through an ice-choked river they worked ahead in the short winter daylight; they tied to tree trunks at night. At Cave in

Rock they found a wrecked flatboat with some weary men trying to salvage cargo. The notorious cave, once a haunt of river pirates, was now barricaded by empty barrels, with potatoes spread on the floor to dry. Devol was luckier than some others.

They crept down from Cairo in endless drift ice, reaching Memphis on the third of February—eleven hundred miles in seventy-one days—"by steam at that." Business was brisk in Memphis, as few boats had come down the ice-clogged river. In two weeks Devol was on the train for home.

Depression collapsed the market in the middle 1870's, and new railroad connections ended the flatboat trade. For some seasons Devol and his neighbors shipped produce to the South by steamboat. But the farm boys stayed at home, and flatboating became a memory. In the 1880's the farmer-boatmen recalled their journeys in a golden haze of reminiscence.

It was just a century since John Pope had made his voyage in the *Smoke House*. Since then the flatboat traffic had risen to a crest and ebbed away, leaving only an echo of an oarsman's song,

>All the way to Shawneetown
>A long time ago.

4

Six Men
and an
Earthquake

IN ST. LOUIS in the fall of 1811 John Bradbury, English botanist and
explorer, slowly recovered from an intermittent fever following the hard-
ships of a two-year expedition up the Missouri. He had sent more than
a thousand botanical specimens down the Mississippi for transshipment
to Liverpool. Early in December he followed them, taking charge of a
flatboat loaded with 30,000 pounds of lead for delivery in New Orleans.
He had a crew of four Creole oarsmen and a steersman *patron*, and he
shared his cabin with a roving Englishman named John Bridge. The
heavy craft carried a dugout canoe in case of accident; there were
frequent mishaps on the Mississippi, especially to boats laden with lead.

Bradbury was a puzzle to his boatmen. Directing them to tie up in
tangled places, he would plunge into swamps and thickets, coming back
hours later with a handful of leaves and seedpods. He gave learned
names to smartweed, burdock, eels and crayfish. He was undisturbed in
a raging windstorm, noting the shrub (*amorpha fruticosa*) to which the
boat was tied. On clear nights he plotted the movement of a comet in
the northern sky while the men crossed themselves and offered a pinch
of tobacco to the river. In his cabin he kept bags of seeds, roots and
dried foliage.

On the chill evening of December 14 they arrived at New Madrid,
some flimsy houses around a bare plain, and bought supplies in the
town's two shabby stores. They were the last visitors to see the settlement on its looping riverbank.

Next day they passed thirteen flatboats bound for New Orleans with produce, and that evening they heard the rush of Devil's Channel, a narrow chute beside a partly submerged island. Wanting daylight to run the channel, they tied up to a willow island just above.

After midnight Bradbury was wakened by a thunderous roar and a violent heaving of the boat. Springing up from his buffalo robe he met his terrified crew. Dimly he saw the river boiling with foam, and he heard the screaming of wildfowl in the willows. *"C'est un tremblement de terre,"* he told the men. As he spoke a mass of riverbank fell into the water. He sent two men ashore with candles to check their mooring. The lights flickered out as a new shock came. Bradbury waded in and groped through thickets on the shelving shore. Shielding a candle he found a long chasm bridged with fallen trees; at its end the sheer bank had caved into the river. Their boat would have been buried had it been moored fifty feet above.

Crouching around a fire at the island's edge, they counted twenty-seven shocks before daylight, when they went aboard their craft. On the riverbank two men were loosing the lines when a shock threw them down and a tree crashed beside them. As the earth yawned open, they freed the moorings and leaped onto the deck.

While Bradbury watched from the roof, the muttering *patron* steered through a tangle of shattered trees. They stopped for breakfast on a slanting bank. Seven shocks spilled their kettle of tea into the fire, with each quake came a rumbling of unseen explosions and a wave of choking, sulfurous air. To brace his mumbling men, Bradbury gave them a round of brandy, and they pushed off. It was touch and go through a racing reddish current, pulling the oars between snags and branches, steering through swirls of muddy foam. At last, with the open river around them, the men dropped their oars, crossed themselves and whooped like Indians.

All day the quakes continued, the forest shores rocking, trees crashing amid the screams of circling geese and swans. At the first Chickasaw Bluff opposite Flour Island (named for the wreckage of many cargoes of flour), they went ashore and found some frightened people. A scientifically minded settler explained that the earth had got caught between the horns of the comet and was now trying to get free.

In his journal Bradbury noted one to five shocks a day as they moved downriver, past the mouths of the Obion, the Forked Deer, the Big

Hatchie, and the Loosahatchie. On Christmas day he was hailed by a St. Louis boatman, M. Longpré, also freighting a cargo of lead. They made camp together and over a dinner of roast swan they compared impressions of the earthquake. Longpré said that the upheaval had centered at New Madrid, whose plain was now a lake ringed with ruined and lifeless dwellings.

On the night of December 16 a fleet of forty flatboats, keelboats and barges from the Ohio tied up at an island below New Madrid. Two hours after midnight Captain John Davis woke to a violent commotion; his boat felt like a runaway wagon on a rocky road. He supposed they were adrift and ramming into snags, but, when he looked out, his craft was lashed to a neighbor under the island shore. Someone cried that the banks were caving, and at that moment a quarter of a mile of bluff collapsed. Seething current drew them to the inside of the island where they held on till daybreak. During that time some fifty shocks kept the boat in agitation.

In the first gray daylight they heard a growing thunder. A convulsion shook the boats. Trees crumpled and water poured through the broken island. The river rose, higher and higher, and the moorings gave way. On a booming current, amid exploding geysers of mud and water, they ran past Flour Island, smashing through muddy logs thrown up from the river bottom. In five hours they covered thirty-five miles, a record flatboat run.

For eight days the battered arks hurried down the river. When Captain Davis reached his home at Natchez on January 5, he told of houses, boats, men and cattle drowned in the swirling waters, of islands swallowed and townsites washed away.

In New Madrid Eliza Bryan, schoolmistress from Boston, woke after midnight on December 16 when her bed banged against the wall. The house was heaving. Outside she heard the cries of her neighbors, the screaming of geese and the bellowing of cattle. Across the town common came a crashing of trees and the roar of the river. In a smoky torchlight the townspeople were gathering. The earth shuddered; with a rending crash a house collapsed. "In one person, a female," wrote Eliza Bryan, "the alarm was so great that she fainted and could not be revived." While people fled across the open plain, a few men stopped to load their wagons and hitch up their frightened teams; they overtook the others halfway to Tywappety Hill, seven miles west of the river. On that high ground around a bonfire they knelt and prayed together—Catholic and Protestant, pleading in English, French and Spanish for God's mercy. Around them pressed bewildered horses, cattle, dogs, geese and chickens that had joined the flight.

Back in New Madrid lay Betsy Masters, a girl of seventeen pinned in her bed by a falling roof pole. Her leg was broken below the knee. They thought of her now but no one was willing to go back. Morning brought new rumblings, a heaving and sinking of fields. Geysers jetted from the earth, erupting sand and water and a black, coal-like shale. The air filled with a strangling sulfurous vapor. Men and animals broke into coughing.

In the Tywappety encampment was a hunter, John Shaw of Marquette County, Wisconsin, who had come by a long route to New Madrid. After two years in Indian country on the Arkansas he had loaded his take—50 beaver and otter skins, 300 bearskins and 800 gallons of bear's oil—in a dugout and floated down to New Orleans. He expected to sell his cargo for $3,000, but the year was 1811 and embargo had ruined the market. He sold for $36 and headed north. He arrived at New Madrid along with disaster.

Though her own people could forget her, John Shaw kept thinking about the girl pinned to her bed by a fallen timber. He went back, with sandblasts erupting around him, to the ruined town. He found Betsy Masters dazed and helpless. He bound up her broken leg, left food and water beside her (she eventually recovered) and returned to the camp. There the despairing people were talking about the end of the world. They supposed that the whole country was in convulsion; either fire or water would burst forth and consume the earth.

A few weeks later they returned to the ruined town and lived as they had done before the calamity. Spring turned the fields and forests green, and though the earth still trembled they paid little heed—"not even," said John Shaw, "checking their dancing, frolics and vices."

John Shaw left New Madrid in 1812 and ran a trading boat between St. Louis and Prairie du Chien. In 1841 he built the first steamboat on the upper Mississippi; it was wrecked in the following year. In 1855, an old man, blind but unclouded in memory, with Lyman C. Draper writing down his words, he recalled the strange dark winter at New Madrid.

Ten miles south and thirty miles downstream from New Madrid lay the settlement of Little Prairie. Here lived the family of a farmer named Ross, who had gone west from Kentucky. Fifteen-year-old Charlie Ross learned a little French and became the hunting partner of young Jean Baptiste Zebon. Their last excursion came in December 1811 when they crossed the Mississippi and tramped through canebrakes to a lake in Tennessee. Charlie shot a deer and dressed it while Baptiste made a brush camp. They ate a big supper and wrapped up in their blankets. Next day they found the lake full of otter and beaver—"swimming like flocks of geese in the water." It promised to be rich hunting.

That night they woke to a rumbling of earth, a surge of water on the shore, the crash of forest trees. It seemed a storm, but the air was still. They lay down and tried to sleep. At daybreak while Charlie was making a fire the ground swam and swayed. Before his startled eyes trees tottered and gaps as wide as a keelboat opened in the lake shore. Baptiste sprang up. Together they watched the lake run dry, its water sinking into muddy chasms. Then the chasms closed, spouting a black ink higher than the treetops. A new shock threw the hunters to the ground.

When the convulsion passed, they stared around them. Their camp with gone without a trace. But they were unhurt and perhaps the world had not ended. They made for the Mississippi, crawling through fallen timber, scrambling around fissures and sinkholes. They heard the river before they found it—a chaos of drowned forest and swirling water. On the far side lay a remnant of Little Prairie. One cow bellowed on the riverbank, the only thing alive.

That night the hunters made a cold camp. There were no stars, the river roared in darkness, a strangling sulfur smell came from the water. In the gray daybreak they made a raft with vines and driftwood, but a surge of current carried it away. Exhausted and famished they watched a canoe creep across the water. In it was Charlie Ross's father; he told them that the people of Little Prairie had fled to high ground. They crossed the river, passed through the ruined village and joined the encampment. Next day the Mississippi cut through the caving bank and flooded the site of Little Prairie.

In his boatman's handbook *The Navigator,* Zadok Cramer described the junction of the Ohio and the Mississippi as "the union of two of the most noble rivers in the universe," but when James McBride steered his flatboat into the Mississippi in the December gloom it was a desolation. "Island No. 1," he read, "is about one mile long, and the channel cannot be mistaken, being at all times on the right side of the island." But the island was either submerged or washed away; there was only the big sullen river, flecked with muddy foam and matted with floating brush and timber.

McBride was an Ohio man, having come west from New Jersey. In Hamilton, Ohio, on the Great Miami, he had loaded his cargo, 350 barrels of apples, flour and whiskey, and hired two oarsmen. Six feet of roofed deck at the stern made up their cabin, smelling of frying pork and drying clothes. They poled, pulled and "cooned" their craft past the shoals and bars of the Miami River. They passed between cooper shops and packing sheds at Cincinnati and swung into the Ohio current. At Louisville McBride heard reports of a great earthquake in the Mississippi valley. A scientific-minded man, measurer of Indian mounds and collector of fossils, he wondered what he would find on the Mississippi.

What he found was chaos, like the beginning, or the end, of creation. The swirling river smelled like brimstone and tasted of sulfur. The shores were ravaged and broken. Old islands were gone, and the river boiled around masses of fallen timber. Above New Madrid, on the Missouri side, the river embraced a three-mile grove of cottonwood and willow. All this timber was bent *upstream*, slanting against the muddy current. As McBride steered past, wondering at the convulsion that had reversed the vast river and then poured it back again, the forest heaved and his boat lifted. The earth was still quaking.

With his oarsmen toiling, McBride steered in toward New Madrid, but there was no landing place. They passed on and in the dusk ran up on a half-drowned island. During the night repeated earth shocks bumped the boat and the current worried it. Then the craft grated on bottom. Torchlight showed the river falling. Every hour they jumped into the water, pushing off the heavy boat and changing the moorings.

At daylight, with a cold rain falling, they let go. In midday they landed at Little Prairie, thirty miles below New Madrid. The town was gone and at the river's edge McBride saw a row of tilted wooden crosses. His mooring place, he realized, was the burying ground, once at the far edge of the settlement. With morbid wonder he climbed past exposed coffins and burial boxes. He found a dozen cabins collapsed or overturned on ground webbed with fissures. A mile across the creviced prairie he came upon a board lean-to where three Frenchmen crouched around a fire.

Their neighbors, they said, had all fled westward. McBride tramped on to a region of circular pits half-filled with water and ringed in coarse black shale. He took some samples to his boat and put them on the fire. They burned with a strong sulfuric smell.

That night he lay under the coffin-studded bank while earth shocks threw pots and pans from his cabin shelves. When they pulled away next morning, the quakes followed them. For a hundred miles they passed shattered forests and shores gashed and gaping. "All nature," McBride concluded, "appeared in ruins, and seemed to mourn in solitude over her melancholy fate."

On the 21st of March *Niles' Weekly Register* in Baltimore gave a summary of the disaster "near the recent city of New Madrid, Missouri." For two hundred miles, it said, the Mississippi River had altered its course. In many places the river bottom had been lifted, great tracts of land were sunken and flooded, lake beds became fields, islands were washed away, a large area in Tennessee had been turned into lake and marsh, a mountain rose during a night from what had been a plain.

When spring came to the valley the earth grew quiet, but strange tales were told in the river towns. A Missouri merchant had bought a boatload of iron castings, which he stored in his cellar. With the first earth shocks, the ground opened under his house and the castings dropped out of sight. After that fearful night a woman went out to get some breakfast bacon from her smokehouse. The smokehouse was gone and the river was at her kitchen door. A Missouri farmer went out that morning with a milking pail; failing to find his cow he heard a lowing from across the river and saw her grazing in Kentucky. With one of the subterranean explosions near New Madrid, a strange skull was thrown up in a geyser of mud. It was eventually sent to the Natural History Museum in New York where it was identified as the remains of a long-extinct musk-ox.

In Louisville that winter a methodic man had kept a daily record of earth tremors, listing them in six classes of intensity. In thirteen weeks following the first quakes he recorded eight of the greatest severity, ten of the second order, and 1874 shocks in all. The tremors diminished steadily until the middle of March. Then the winter of the earthquake was over, but it would be a wonder and a legend for many years to come.

II

~~~~~

Two Thousand Packets

It was always the custom for the boats to leave New Orleans between four and five o'clock in the afternoon. . . . Steamer after steamer falls into line, and the stately procession goes winging its flight up the river.

MARK TWAIN

5

Smoke on the Rivers

THE YEAR 1811 was a time of wonders in the West. It began with flood-waters on the Ohio, all the side rivers out of their banks and settlers scrambling from the bottoms while their cabins washed away. It ended with an eclipse that darkened the sun, a comet trailing ghostly fire across the midnight sky, and earthquakes changing the course of the Mississippi. In Missouri the Sacs daubed themselves with vermilion, in Detroit tribesmen whooped around the war post, and at Tippecanoe Creek on the Wabash Tecumseh's warriors stormed across the marshes at Harrison's frontier army. In 1811 the future was hurrying into the wild Western country.

In that portentous year a consumptive bookbinder from Pittsburgh went down to Natchez for his health. It was his first long river journey, though as author of *The Navigator* he had guided countless boatmen. Using the journals and reports of river travelers, Zadok Cramer had compiled a mile-by-mile pilot's manual, describing the river channel all the way from Pittsburgh to New Orleans. In the 1811 edition of this boatman's Bible, Cramer noted the greatest wonder in that wonderful year. "There is now on foot a new method of navigating our western waters, particularly the Ohio and Mississippi rivers. This is with boats propelled by the power of steam. . . . It will be a novel sight, and as pleasing as novel, to see a huge boat working her way up the windings of the Ohio, without the appearance of sail, oar, pole, or any manual labor about her —moving within the secrets of her own wonderful mechanism and propelled by power undiscoverable!—This plan, if it succeeds, must open to

5 3

view flattering prospects to an immense country, an interior of not less than two thousand miles of as fine a soil and climate as the world can produce, and to a people worthy of all the advantages that nature and art can give them. . . . The immensity of country we have yet to settle, the vast riches of the bowels of the earth, the unexampled advantage of our water courses, which wind without interruption for a thousand miles, the numerous sources of trade and wealth opening to the enterprising and industrious citizens, are reflections that must rouse the most dull and stupid."

While Zadok Cramer, coughing into a stained handkerchief, was writing his prophecy, there was clatter and commotion on the Pittsburgh riverbank. At Beelen's Iron Foundry on the Monongahela, with a creaking of ropes and a thudding of hammers, the steamboat *New Orleans* was taking shape. She had a long deck—more than a hundred feet—a spacious cabin surmounted by a boxy pilothouse, a lofty smokestack, two masts and a pair of big side-wheels. Accounts of this wonder spread and grew. In Baltimore *Niles' Register* caught the excitement. "A ship of 450 tons has lately been launched in the Scioto River! The steamboat of *Ohio* to carry 450 tons!!" It was the wrong place, the wrong name, the wrong size; but the first steamboat had slid into the Western waters. She made a trial run up the Monongahela and then prepared for the long voyage to New Orleans.

That voyage is now the most familiar episode in river history. It is an eventful story—crowds lining the landings where the steamboat passed, Indians running from the sight of "Penelore," the smoking canoe, wonder-struck farmers thinking the comet had fallen into the river. At Louisville the vessel waited for high water to run the falls, and Commodore Nicholas J. Roosevelt (the brother of Theodore Roosevelt's grandfather) entertained the town officials a few days before a child was born, in the ladies' cabin, to his young wife. In the last week of November rains swelled the river and the steamer swirled through the falls. On a December night the boat caught fire from wood placed beside the cabin stove. That peril was forgotten when the shores shuddered with an earthquake. Islands vanished, bluffs collapsed, and the vessel groped through a chaos of drowned and ravaged forest. On January 12, 1812, the first steamboat arrived at the levee in New Orleans.

The odd thing is that the story of the *New Orleans* was not fully told for sixty years. In 1871 in Baltimore, John Hazlehurst Boneval

Latrobe read a paper to the members of the Maryland Historical Society. Lawyer, inventor and civic leader, Latrobe had once served on a committee that gave a prize to Edgar Allan Poe for his first published story —"MS. Found in a Bottle"—a tale of a perilous voyage in polar seas. Latrobe's subject in 1871 was "The First Steamboat Voyage on the Western Waters." The writer was eight years old in 1811, but his oldest sister was Mrs. Nicholas Roosevelt, and he had heard the voyage recounted many times in his childhood. Since its publication in 1871 Latrobe's narrative has often been reprinted. It is the Genesis of steamboat history on the Mississippi.

Behind the voyage of the *New Orleans* lay a complex web of influences, enterprise and heartbreak. As a farm boy on the Hudson, Nicholas Roosevelt was excited by anything that moved by wheels. Between chores in the barnyard he built a model boat with paddle wheels turned by an axle cord attached to springs of hickory and whalebone. A few years later in Philadelphia he met a London inventor, Benjamin Henry Latrobe, who was designing a municipal water system. Roosevelt built steam engines for the waterworks, and became acquainted with Latrobe's daughter. Meanwhile a young Pennsylvania artist named Robert Fulton was studying painting in London. While he mixed his paints and sketched still life, his mind wandered. Soon he went to Paris where he built a steamboat that ran successfully on the Seine. The French government, coping with a revolution, was not interested in his patent, but the American ambassador was. Robert Livingston, the Minister to France who had negotiated the Louisiana Purchase, became Fulton's partner. In 1807 they launched the *Clermont* on the Hudson. She ran from New York to Albany and back in sixty-two hours.

In the uncertain providences of history, this invention seemed made for the American frontier. It came at the very hour when the first great tide of migration and commerce was rising in the West. To that vast and roadless country the steamboat was a godsend; for its builders it could be a gold mine. In 1809 Livingston and Fulton sent Nicholas Roosevelt on a survey trip from Pittsburgh to New Orleans. For Lydia Latrobe Roosevelt it was a bridal journey, floating down the rivers in a houseboat in summer weather. But on that honeymoon her husband was gauging currents, studying channels and landings, marking fueling stations. In 1810, back from his survey, Roosevelt opened an office in Pittsburgh and began building the first steamboat west of the mountains.

5 5

Fulton and Livingston had obtained from the officials of Orleans Territory a fourteen-year monopoly for steam navigation on the lower Mississippi.

Already another dream had ended in the West, when a gaunt shabby man died in Kentucky asking to be buried beside the Ohio where he might hear steamboats passing "when men are wise enough to journey those waters in such vessels." John Fitch of Connecticut had gone West in 1780 to locate land claims in Kentucky. Floating down the Ohio he was captured by Indians. When he escaped, two years later, and crossed the mountains to civilization, he had a dream steamboat in his mind. Few men had more ingenuity and perseverance than John Fitch, and none had worse fortune. By 1790 he had built three successful vessels driven by steam-propelled oars, and had secured from Virginia officials exclusive rights to operate steam craft on the Western rivers. Then the bad luck came. His new boat was wrecked in a storm at Philadelphia and he could raise no more money. He took his plans to France and met indifference there. But his designs were studied by Robert Fulton, who appropriated their principle of power transmission. Fitch worked his passage home as a common sailor and went out to his claim in Kentucky. His land was occupied by squatters. In a boardinghouse in Bardstown he built a model steamboat that ran on the town creek. But no one caught his dream of steamboats on the Ohio. Penniless and disheartened—"It was useless for me to work against Wind, Tide & Ignorance. The first two were completely overcome but the last is an overwhelming Flood"—he gulped a glass of poison on a summer night in 1798. He was buried behind the Bardstown jail.

But the steamboats came, as Fitch predicted. A procession of them followed the *New Orleans*—stubby, high-stacked little steamers, churning the waters, fuming and thumping and seething, running aground and blowing to pieces, taking their place in history. They are recorded in the old Wharfage Book at New Orleans, the first of four thousand before the century was past—*Comet, Vesuvius, Enterprise, Aetna, Pike, Dispatch, Buffalo,* and all the rest. In the eight years after 1811, sixty-three steamboats trailed their smoke over the Western rivers. Each one had a story of venture and hazard and a violent end. Each one carried excitement with her and brought the world to lonely places.

The average life of a Mississippi steamboat was five years. The first one's life was shorter. For two years she paddled profitably between

Steamboats at Yankton, South Dakota (Way Collection)

Steamboat to the Rockies. The levee at Fort Benton, Montana, *ca.* 1870 (Audio-Visual Service)

New Orleans and Natchez (she was planned for this trade on the deep broad lower river), earning her cost and something over. On a July night in 1814 the *New Orleans* landed two miles above Baton Rouge and took on wood. At daylight the engineer raised steam, the paddle wheels turned, but the vessel did not move. The river had fallen during the night and her hull was resting on a submerged stump. When she worked free, water poured into the boiler room. There was barely time to run against the bank; the boat was sinking while the passengers scrambled off.

To exploit their river monopoly, Fulton and Livingston launched new boats at Pittsburgh—*Vesuvius, Aetna*, a second *New Orleans*, and *Buffalo*. They had rough fortunes. The *Vesuvius* ran down to New Orleans in the spring of 1814. Bound back upriver for Louisville, she beached herself on a bar below Memphis. All summer and fall she lay there, until high water floated her off in December. Returning to New Orleans she went aground again, for ten weeks this time. The next year she caught fire and burned up. *Aetna* fared somewhat better, running a schedule on the lower river, but in 1815 and 1816 on successive trips to Louisville she broke both her paddle-wheel shafts. The *Buffalo* was built for the upper Ohio; with a draft of but thirty inches it was hoped she could run all summer. A Philadelphia paper described her as "a fine and uncommonly well built vessel. . . . She has two cabins and four staterooms for private families and will conveniently accommodate one hundred persons with beds." But she was snagged by financial troubles. At a sheriff's sale in Louisville she was knocked down for eight hundred dollars.

In these years the only populous parts of the Ohio-Mississippi valley were the segments at either end, from New Orleans to Natchez and from Pittsburgh to Louisville. Beyond frontier Louisville, a stump-studded town of fifteen hundred, lay eleven hundred miles of wilderness-framed river, with a few lonely settlements on the way to Natchez. The Fulton-Livingston firm had provided steamboat service between Natchez and New Orleans, but it had not brought steam navigation to the great valley. The monopoly would soon be contested by other men.

At Brownsville on the Monongahela, fifty miles above Pittsburgh, Daniel French and Henry Miller Shreve launched their first steamer in 1813. They began with a bold name and a small boat; their *Comet*, 25 tons, a cabined skiff with a stern paddle wheel, splashed down to

5 7

New Orleans in the spring of 1814 and was put on the run to Natchez. It was a small threat to Fulton-Livingston and small profit to the owners. After a few trips on the lower river, the *Comet* was sold to a Plantation man who used her engine to work his cotton gin.

In 1814 the Brownsville men did better with their 75-ton *Enterprise*. After a summer trade between Pittsburgh and Louisville, this vessel loaded military stores at Pittsburgh. With a smooth run to New Orleans, Captain Shreve delivered his cargo to General Andrew Jackson who was defending that port from the British. The *Enterprise* then served Jackson as a patrol boat and troop transport on the lower Mississippi. In 1815 she made a 25-day passage to Louisville, and went on to Pittsburgh—the first steamboat to complete the return trip up the rivers. Though she was soon afterward wrecked on the rocks at Shippingport (Louisville), the *Enterprise* had left a record and had defied the monopoly. Her example led other men into the packet business.

The *Zebulon M. Pike*, built at Henderson, Kentucky, made river history, panting up to St. Louis in 1817. In the Mississippi current her low-pressure engine was helped by the crew, pushing against setting poles as on the keelboats. She landed at the foot of Market Street on a hot day in August, and the whole town turned out. For a season this pioneer steamer plied between St. Louis and Louisville; the next year she went into the Red River trade where she was promptly snagged and sunk.

In 1816 came the 400-ton two-decked *Washington*. Designed by Henry M. Shreve and built at Wheeling, this historic vessel established the pattern of all future steamboats on the Western rivers. The *Washington's* timbers were well seasoned—they came from Wheeling's old bastion of Fort Henry—and her lines were well conceived. A former keelboat man, Shreve designed a shallow-keeled hull to ride the river currents and to rub over the shoals. On the floored hull he installed his engines—four boilers and two cylinders—horizontally. Having used his main deck for the engines, he added an upper cabin deck, with a pilot-house on top. Two tall chimneys, cross-braced, completed her silhouette. The *Washington* was the biggest boat yet launched and the first two-decker on the rivers.

From her jack staff flew a banner showing Fame blowing a trumpet, but the *Washington's* first fortunes were hard. Steaming down the river, she stopped just below Marietta and her crew went ashore to cut firewood. On her way again in fine June weather, she went aground on the Virginia (now West Virginia) side. There, with a thunderous blast of steam and rending metal, a boiler exploded. Captain Shreve was blown into the river, along with some of his crew. They were luckier than the maimed and scalded left on deck. Six passengers and three of the crew were killed, twenty more were injured.

Repairs took all summer. Then the *Washington* went smoothly down the rivers, reaching New Orleans in mid-October. Both Fulton and Livingston were dead by 1816, but their heirs had deprived Shreve's boats of cargo and had twice seized the *Enterprise*, which the court released on bail. Now they brought suit against the *Washington* for navigating restricted waters. While lawyers wrangled in the courts, Shreve lined up cargo for his return voyage. The frontier was not impressed by the technicalities of monopoly and patent, and Western sentiment was on Shreve's side. Could the officials at New Orleans grant exclusive rights to the use of the great river, or did the river belong to the people? For two years the question was argued in the courts, but the answer was foreknown, even to the monopolists. Shreve had already broken the blockade. While litigation was going on, the Livingston-Fulton interests sold their vessels to the Natchez Steamboat Company and retired from the river.

Meanwhile the *Washington* steamed up to Louisville in the fall of 1816. Ice kept her at the Falls till March, when she returned to New Orleans. Then came the great run, upstream, breasting the full spring current, testing the boat's strength, stamina and maneuverability. She made a historic trip—four days to Natchez, fifteen days to Memphis, nineteen days to Cairo. Twenty-one days out of New Orleans, Captain Shreve blew a trumpet blast at Shippingport on the edge of Louisville. Steam had come to stay.

Now the river trade was free and the future was bright. Though the next two steamboats came to grief—the *Franklin* was snagged near Ste. Genevieve in a hazardous stretch of the Mississippi and the *Oliver Evans*, four months off the ways, burst a boiler and killed eleven men— the shipyards throbbed with life. By the year 1820 sixty-two steamers had slid into the water. They were little boats on the big rivers, steaming through solitude, occasionally sighting another smoke and blowing a trumpet greeting as they passed. More and bigger vessels were coming, two hundred in the next six years. They carried a growing trade between

5 9

the growing cities, and they pushed up the side rivers, bringing the future to remote places.

In the summer of 1818 the *General Jackson* bustled up the Cumberland with New Orleans cargo for Nashville, to the joy of all its people. For a keelboat that was a formidable trip, five months of toil and trouble; the *Jackson* did it in thirty days. A group of Nashville merchants promptly formed a steamboat company and invested in the new age. By 1824 they had a dozen packets on regular run to Louisville and New Orleans. Nashville cotton, tobacco, pork and lard went down the rivers; groceries, hardware and dry goods returned. With steamboats on the Cumberland, Nashville housewives bought sugar, salt and coffee at one-third the former cost.

In 1821 the chesty little *Osage* inaugurated a new run, up the winding, hill-framed Tennessee. She steamed through a beautiful wild country where history would come—Cerro Gordo, Pittsburg Landing, Shiloh—and pulled up at Waterloo, a town without houses, where the flatboatmen on the Natchez Trace crossed the river on George Colbert's ferry. After unloading some barrels there, the *Osage* thrashed on to Muscle Shoals where a town had been laid out by the Cypress Land Company. A bright venture in the wilderness, Florence was plotted with broad avenues and leafy parks; it was designed by an Italian engineer who named it for his native city on the Arno. After the *Osage* came the sizzling little *Rocket,* then the *Courier* and the *Velocipede.* These pioneer arrivals were good news for northern Alabama farmers with cotton ready for shipment, and bad news for the Creek tribesmen who would soon have a one-way ride to Indian Territory up the Arkansas. Steamboats carried the future to Muscle Shoals. The splash of their paddle wheels set off land speculation in Florence, Eastport and Tuscumbia and brought a rush of settlement that would crowd the Indians out.

The largest river entering the Ohio from the north was the Wabash. It flowed through Indian country; Tecumseh's stronghold had straddled the mouth of Tippecanoe Creek. But its rich bottomlands attracted settlers, whose produce went out in hundreds of flatboats every fall. By 1830 riverside farmers had a new business, selling steamboat fuelwood at their landings. Around the bend came the *Florence,* the *Ploughboy,* the *Josephine,* the *Decatur* and the tall-stacked *Belvedere.* Occasionally on the spring freshet Wabash steamboats pushed up the tributary White River to the new capital of Indianapolis.

Far up the Mississippi went the pioneer *Virginia* in 1823, taking military supplies to Fort Snelling just below the Falls of St. Anthony. It had been a sixty-day trip by keelboat. The *Virginia*, lying up at night, cutting her own fuel on wooded points and islands, rumbling through the rapids and backing off of shoals, made it in twenty days. Within a few years a busy packet trade linked St. Louis to the lead mines at Galena, and steamboats ceased to astonish the Indians on the upper Mississippi.

From the roof-deck of a St. Louis steamer in 1827, Timothy Flint saw a dozen steamboats starting out for as many destinations. They were bound for trading posts up the long Missouri, for Prairie du Chien and the Falls of St. Anthony, for the highest points of the Illinois, for army forts up the Arkansas, for Pittsburgh, Nashville and New Orleans. By then nearly three hundred steamboats had been built on the Western rivers, and their trade extended through the heart of the continent.

Military transport sent the first steamboats up the Arkansas. On spring water in 1820 the *Comet* (No. 2) arrived at Arkansas Post with trade goods and supplies. Two years later the *Eagle* unloaded at Little Rock, and the *Robert Thompson* delivered cargo from Pittsburgh to the garrison at Fort Smith. In 1824 the *Florence*, scratched by branches and dented by floating timber, worked all the way up to Fort Gibson with military stores and 102 recruits. Fort Gibson had seemed beyond the edge of nowhere until the steamboat came.

While flatboats were unloading settlers and loading salt at Shawnee-town, steamboats thumped past on their way to far new places. Said the *Missouri Gazette* in November, 1818: "The new steamboat *Johnson* passed Shawneetown the first of this month bound for New Orleans. She is intended as a regular trader from Kentucky on the Mississippi and the Missouri as far up as the Yellowstone River."

In bright spring weather in 1819 the first steamer crept up the turbulent Missouri. Thirteen days out of St. Louis (six days sailing and seven days aground), the *Independence* arrived at the cheering town of Franklin, the head of the Santa Fé Trail. One of her welcomers was ten-year-old Kit Carson. A few days later she went on up to Chariton, where her arrival touched off another celebration. At a banquet for the steamboat men, an excited editor declared that soon a trip to the Pacific would be more commonplace than a trip to Kentucky or Ohio had been twenty years before.

In these years three centers of steamboat-building had developed on the Ohio—at Pittsburgh, Cincinnati and the Louisville district. Boat timber was plentiful in the Ohio valley, foundries smoked beside the river, and Eastern engineers and mechanics came over the mountains. At Jeffersonville, Indiana, across from Louisville, there arrived from Philadelphia in the summer of 1818 twenty-five ship's carpenters who began building the *United States*. This vessel, 700 tons, was the leviathan of the early trade and the first of hundreds of steamboats to be built at Jeffersonville. At neighboring New Albany another crew of workmen were launching the *Post Boy*, built by Henry M. Shreve for use as a mail carrier between Louisville and New Orleans. An Act of Congress in March 1819 authorized mail service on the rivers.

The *Cincinnati*, built in that city in 1818, got hung up on a bar six miles below Shawneetown. That summer the new double-decked *Vesta* swished past her on a fast voyage to New Orleans. But on her return, the *Vesta* went aground opposite the mouth of the Red River and stayed there till the June rise. After that the *Vesta* made a name for speed on the run between Louisville, Cincinnati and Maysville. She had a rival when the *General Pike* slid into the water at Cincinnati. The first Western steamboat built exclusively for passenger traffic, she had crimson berth curtains, gleaming mirrors and chandeliers, and eight cabin columns painted like cloudy marble. She was a fast boat and her races with the *Vesta* became a part of river lore. At evening in Cincinnati boys raced through the streets crying, "Go ahead *Vesta*, the *Pike* is coming!" Their game outlasted the rival packets.

In 1826 Pittsburgh builders launched a stubby craft with an elegant figurehead and a fancy name. At the prow of the *Lady Adams* was a likeness of "her highness," complete with earrings and necklace. A thousand people crowding the wharf to watch her departure were puzzled to see GENERAL COFFEE boldly lettered on her nameboards; then they saw on the prow the scowling likeness of a frontier soldier. At the last moment patriotism had replaced elegance, and "her highness" gave way to a military figure. Up and down the river the new steamer carried the memory of a hero of the Battle of New Orleans.

Early steamboats took the river as they found it, with only trees, rocks and towheads to steer by. The engineer fed river water into his boilers, which often choked up with sand and silt; on some runs there was a daily stop to clean out the boilers. The Mississippi was bad, but the Missouri was worse. After twelve days on the Missouri, an engineer figured he had removed two hundred tons of mud from his boilers.

Crew and passengers drank water straight from the river, and tried to make a virtue of it. Zadok Cramer observed that the muddy Mississippi became more palatable if its water was allowed to settle overnight. But he added that full-strength Mississippi was good medicine—"having performed cures for [various] diseases, operating on some as a powerful cathartic and as a purifier of the blood. . . . And I have known those distressed with a sudden attack of a violent intermittent fever whose pulse was very quick and skin dry and hot to get relief in a few minutes after drinking freely of this water; two or three tumblers full throwing the person into a fine and free perspiration."

Early steamboating had no vexing regulations. Any man who could get himself hired became a pilot or an engineer. Not until 1852, after a long list of accidents and disasters, did Federal law require examination and licensing of steamboat officers. The first pilots were former keelboat men who navigated by memory, instinct and intuition. Instead of a chart they read the water—its color, its shadows, its swirls and eddies. They knew where the current was strong and where it gave way to slack water. They knew where the channel crossed—there were 390 crossings between Cairo and New Orleans. "The channel runs from bend to bend," said Cumming's *Western Pilot*, "and the sharper the turn of the bend the squarer the crossing at the foot of it." They did not dream of scaled charts or of the parade of daymarks and range lights that were to come.

Behind the marked and posted modern waterway lies the wilderness river that Cramer traced in crude segmented maps with the channel marked by anonymous islands, points, passes, bars and bends. His was the only guidebook until 1820, and it was of little use to steamboat men. Cramer's landmarks were an endless sequence of *Willow islands . . . a long willow bar . . . large willow and sandbar . . . a willow point . . . a willow beach and bar*, which he varied with an occasional glimpse of history or folklore. "Opposite the bluff there used to stand a Spanish fort, now demolished. The commandant had a road cut in a straight line from the mouth of Chickasaw Creek to Wolf River for the purpose of taking exercise on horseback. . . . At the right hand point just below Seary's island is a large scraggy sandbar, to which has been given by some wag the name of GENERAL HULL'S LEFT LEG. It was formerly a dangerous and deceptive enemy; it is now harmless, providing you bear well to the left and keep a good look out." Once in a while Cramer gave a startling picture of lower Mississippi wildlife before the land was tamed. "There [Island No. 88] and lower down are to be seen pelicans, swans, geese and sandhill cranes and ducks, in millions. The sandbars for miles are covered with them, and at night their noise is so great that you can scarcely sleep for them. They sometimes rise from the small lakes adjoining the river in such immense numbers as almost to form a cloud over your head, the sandhill cranes particularly, whose voice you hear when you can no longer see them, their flight being so high." After this excitement *The Navigator* comes back to business. "Island No. 89 is a small wood and willow island lying close to the right shore—channel left side at all times."

Since that writing, 150 years of history and change have given names to the successive features, all of them now marked by diamond dayboards and beacon lights. The names are a grab bag of river memory: names from industry, politics, local characters, folktales and superstition. Below Cairo a pilot steers for Quaker Oats Light, then he picks up Bessie Light, Riddle Point, Bixby Light, Cherokee, Skullbone, and the River Styx. Robinson Crusoe Light is incongruously near the Memphis riverfront. Then comes Vice President Light, Dutch Smith, Reverie, Sunrise Chute, Kangaroo Point and Sunflower Cutoff. Battle Axe is an echo of Chickasaw warfare, and General Pillow Light is for a military hero from Tennessee. But Caving Bank Light is as indiscriminate as Cramer's Willow islands.

Fuel supply was no problem to the early steamboatmen. The rivers were lined with timber, there for the taking. Twice a day crews scrambled ashore to cut firewood, swinging an ax in tangled timber in sun, rain, snow or clouds of mosquitoes. As the steamboat trade increased, a woodyard business developed. Some woodmen were squatters, living on islands or riverbanks and cutting off government timber. Many riverside farmers made a steady income from their wood racks.

NOTIC
to all persons takin wood from
this landin please to leav a ticket
payable to the subscriber, at $1.75
a cord as heretofore.

Amos Sikes

The best fuelwood came from the hardwood forests of the Ohio and upper Mississippi valleys. Avoiding the sycamore and willow shores, a woodman located his yard near stands of maple, oak, beech, ash and chestnut. On the lower Mississippi were miles of cottonwood, which burned like a bonfire and was quickly gone. The lower reaches of the river offered a hot, resinous pine, the engineer's favorite fuel. This was a tantalizing memory to boatmen on the treeless upper Missouri, where they cut up snags and driftwood to feed the furnaces.

Steamboats ate up wood at a hungry rate—even the little 75-tonners burned twenty to forty cords a day—and woodyards became established every few miles on the main rivers. Even so, engineers sometimes ran out of fuel. Coming up the Mississippi on the *Phoenix* in 1826, Prince Bernhard Karl, the young German nobleman from Saxe-Weimar, saw firemen cutting up barrels, spars and floor planks to get to the next woodyard. At the height of the trade, wood-supplying was a big business. One woodyard on the Mississippi had 20,000 cords of fuel, worth $70,000. Enterprising woodmen kept wood scows loaded at their landing. The steamer came in, lashed on a scow and steamed away, and the fuel was loaded in passage—like midstream fueling of diesel towboats a hundred years later. The empty scow was cast adrift, to float back to the woodyard.

After the Civil War coal became a river fuel, but during the early years millions of trees were consumed in the steamboat furnaces. In the frontier West trees were something to get rid of; no one thought it a waste of timber. Whole forests became smoke on the rivers, and towns sprang up in the stumplands of the old wooding stations.

6

~~~~~

Captain Shreve Was There

In *The Western Pilot* in 1830 James Cummings described the Ohio
channel at Hurricane Island and Cave in Rock with one of his chatty
comments: "If Captain Shreve would take out the logs it would be in a
short time the best channel. . . . You pass close by this cut bank of the
bar and square in to the right shore just above the lower end of the
hill to the right, or in to the Widow Sprock's spring, you can see it very
plain when the banks are dry . . . cross in to the left hand bend opposite
to Irish Jimmy's bar."

Since then the Widow Sprock is gone beyond all recollection and
time has taken both Irish Jimmy and his bar, but Captain Shreve remains. He created the permanent design of Western steamboats, he
broke the Fulton-Livingston monopoly, and he freed the rivers from
thousands of obstructions. Henry Miller Shreve was a slight, straight
man, a bare six feet in his black Quaker hat, but he cast a shadow over
15,000 miles of river channels.

All his life was lived beside flowing water. As a boy on the hill-
framed Youghiogheny he watched the boats swarming past—pirogues,
flatboats, arks, and barges, boats with oars, sails and poles, loaded with
barreled cargo, with horses, cattle and poultry, with trading men and
emigrant families—all going West on a one-way journey. Pennsylvania
men had taken flatboats all the way to remote, exotic Louisiana. His own
oldest brother had sailed from Brownsville with a cargo of flour for the
West Indies. He grew up on tales of the river.

When he was twenty-one Henry Shreve built his own sturdy keelboat, thirty-five tons, with a movable mast, a square sail and a long-armed rudder. With a crew of ten French boatmen he cast off on the high water of October, 1807. Soon his men were loading cargo in Pittsburgh. He meant to deliver it in St. Louis where no Pittsburgh goods had ever gone.

Swinging down the Ohio the young captain learned his first lessons about currents, channels, and the timber snags that the French boatmen called *chicots*—teeth. At the cry *Chicot!* the steersman pulled on the long rudder oar and the men sprang up with their prodding poles. In years to come Henry Shreve would operate steam snag boats—"Uncle Sam's teeth-pullers"—on this obstructed channel. The Ohio led at last to the Mississippi where Shreve turned north against the current. It was a headlong river, swirling with rips, troughs and eddies, studded with logs and sunken trees. His men toiled with oars and setting poles; at times they bushwhacked under the shelving bank, pulling at branches on the shore. At night they tied to sycamore trunks, and they toiled on in the first gray light of morning.

Early in December, six weeks out of Brownsville, they pulled up to the sloping riverfront under the streets of St. Louis. This was a foreign-seeming town of gray stone shops and galleried cottages. In the taverns were plaid shirts, *capots*, the clump of boots and the whisper of moccasins, and a buzz of many voices. Through narrow streets passed Creoles, Frenchmen, Spaniards, Negro roustabouts, half-breed boatmen, feathered Indians from the forest and blanket Indians from the plains. Outside the fur shops crouched piles of dusty pelts; the inside dimness was rank with musk and mold. Bearskins and deer hides hung from the rafters, shaggy buffalo robes were stacked to the roof. Bundles of beaver spilled over the long counter. With a boatload of baled peltry, Shreve started back for Pittsburgh.

In the short winter days they drifted past the old Spanish fort at Ste. Genevieve and the village of Cape Girardeau on its bare white bluff. The Mississippi sucked them southward, but with oars and poles the men worked in to the Ohio. Then began the long pull, a thousand miles against the winter current, to Pittsburgh. As spring came they pulled and poled against the cresting river, while the woods turned green.

In Pittsburgh Shreve bundled his peltry onto freight wagons for Philadelphia. For the first time St. Louis furs were going over the mountains. In the long summer days Shreve loaded another cargo for St. Louis.

Two years later he started West with a new destination. That spring his men toiled past St. Louis and on up the Mississippi. Beyond the swirling mouth of the Missouri they found a clear river, flowing past green bluffs and wind-rippled prairies. For miles it was a boatman's idyll, with sail catching the wind and the wild shores passing. Other miles were toil and travail, the men wading on reefs and ledges, inching the boat through the long rapids. They turned into Fever River and tied up in a steep valley pocked with lead mines. Indians came down to see the keelboat, a strange big craft amid the canoes, pirogues and mackinaw boats of the upper river.

The Sac tribesmen looked glumly at Shreve's stock of farming tools and waited for the gurgle of whiskey. They had lead to trade for liquor, but sober Henry Shreve was not in that business; the kegs the Indians pointed to contained only nails. He waited. He shared salt, tea and tobacco with them; he gave them gunpowder and feasted with them when the hunters came in from the prairie. Then the trading began, and Shreve had more lead than his keel could carry. After building a flatboat and trading goods for a mackinaw boat, he had three heavy cargoes. They could never freight that lead up the Ohio, but they could ride the river down to New Orleans.

Twelve days out they were in St. Louis with the first load of lead to come down from Galena. After selling some cargo for fresh provisions, Shreve took his little flotilla on. Below the mouth of the Ohio he was in water he had never seen before—sometimes a vast broad sweeping river; sometimes a maze of islands, towheads and timber-choked channels. Back and forth, twisting and turning between dense green shores, the river serpentined. At night they pulled in under leaning cottonwoods and sycamores. Pigeons and parakeets and little fly-up-the-creeks chorused around them at daylight, while their breakfast smoke turned rosy in the sunrise. They stopped at Natchez, tying up in the raffish lower town and climbing the hill to the serene streets above. They passed the mouths of the Arkansas and the Red rivers; they skirted points and bayous where they saw wrecked boats enmeshed in vines and driftwood. On a river with no bottom (the channel was a hundred feet deep at Baton Rouge) they drifted down to New Orleans.

Here were tall ships from Mobile, Baltimore and Philadelphia and low-roofed arks from the Ohio and the Tennessee. Shreve sold his three craft, loaded his lead onto a brig for Philadelphia and climbed aboard. As a supercargo he traveled down the jungle-lined delta into the Gulf of Mexico; long after land was out of sight the coffee-colored tide turned blue. A month later Shreve sold his lead in Philadelphia. He returned to Brownsville from the East this time, rocking over the mountains in an Allegheny stagecoach.

The spring of 1811 saw the steamboat *New Orleans* building, but Henry Shreve was on his way in a new keelboat, ninety-five tons, taking Pittsburgh hardware to New Orleans. In summer heat and languor he loaded New Orleans cargo, and with a crew of forty men began the long pull up the Mississippi. Some days they plodded on the riverbank, dragging the boat behind them. Again they took a rope ahead in the yawl, made fast to a tree trunk and pulled the craft upstream. They poled in shallow places and bushwhacked through narrow ones. So they crept up the river, past the infrequent towns, and turned into the hill-framed Ohio. At Louisville they saw the river's first steamboat, smoke sifting up from its chimney and paddle wheels idle; the *New Orleans* was waiting for a crest of water to run the falls. The woods were bare, and frost whitened the bottom fields when Shreve tied up in Pittsburgh. A few weeks later came news of an earthquake that had convulsed the Mississippi. Next spring, taking another cargo to New Orleans, Shreve saw the raw new riverbanks and the drowned forests at New Madrid.

Two years later, on the downstream voyage, Shreve passed the steamboat *Vesuvius* marooned on an island near Natchez. New Orleans was a dead city in 1814. The British had cut off its ocean trade, and the new steamboats could not run upstream above Natchez. Shreve said nothing, but on his next trip he would be a steamboat captain. Back at Brownsville his friend Daniel French was building the *Enterprise*, which Shreve would oppose to the Eastern monopoly and the British blockade.

In December, 1814, the *Enterprise* cast off from Pittsburgh, loaded with guns and ammunition for General Andrew Jackson. When he arrived in New Orleans, Shreve faced two kinds of warfare: the court ordered him to surrender his boat for infringement of the monopoly, and General Jackson told him to search for three lost flatboats of military cargo. With government service nullifying the court order, Shreve steamed up the river and found the flatboats loafing along near Natchez. He lashed them alongside the *Enterprise* and returned to New Orleans. Armoring his boat with cotton bales he ran the British batteries with supplies for Fort St. Philip in the delta below New Orleans. When the Battle of New Orleans was won, Shreve loaded cargo for the Ohio. It was spring with all the rivers brimming and the great current booming down. Shreve cut across submerged bottoms and ran through sheltered chutes. With throbbing engines he made the crossings and pushed on. When he tied up in Louisville at the end of May, the first steamboat had ascended the rivers.

That feat made him restless for another one—to bring a steamboat upstream in low water. In his mind was a shallow-draft steamer, a new design, flat-hulled with boilers on the main deck and side wheels each powered by its own engine. Such a vessel could navigate shallow water, maneuvering through crosscurrents and intricate channels. Early in 1816 he began building the *Washington* on the Wheeling riverfront.

The next year, 1817, was a notable time for American transportation. While the National Road was reaching over the mountains from Baltimore to Wheeling and an army of Irish shovelmen began digging the Erie Canal, the *Washington* made history on the rivers. Taking his vessel down to New Orleans, Shreve again encountered the Fulton-Livingston company. This time they offered to buy him off with a half interest in their monopoly. But Shreve wanted a free river, and the public was on his side. While court action hung fire, he loaded cargo for Louisville and steamed north, proving that a shallow-draft, river-designed steamboat could run both up and down the great valley. His next vindication was legal; the suit was dismissed, and, when the *Washington* again arrived at New Orleans, she was saluted by a cannon signal from the rival *Vesuvius*. In 1818 the Fulton-Livingston company gave up its claim of exclusive right to steam navigation. The rivers were free, and in the busy boatyards new vessels were taking shape.

On her trip down the Mississippi early in 1817 the *Washington* met three steamboats in 1300 miles—the *Aetna* with sail catching the wind at the foot of Beech Island, the *Harriet* taking on wood at a muddy landing, and the *Buffalo* aground on Island No. 57. Ten years later, when Captain Shreve was running his big new packets *George Washington* and *President*, more than two hundred steamboats churned the rivers, though the channels were as treacherous and obstructed as when he had made his first keelboat voyages. In the five years after 1822 the loss in snagged boats and cargoes totaled $1,362,500, and in 1827 Henry Miller Shreve became Superintendent of Western River Improvement, under authority of the War Department.

Using Shreve's design for a twin-hulled snag boat, carpenters at New

Albany began building the *Heliopolis*. Meanwhile the new superintendent was already at work; with hand-operated winches on a flatboat he was yanking sawyers and planters out of the steamboat "graveyard" between Cairo and St. Louis. In the spring of 1829 he took the *Heliopolis* down to Plum Point, Tennessee, and began work on a notorious stretch of river.

The *Heliopolis* had a massive M-shaped bow, plated with iron and bristling with derricks and spars. Wedging a snag in those iron jaws, she either wrenched it free or broke it off from the river bottom. Grappling hooks lifted the timber and a clanking windlass dragged it aboard. Power saws cut it into disposable lengths, and rollers passed it through the tunneled vessel and out the stern. Waterlogged roots and stumps sank harmless to the river bottom; salvaged cordwood was fed into the furnaces. A day's work cleared out snags that had imperiled navigation for thirty years.

The snag boat was an ugly craft, half machinery and half living quarters. On the hurricane deck a clerk tallied the removals. At the end of the season Shreve would report to Washington his totals in five digits—"of snags, rigidly speaking"; "of roots logs and stumps"; "of impending trees and trees liable to fall in the rivers." To the snag boat each of those thousands was a shock and a crashing, a clanking of chain and cable, a screaming of saws and a rumble of rollers. Each was a safe passage past a once-menacing ripple or an unseen disaster. During the first five years of snag removal, steamboats multiplied on the river and wrecks diminished. In 1832 not a single boat was lost from snagging. By 1834 boats ran at night through channels that had been dangerous by daylight.

Downriver steamed the *Heliopolis* to another pilot's nightmare, Islands 62 and 63. In these lonely reaches Shreve frightened the herons with the din of heavy labor. With a puffing of steam and a creaking of cables, mats of logs and vines were hauled from towheads, and old rooted sycamores were dragged from the mud. Behind the *Heliopolis* lay a safe clear river channel.

At the Grand Chain of Rocks near the mouth of the Ohio, Shreve went to work on the obstructing reef. Tied to the bank were houseboats and messboats for his crew, with kegs of blasting powder cached on the shore. When the river dropped to low water they drilled, blasted and hauled up the broken reef. With 3000 tons of broken rock they made the first wing dam on the rivers, throwing out a dike from the Illinois shore. A bank of riprap kept the current scouring out its own improved channel.

In these years Shreve traveled up and down the rivers directing his work crews, improving their machinery, planning new projects. Between tours he was back at Louisville, facing a desk piled high with paper work. He could more cheerfully attack a snag-snarled channel than the stack of vouchers, receipts, requisitions and reports for the Corps of Engineers in Washington. To work in channels denied the big *Heliopolis*, he built the compact twin-hulled *Archimedes*. By 1833, after six years of toil in summer's heat and winter's cold, the busy rivers were cleared of obstruction. Then came orders to open the Red River—the biggest task of all.

Explorers up the Red River valley had found the stream impassable. Beyond Natchitoches the river disappeared beneath a solid mat of logs, vines and driftwood. This notorious "Red River Raft," hundreds of years in the making, choked the river for 160 miles. In places it was solid as a bridge; hunters and horsemen crossed it unaware of the stream beneath them. Decaying wood and foliage made a seedbed for weeds, gaudy flowers and willow thickets. Choked by this mass of vegetation, the spring waters spread over a marshy basin twenty miles across. Keelboats and small steamers made circuitous trips up to Fort Towson, following a maze of interlacing lakes and bayous. Some of them, stranded by falling water, waited on sandbars through the long dry season.

In 1832, when Choctaws from Alabama were assigned to lands in Indian Territory, army men took a hard look at the Great Raft. At its upper end the mass of vegetation rose and fell with the river; farther down it was as solid as the earth, locked with its mesh of vines and creepers—there the choked river spread over miles of swampland. Some surveyors doubted that it could ever be cleared. But Shreve got an expedition ready.

At. St. Louis he recruited 160 men and assembled his snag boat *Archimedes*, the government steamers *Java*, *Pearl* and *Souvenir* and a dozen flatboats. They went down the river in the spring, steaming past Natchez and into the Red River through a land of pleasant settlements and rich cotton fields. The town of Natchitoches, older than Philadelphia, was the end of steamboat travel. Beyond the last plantations lay a

7 3

somber gloom and silence. Vines and branches drifted in the slow current. Then the current ceased and there was only a mass of growth and decay wedged in walls of cypress and cottonwood. From rotting logs, alligators stared at the intruding vessels.

Into this spectral place Shreve brought the clank and clatter of machinery, the snort of steam engines, the cries of workmen, the thud of axes and the scream of saws. From skiffs and flatboats men hacked at the edge of the obstruction, pushing freed timbers into the current; a steamboat herded them into the mouth of a bayou. As he advanced into the raft Shreve used severed timbers to wall the riverbanks. With harsh cries herons and pelicans flew out of the thickets. The snorting *Archimedes* pushed into a chaos where uprooted trees lay like a mass of giant jackstraws.

In the summer dusk the swamp silence returned. Candles gleamed on the long tables in the messboats. After supper the men lit their pipes, smoking the mosquitoes away. They slept under mosquito bar. Midnight was black and soft with a barred owl *hoo-hooing* in the swamp.

After two days Shreve had probed five miles into the raft. He wrote to Washington: "I hope to effect more than was believed . . . possible." From a flatboat came the din of the blacksmith's hammer, pounding new points on the pike poles and forging new links for the log chains. Day after day the *Archimedes* pushed into the jungle green. Grappling hooks wrenched up submerged trees and masses of vine-locked timber floated free. By early June sixty miles of channel were opened. Matted timber came down the current and the little *Pearl* and *Souvenir* prodded it into the mouths of bayous. Repeated buffetings made an embankment, and the confined current scoured a channel. The river did its own work when the raft was cleared.

At the end of June low water halted the snag boats; work would have to wait for the fall freshet. Shreve took his battered boats downstream, stopping at Natchitoches where his men celebrated their return from the swamp. Aboard again and bound for the Ohio, they carried an unseen pestilence. They had survived the miasma of the swamps, the perils of snapping cables and broken chains. But four men were dead of cholera when Shreve paid off his crew at Louisville.

There, for a few weeks, Shreve was a family man, getting acquainted with his small daughters between stints of paper work at his desk. At the end of the summer he was back on the Red River, making his camp on Bennett's Bluff and planning the new assault on the raft. That season they made dramatic progress. Whole sections of the barricade broke up when key logs were removed. Already settlement was following his snag boats up the reclaimed river. Soon Bennett's Bluff would become Shreveport, with cotton bursting white on thousands of acres of former swampland.

In the spring of 1838 snag boats broke through the last log jam and the Red River was open. Until then the upper valley had only one settlement, the Caddo Indian Agency. Now packet boats steamed up the river to some of the richest corn and cotton land in the nation. Shreve's undertaking had cost $300,000. He estimated that the opening of the river added fifteen million dollars to the worth of the public domain—a sober figure that would soon be multiplied. A generation later a digit-loving statistician figured the money value of the Red River at $106,813,440.

Other labors waited, and Shreve hurried from one project to the next. With the powerful snag boats *Eradicator* and *Henry M. Shreve*, he cleared the upper Arkansas, letting commerce into a rich and spacious region. On the upper Mississippi he made channels through the Des Moines and the Rock Island rapids. Wherever navigation was impeded, Captain Shreve was there.

St. Louis, with all its river commerce, had no natural harbor. In 1817, when the first steamboat came up the river, a sandbar began forming at the southern end of town; soon another was growing at the northern edge of St. Louis, west of Bloody Island. These bars turned the current eastward; every year the river ate into the Illinois shore and edged away from the landing. In place of a harbor, St. Louis was being given a naked beach of sand.

In 1833, when Shreve was beginning his attack on the Red River, the city of St. Louis hired John Goodfellow to plow up the unwanted sandbar. In midsummer Goodfellow splashed oxen across the shrunken channel, ran a plowshare up and down the island, and waited for high water to wash it away. Instead, the rising Mississippi smoothed over the plowed field and left a fresh layer of silt; the bar had a good growth that season. What had formerly been the main river channel was now a long gray hummock of silt and sand, stretching for two miles along the St. Louis riverfront.

Up and down the riverfront Shreve studied the river bottom and the

7 5

shores, measuring the current at changing stages. He planned dikes from
the Illinois shore and Bloody Island to throw the river back toward
St. Louis. When he requested more help, the War Department sent a
young engineer, Lieutenant Robert E. Lee, to do the job. Lee made a
beginning, with a dike extending downstream from Bloody Island, but
government funds ran out. Eventually the work was done, as Shreve
had planned it, at the expense of the city. Within rugged dikes laid
down upon stone foundations, the confined river swept the harbor clear
and boats steamed safely into the St. Louis levee.

In 1840 hard times troubled the Congress and river improvement was
halted. In 1841 Shreve was released from office. There was more work
to do, but the great tasks had been accomplished. A graying man of
fifty-six, he put his family on a steamboat and traveled as a passenger
from Louisville to St. Louis. On Grand Prairie, outside of St. Louis, he
built a plantation house and called himself a farmer. But he was still a
riverman. Steamboat builders, owners, pilots, retired engineers and captains sat with him on the gallery. The talk was full of rivers and their
subtlety and danger, of a brown current sliding past the islands and a
clear channel leading through. At his death in 1851 Captain Shreve was
buried on Bellefontaine Bluff where the packets passed, white in the
sunlight and glimmering under the stars.

7

Travelers' Tales

WHEN THE MARQUIS DE LAFAYETTE, Marshal of France and former major general in the American Revolution, boarded the steamer *Natchez* at the Natchez Landing in April, 1825, he must have heaved a grateful sigh. Ahead of him stretched a thousand miles of river wilderness. Behind lay an endless round of parades, receptions, illuminations, concerts, collations, balls and banquets. At New Orleans, in the Place d'Armes (now Jackson Square), he had passed through an Arch of Triumph, decorated with statues of Justice and Liberty, to his sumptuous quarters in the Cabildo. He had departed that city in a six-horse carriage, through ranked troops and streets massed with people. When he boarded the *Natchez*, artillery boomed from the levee. At Baton Rouge he was greeted by a salute of twenty-four guns and escorted through the cheering town. After a civic banquet citizens sang from the riverbank while the vessel steamed away. At Natchez a procession in carriages, on horseback and on foot passed along the promenade overlooking the Mississippi, where the youth of the city were assembled for his blessing. At dinner in the Steamboat Hotel thirty toasts were offered to Liberty and all its synonyms and supporters. It was past midnight when the famous visitor waved farewell from the guardrail of his steamer.

General Lafayette, a stout, stalwart, florid man of sixty-eight, was touring America as a guest of the government. He walked with a limp which reporters traced to a wound from the Battle of Brandywine, though it came from a fall in Paris twenty years later. With him on tour were his son George Washington Lafayette, his secretary Colonel V. Lavasseur, his valet Bastien, and a little black-and-white dog that had been given him by a young American admirer. When they left Natchez, no United States dignitaries were aboard. Now the general could write to his family, catch up on his endless correspondence with American editors and officials, play with his dog and watch the wild river shores.

To leave Natchez, northward bound, in 1825, was to leave the civilized world. Between that city and St. Louis stretched the dense Mississippi forests. Down the river came trees, logs, branches, mats of driftwood, tangled flotsam from wrecked boats and barges a thousand miles away. In the pilothouse Captain Davis told his visitor about towheads, river currents and changing channels. As they nosed into a woodyard, he pointed out snags and shoals. Sawyers, floating submerged in the current, and planters, rooted in the river bottom—either could pierce a vessel's timbers and add its wreckage to the stream. While fuel came aboard, the drawling woodman described a recent steamboat explosion that had killed forty travelers. Soon afterward, on the way again, they passed a steamer patching a stove hull while its passengers fought mosquitos on the bank.

It was the end of April now, past the flatboat season, and the great river was a solitude. Day after day the dense green shores crept past. Beyond the forest wall the land lay vast and empty, waiting for the future. Some of that land belonged to General Lafayette; Congress had voted him 11,520 acres of the public domain. At the mouth of the Ohio they loaded fuel from a wood barge, and a new pilot came aboard for the ascent to St. Louis. Another steamboat lay at the landing, the boxy little *Mechanic* that was to take the party up the Cumberland to Nashville. She waited there while the *Natchez* pushed on to St. Louis.

Now the shores lifted into bluffs with villages clinging to them. The names—Cape Girardeau, Lake La Croix, Fort de Chartres—marked it as a French country; this region had been explored and thinly settled by the French from Canada. At Carondelet the habitants told Lafayette that the farms they had cleared were now on sale at the United States Land Office. When the general promised to explain their plight to Federal officials, they brought him presents—a pair of squawking geese, a tame fawn, a collection of fossils and river shells.

Next morning General William Clark and Colonel Thomas Hart Benton came aboard to escort the visitor to St. Louis. Protocol had returned and Lafayette was ready; he throve on adulation. In midstream the *Natchez* was met by the steamer *Plough Boy* with a salute from its signal cannon. All St. Louis was on the levee when they landed.

Next day the *Natchez* swung down to the old French post of Kaskaskia (sixty years later it would be buried by the Mississippi) where Indian traders had come in with their winter peltry. After a hearty frontier reception they were aboard again, sweeping down to Cairo where the *Mechanic* had been waiting.

With fuss and flutter, jolt and joggle, she churned up the Cumberland, past skiffs and flatboats filled with waving people. News traveled mysteriously on the rivers. General Andrew Jackson met the visitor at Nashville. With a clatter of cavalry they passed through a civic arch of welcome to some of the longest speeches of Lafayette's whole tour.

In the bright sunrise of May 7, the *Mechanic* fired its cannon, clanged its bell and headed down the river. The next afternoon she stopped at Shawneetown, to a salute of twenty-four guns that filled the hills with echoes. Through lines of men, women, children, dogs, geese and chickens Lafayette limped to a reception at the Rawlings Tavern. The party returned through the long shadows of afternoon while cannon shook the cottonwoods. Dusk brought an overcast, and a light rain came with darkness. It fell in slanting ropes around the torchlights. Lafayette was behind schedule and Captain Hall kept full speed, his little steamer butting up the dark river.

At midnight the *Mechanic* stopped with a shudder. Out of their quarters poured crew and passengers. Above hissing steam rose a clamor of voices. Captain Hall came into the cabin. The boat, he said, was snagged and sinking. He ordered everyone ashore.

General Lafayette had been sleeping in the ladies' cabin in the after-end. He pulled on some outer clothing while his valet began packing trunks. Lavasseur burst in and hurried the general out. Halfway through the main cabin Lafayette remembered his snuffbox with its enameled portrait of George Washington. Lavasseur ran back to find it. By guttering torchlight, in shadows and confusion, Lafayette limped over the listing deck. Captain Hall had the yawl ready and Lafayette was helped aboard. He was landed on the dripping riverbank, and the yawl went back for survivors clinging to the pilothouse roof and the tilted texas. Through the rainy darkness gleamed the furnace fires. With a hiss and rumble the *Mechanic* went down.

On the brushy riverbank, fires licked through wet wood and grew brighter. A mattress floated ashore, "almost dry on one side." Under a salvaged umbrella General Lafayette lay on the sodden mattress until the gray daybreak. Two hours later smoke showed beyond the river bend and soon the steamer *Paragon* appeared. She was hailed and halted. The yawl brought the castaways alongside and Lafayette was lifted aboard. It was his only embarkation without fanfare.

Behind, on the river bottom, were his papers, his fine carriage and his pet dog, along with the pair of geese, the fawn and the collection of fossils from Carondelet. With all the survivors aboard, the *Paragon* got under weigh at noon. The next night she landed at Louisville. Reporting the wreck and the rescue a few days later, the Shawneetown newspaper softened the facts of river travel by misstating that this was the first accident of its kind on the Ohio.

The rest of Lafayette's trip was triumphant. At Louisville, Lexington and Cincinnati he was fed, followed and feted. In fine weather on the steamer *Herald* with a GEN. LAFAYETTE banner on her guards, he voyaged up the Ohio with festive stops at Maysville, Marietta and the old French town of Gallipolis. He arrived at Wheeling to band music and the clangor of church bells. From there he hurried eastward by stagecoach, past streams of emigrants for the Western country, to lay the cornerstone of the Bunker Hill Monument.

In the 1840's two million people traveled annually on Ohio River steamboats. Flush times had come to the valley. Pittsburgh skies were stained with the smoke of forges and foundries; the streets of Cincinnati milled with hogs, cattle and market wagons; across the river from Louisville's distilleries and tobacco sheds rose the din of shipyards building bigger steamboats to carry the restless trade. Down the river came sidewheelers with scrollwork on the cornices, brass balls on the crossbars between the lofty stacks, gaudy colors on the big paddle boxes. Through the main cabin, which doubled as a dining salon, ran a long table, with iron stoves at each end. Off the cabin opened stateroom doors, each one ornamented with a floral or landscape painting. The packet boats were wonders in the frontier West.

One of the multitude of travelers in 1842 was a young English novelist, just turned thirty, on the first crest of his fame. Charles Dickens was not impressed by the "floating palaces"—except for their threat to life

and limb. In the caustic *American Notes*, which would soon tell the
world about his travels, he reported that "Western steamboats usually
blow up, one or two a week, during the season."

From the Pittsburgh riverbank the packets looked alike—rows of
flimsy staterooms above glaring furnaces and thumping engines. Dickens
inquired for the safest vessel and settled on the *Messenger*. She had
been advertised, he said, to start for Cincinnati every day for two weeks.
Still announcing IMMEDIATE DEPARTURE, she had steam up and
bells clanging when Dickens and his wife went aboard on April 1. They
were soon on the way.

The *Messenger* had forty cabin passengers and twice as many
crowded around the cargo and machinery on the lower deck. Dickens
was pleased to be in the stern, at the far end from the boilers. His outside door opened onto a narrow gallery where he could watch the shores
go by. What he saw was miles of forest solitude, of beetling cliff and
shadowed valley, marked by an occasional Indian mound or a lonely
settler's cabin.

It was three days, barring accident, from Pittsburgh to Cincinnati.
Each day the steamer put in where a woodyard showed in a clearing.
Sometimes she stopped at a cluster of huts that had taken the name—
Glasgow, Liverpool, Syracuse, Manchester, Moscow—of an Old World
port or capital. Once a family of settlers was rowed ashore where a path
led into a thicket. With them went all their possessions—a bag, a chest
and a cane-bottomed chair. On the weedy bank the old woman sat on
the chair, watching the *Messenger* churn away.

Dickens found the steamboat as cheerless as the dark and tangled
shores. Meals were eaten in silence, and after dinner men stood around
the stove, spitting; this, he said, was the only sociability on the voyage.
One of the passengers was a young emigrant with a heavily bandaged
head; his stagecoach had overturned in Pennsylvania. Travel was risky,
Dickens saw, by water or by land. And the American interior seemed
endless. In his cabin, away from the roar of the engines and his glum
companions, he wrote a letter to England. "Think what rivers are in this
country! The Ohio is nine hundred miles long and virtually as broad as
the Thames at Greenwich—very often much wider." Outside, the wild
shores slid past and the boat moved deeper into the New World
solitude.

At Cincinnati, a handsome city which evoked his admiration, he transferred to the mail packet *Pike*, and on the 12-hour run to Louisville he found a congenial traveler. This was a Choctaw chief on his way home from a visit in the East. A cultivated savage, educated in a frontier academy, he had read Cooper and Scott, and, if he had not read *Oliver Twist* and *Pickwick Papers*, he knew the fame of their author. He "sent his card" to Dickens in his stateroom and the two had a warm conversation. The chief had been to Washington on tribal business; it pleased Dickens to hear that the U.S. Congress lacked dignity. With mutual pleasure they exchanged invitations, Dickens saying he must come to England and his friend proposing a buffalo hunt on the Arkansas. At Louisville, sorry to part with this urbane tribesman, Dickens shook his hand and went back to his stateroom to record the encounter.

By the time of Dickens' journey a canal had been built around the Falls of the Ohio—the first improvement on the Western rivers. The "falls" were more properly rapids, a section of rocky, irregular channel where the river fell twenty-three feet in two miles. At low water the falls were impassable even by keelboats; with a normal stage nervy falls-pilots steered through the hurrying chutes. Until the canal was opened steamboats had to wait for high water, and it was a touchy passage then.

There were dramatic memories of the falls, tense passages, accidents and disasters. Had Dickens inquired he would have been told how in the spring of 1807 three tall-masted ships, built at Marietta for ocean commerce, tried to run the rocky gantlet before the summer drought. First in line was the *John Atkinson*. With pilots on the bow and at the wheel she eased into the stream where the current caught her. She bore down the chute on the Indiana side, her bow pitching and her tall masts sawing the sky. Three times she rubbed the rocks and shuddered, but she kept the channel. With cheers from the riverbank she coasted into the lee of Sandy Island and dropped anchor. Behind her came the *Tuscarora* and the *Rufus King*. Barely into the chute the *Tuscarora* smashed against a rock. She recoiled, lost steerageway and was thrown upon a ledge. In the 15-mile current she rolled, battered and breaking, and her masts came down. Behind her the frantic *King* dropped anchor, but the hook did not hold. She was flung against a rock, her bow was broken and her hull stove in amidships. Then the *Atkinson's* anchor cable parted and she went aground on Sandy Island shoal. These disasters and the embargo put an end to ocean shipbuilding on the upper Ohio.

For twenty years, while river traffic grew and carting cargoes around the falls became Louisville's chief business, men talked of a canal. At last in 1825 the Louisville and Portland Canal Company went to work. They dug a mile-long ditch across Louisville's riverfront, past the old landing of Shippingport to Portland, then a separate town, rejoining the river abreast of Sandy Island. Work began in 1825 with gangs of slaves manning shovels and wheelbarrows. In December, 1830, the steamboat *Uncas* locked through to a clangor of bells and a boom of cannon. At tolls of twenty cents per ton for steamboats and four dollars for flatboats, the canal made fortunes for its builders and spurred the river trade. By 1840 fifteen hundred steamboats and hundreds of keels and flatboats passed through the locks each year. Steamboats soon outgrew the original chambers, which were successively enlarged. The canal was taken over by the Federal government in 1872.

Dickens was a strangely uncurious traveler, heedless of the past and bored by the present. Leaving Louisville, on America's great interior highway, he talked to just one passenger, a young man who stooped under the doorways and sat sideways at the table. This was the Kentucky Giant, nearly eight feet tall. He told Dickens his story. At fifteen he had been undersized, then he shot up like a stalk in a canebrake. A mild, slow-speaking, long-faced youth, he now carried a pistol with boyish pride.

The hills flattened out as the Ohio neared the Mississippi, and it was low, bushy land where the rivers merged. Here the novelist used his strongest language. This "breeding place of fever, ague and death" he said was vaunted in Europe as a mine of Golden Hope. A land speculation had pictured Cairo as a future metropolis, and some English investors had grasped at a bubble which burst in their faces. Dickens was one of them; now with a personal grievance he described "the hateful Mississippi pouring its muddy flood past dismal Cairo."

This was the picture he gave in *American Notes*, a picture enlarged, in fiction, two years later. In *Martin Chuzzlewit* he took Martin and his friend Mark Tapley on a steamboat journey "through great solitudes where the trees upon the bank grew thick and close; and floated in the stream; and held up shriveled arms from out the river's depths; and slid down from the margin of the land; half growing, half decaying in the miry water." At last they came to Eden (the counterpart of Cairo) where they found a few wretched settlers in dank, decaying cabins. Like his author, the fictitious Chuzzlewit was an investor in this city of the future, but, shaking with chills and fever, he decided to sell his shares in Eden. There were no takers. "Nobody but corpses to buy 'em," said Mark Tapley ruefully, "and pigs." When a steamer came up the river they were waiting. As paddles churned the muddy water, they tried to forget their brief sojourn in the land of promise.

From Cairo, Dickens traveled up the Mississippi—"an enormous ditch . . . choked and obstructed everywhere by huge logs and whole forest trees." After a week in St. Louis he returned, with a lookout banging a bell to stop the engines when a menacing log appeared. To Dickens it seemed the bell rang all night long, and at each alarm he braced himself for shock. He was glad to leave the Father of Waters, "dragging its slimy length and ugly freight toward New Orleans," for the Ohio. At Louisville he changed to the fine mail boat *Ben Franklin* which brought him to Cincinnati. There he walked across intervening steamboats, past hissing boilers and leaking casks of molasses. With sticky feet he stepped ashore, his river travels ended. The world would soon read about them in the caustic *American Notes* which he could hardly wait to publish.

A more genial and generous Englishman came up the river a few seasons later. Years ago in London I became familiar with the bearded face of Sir Charles Lyell; each morning I passed his portrait in the hallway of King's College where he had been the first professor of geology. I knew that this great scientist had traveled to far places, but I never then thought of him in America. I did not know that he had measured the age of the rivers of my boyhood.

When Sir Charles Lyell reached New Orleans by way of the Gulf in February of 1846, he found a carnival city. Everywhere he looked were masked and costumed processions, troops on horseback, plumed horses and decorated carriages, marching bands filling the streets with music. For Sir Charles this Mardi Gras revelry was a new sight in America. In the hurrying Eastern cities it had seemed the national motto was "Work, work, work," but here the rule was gaiety. Then the gaiety was interrupted. Through a street corner a Negro teamster drove a load of baled cotton toward the river. The carnival procession halted while the wagon passed. To the English visitor here was a sign of the future, when American commerce would overcome the music even of the old Creole capital of Louisiana.

On the riverfront he found a clamor of hoofs, carts, wagon wheels, teamsters' cries, steamboat bells, the chants of roustabouts and stevedores. Tall ships unloaded Swiss muslins, Paris cologne water, umbrellas from Naples, Spanish cutlery, New Bedford sperm candles and Italian silk and marble. From riverboats on the upper levee, files of stevedores rolled bales and barrels. Steamers were loading for Shreveport, Little Rock, Natchez, St. Louis, Nashville, Evansville, Wheeling and Pittsburgh, and for army posts far up the Red River and the Arkansas. With clang of bells and splash of paddle wheels a boat backed into the current. Voices came over the water—

> On de levee by de river side
> I left my gal in New Orleans—

From the rail of the *Rainbow*, the Lyells watched the big sugar plantations pass. Downstream came boats bulging with cotton from the Red River, the Ouachita, the Sunflower and the Yazoo. At a wooding station a store boat was peddling lard, cheese, beef, bacon, flour and whiskey. The woodmen intercepted drifting trees, towing them in and cutting them up for fuel. Trees that had grown in Wisconsin, Missouri, Pennsylvania and Alabama were fed into steamboat furnaces at Baton Rouge.

At Natchez Sir Charles and Lady Lyell boarded the new steamer *Magnolia*, fitted with mahogany and velvet furniture and glass chandeliers. The bill of fare was sumptuous—soup, two kinds of fish, a chain of entrees and desserts. The claret was excellent, and Lyell was puzzled to see his neighbors drinking river water. Being told it was a healthful drink, he tried some, finding it pleasant enough if one closed his eyes. The geologist's sight was dim anyway; he peered closely at the suspended silt, wondering how far those minute particles had come and how far they would go.

From Vicksburg they took the steamer *Andrew Jackson*, paying six dollars for board, lodging and a 400-mile journey. This vessel had a cargo of molasses and drew eight feet of water. To avoid drifting logs in the channel, the captain took a cutoff through the chute inside Island No. 84. As they moved up the forest-framed river, in vastness and solitude, a white flag by day or a bonfire at night signaled them in where a new passenger waited. Between the infrequent stops Sir Charles went down to the lower deck and found immigrants camping there amid machinery, cordwood, livestock and cargo. At night he read American and English periodicals at the cabin table. A steamboat clerk, recognizing his name, asked if he was the author of a work on geology and wondered if he were acquainted with Mr. Macaulay whose article on Addison in the *Edinburgh Review* he had been discussing with a passenger that evening. As though to answer Dickens' diatribe, Lyell observed that because there was so much civilization in the Western states foreigners contrasted them with the highest standards in older countries and so judged them unfairly.

But not all his fellow travelers were scholars. Sir Charles was near-sighted, and to strengthen his vision he carried a pair of short-sight glasses hung from a ribbon around his neck. As he paced the deck, sometimes a passenger seized the glasses, without leave or apology, and bumping Lyell's head out of the way peered through, and then complained that they showed nothing. Meanwhile in the ladies' cabin, women passengers snatched Lady Lyell's embroidery out of her hands and examined it with muttered comments. In his notebook the patient scientist remarked that one who is studying the geology of the Mississippi ought to remember that these people support the noble steamers without which his researches could not be pursued.

At Memphis, a bustling new town with an ancient and venerable name, Lyell examined the bluff, peering through his glass at the successive bands of loam, quartz and clay, and drawing a cross section in his notebook. At New Madrid he studied scars and sinkholes left from the earthquake thirty-five years before. He borrowed a horse and rode over the "sunk lands," dismounting to examine the grass-healed fissures and peering at flakes of slate and coal. In the forlorn settlement, the houseguest of a German settler, he talked with a fellow lodger, "Uncle John" by name, an old river pilot and sailor who had been to France and Italy where Lyell had done his first geological surveys. Uncle John told him that the 1811 site of New Madrid, before the quake, was now the channel of the Mississippi. The river had been heaved out of its former course, and the old Missouri graveyard was now in Kentucky. The channel was still changing; just a few days ago a house had fallen into the stream. In a few years, Lyell reflected, the river would be passing over the cabin that now sheltered him.

After New Madrid the Lyells' destination was New Harmony on the Wabash. The channel ran close to the New Madrid shore, and they waited on the half-built wharf boat to hail a steamer. The first one proved to be bound for St. Louis; the next for the Cumberland. A third was fully loaded and did not come in. By that time night was falling. They spread blankets on the floor and slept, leaving a Negro handyman on watch. Some hours later, while the watchman was sound asleep, Sir Charles woke to the puffing and splashing of a steamboat. Too late to intercept it, he read NIMROD on the passing paddlebox. (Three days later the *Nimrod* was snagged, her boilers pierced, her chimneys toppled, and half her people killed or injured.) Watching her lights diminish up the river, Sir Charles complained to the wharf-boat keeper. He roused his handyman, who was asleep again, and made a bonfire on the bank. Soon came the wink of furnace fires and the surge of paddle buckets. A boat drew alongside, Negro stevedores snatched up the luggage and the clerk led the Lyells to a bright saloon where an orchestra was playing. Already the sunk country seemed far away.

Of all her countless travelers none saw the vastness of the Mississippi more clearly than the close-sighted Lyell. His mind pictured the ancient river forming its vast delta which rose from sea level to 200-feet altitude at Cairo. Farther back he saw the heave and fall of continental land masses, the creeping of ice sheets, the changing river course. He drew cross sections of the valley and made calculations that reached into the depths of time. "The area of the delta being about 13,600 square statute miles," he wrote, "and the quantity of solid matter annually brought down by the river 3,702,758,400 cubic feet, it must have taken 67,000 years for the formation of the whole." For this reverent, kindly, soft-spoken scientist, the Mississippi was one of the wonders of the world.

At New Harmony he discussed geology with David Dale Owen and admired the collection of Wabash rocks and fossils in the museum. Then he went on up the Ohio in the fine new packet *Sultana*. A fellow traveler from Cincinnati talked to him about the pork business and asked abruptly, "How many hogs do you think I killed last season?" Lyell guessed three hundred. "Eighteen thousand," was the answer, "and all of them dispatched in thirty-five days."

At New Albany, across the river from Louisville, Sir Charles visited a Hoosier geologist, Dr. Clapp, who showed him a coral reef in the river-bed. In his study Dr. Clapp had a collection of river corals older than the Alps and the Pyrenees. Studying those stems and pores, the two men saw the tropical ocean that once had washed the Ohio hills.

From Cincinnati the Lyells journeyed up to Pittsburgh on the steam-boat *Clipper*. She made ten miles an hour, steering past big timber rafts

floating down on the spring crest. They saw another steamboat en-
tangled in a raft; bound for Pittsburgh the vessel was now drifting
downstream toward the timber's destination. On a foggy night the
Clipper's bell was silent, being supplanted by a new signal which the
English geologist was one of the first to describe. "In place of the usual
bell," he wrote, "signals are made by a wild and harsh scream, produced
by the escape of steam, as in locomotive engines; a fearful sound in the
night, and which, it is to be hoped, some machinist who has an ear for
music will find means to modulate."

Soon steamboat whistles would become the voice of the river, a voice
well modulated, of varied pitch and mellow resonance, and the hills
would give back their music.

At Pittsburgh the English visitors exchanged the steamboat for a
carriage. In June they sailed from Boston on the Cunard Liner *Britannia*
for Liverpool. A week out, off the coast of Newfoundland, they passed
towering icebergs and steered through fields of drift ice. As the ship
veered and swung, Sir Charles' memory went back to the hazards of the
Mississippi, where the lookout cried and the steersman clawed at the
big wheel while the boat thudded into drifting logs. Perhaps then he
recalled his thought while peering at the silt suspended in a glass of
river water: its minute particles might be added to a towhead in the
river, or they could be carried into the Gulf Stream and so into the
Atlantic; they might easily travel to the banks of Newfoundland. Silt
from the headwaters of the Missouri in the 49th degree of north latitude
might wander for a distance as far as from the pole to the equator, and
return to the same latitude from which it had set out. All the waters
of the earth are one.

At New Orleans on New Year's Day, 1847, a man from Berne, Switzerland, carried a portmanteau and a large sketching pad aboard the
steamer *Amaranth*. Rudolph Friederich Kurz, just past his thirtieth
birthday, was at the beginning of the great adventure of his life. From
a land of steep valleys and walled horizons, he had come to a country as
vast and primordial as the sea. As he looked up the Mississippi he saw
space and sky and forest, and his mind went deeper and deeper, farther
and farther, to the remote wilderness where the streams began. America
was all distance, without boundaries or barriers. The rivers came from

Loading cotton, New Orleans (The Mariners Museum)

Mixed cargo on the *Jas. T. Staples*
(Reproduced from the Collections of the Library of Congress)

far places, flowing through varied and violent climates on their long way to the sea.

For twelve years Rudolph Kurz had been preparing for an artist's field trip on the frontiers, studying languages, science and geography and hardening himself for the wilderness. Ahead of him that New Year's Day were six years of exploration and discovery on the far reaches of the rivers and some close acquaintance with hardship, danger and death.

In a few days the *Amaranth* passed from languorous Louisiana to wintry Illinois—from orange trees and Spanish moss to leafless willow islands and forests deep in snow. It was a cold January. Beyond Memphis passengers hugged the cabin stoves and on the lower deck immigrants huddled against the boiler bulkheads. At Cairo the river was a long gray waste with a ragged ice-clogged channel. Slowly the steamer pushed through drift ice in midstream.

On January 12, in the blackness of night, they stopped at Devil's Hole for firewood. By torchlight the wooding crew lugged cordwood over the ridged and rugged ice. When that job was done the *Amaranth* was frozen in. Roustabouts prodded the ice with pikes and poles; with steam hissing from the exhaust the engineers worked the ponderous rudder. The boat would not budge. After a week pantry stores ran low and the passengers were reduced to two meals a day. While they waited for a thaw, the river fell and the *Amaranth* was stranded. It looked like a long stay.

On a bitter day Kurz went ashore with his sketching pad and pencils. In the snowy forest he found his first American log cabin, but his hands were too numb for drawing. Inside, he thawed out by the yawning chimney mouth and shared a backwoods meal of corn bread, hominy and ham gravy. Then he tramped back to the marooned steamboat.

After a cold and hungry week the river rose. With a crackling din the ice broke up, but only in mid-channel. To cut a path to live waters, the mate sent his crew onto the ice with axes. They chopped an opening for the yawl and dragged it back and forth against the ice crust; after a long day's toil they had a path to mid-river. Hissing and rumbling, her decks and timbers shuddering, the *Amaranth* crept into the channel. She went up to St. Louis with ice pounding her bow and thudding under her paddle wheels.

For Rudolph Kurz it was a bleak introduction to America, but a better season was coming. In April he went on up the Mississippi in the steamer *Providence*. It was fine weather, blue sky arching over the green shores and a west wind smelling of prairie distance. At Rock Island, while the boat toiled through the rapids, Kurz set up a makeshift easel on the gallery and began to sketch old Fort Armstrong. He had just made his first quick outline when his easel collapsed with a thunderous roar. Steam and water gushed up from the main deck. Out of the cabin poured startled passengers, and up the stairways came scalded and blackened immigrants. A German girl and her small brother were carried into the stern cabin where their burns were dressed with oil and poultice of raw potatoes. The engineer had forgotten to check the water level in his boilers. Four victims died that night.

When a rescue vessel came, the shattered *Providence* was towed back to Rock Island where the passengers went ashore. Kurz had one satisfaction; he had not paid for his passage in advance. Next morning a cloud of smoke grew up against the lower forest shore; through his telescope Kurz could read the name *Red Wing* on a steamer's paddle box. Aboard the *Red Wing* he resumed his sketching of Fort Armstrong while that steamer toiled through the upper rapids and steered into the winding Fever River. After a couple of days visiting Indian camps in the Galena hills, he caught the *War Eagle* for a fast run down to St. Louis.

For months Rudolph Kurz traveled the rivers, going ashore at frontier landings and making field trips into wild territory. He had prepared well for his New World tour, reading about Indian life, studying botany, zoology, ornithology. Now he filled his sketchbook with romantic drawings of forest, prairie and riverbank, and of tribal life in camp and on the trail. A voyage south in November brought him to New Orleans in time for the frenzied reception of General Zachary Taylor, fresh from his triumphs in Mexico. Riding Old Whitey at the head of his troops, the general saluted crowds who would not be satisfied until Old Rough and Ready was on his way to the White House.

With some new sketches in his portfolio—Choctaw squaws and hunters selling herbs and game in the New Orleans market, forest and river scenes in Louisiana and Arkansas—Kurz voyaged north on the steamer *Hannibal*, whose pious captain did not travel on Sunday. On Saturday evening he beached his boat at the head of a lifeless island and stayed there till Monday morning. The captain offered three sermons during the Sabbath, but Kurz went ashore to sketch moss-hung live oaks in the river mist. A crashing thunderstorm hurried him back to the boat in midafternoon.

At Cairo, hearing that the upper river was frozen over, the religious captain ignored his contract and put his passengers ashore. After a day's wait they boarded the grimy little Ohio stern-wheeler *Oswego*. On high water, amid floating sheds, wreckage, fences and dead cattle, with river pirates scouring the channel for salvage, they entered the Mississippi. The booming Ohio current held back the Mississippi whose slack water was crusted with ice. The *Oswego* made frequent stops for repair of her machinery and her battered paddle wheel. At Chester she ran aground and her engine gave up. There, after bringing her people a scant sixty miles, the *Oswego* was abandoned. Next day along came the *Boreas* (No. 3) from New Orleans, with a crowd of German immigrants. In the bleak wind they cowered between an iron stove and a flapping wing of canvas. Some giggling German girls promenaded the main cabin, off limits for deck passengers, where they hoped to attract husbands. Bachelor Kurz watched them from a distance. They were quite ready to be married to an American, he noted in his journal, even though they could not converse with one.

Working up the ice-clogged river, the *Boreas* found a distressed vessel, the *Atlantic*, her paddle wheels dead and the ice tightening around her; she had burned up her fuel two days before and her furnaces were cold. The *Boreas* pushed her into live water and gave her some cords of fuelwood. On the day before Christmas, 1847, Kurz stepped ashore in St. Louis. In his first year in America he had seen thousands of miles of river valley.

But his travels were only begun. In the spring of 1848 he went up the Missouri on the steamer *Tamerlane* with veteran Joseph La Barge standing pilot watches. It was an intoxicating trip to Kurz, daily drawing nearer to the wild land of elk, buffalo, antelope, and the roving Indians of the plains. At bustling St. Joe he saw his first bear—chained to a tree in a circle of yapping dogs.

In 1848 St. Joseph was an artist's paradise. Through the muddy streets went mountain men in fringed buckskin, blanketed Indians, immigrants bound for Oregon. Tents, tepees, carts and wagons dotted the riverbank. Over the trampled ground came the clang of anvils, the creak of wagon wheels, the bellowing of cattle and the braying of mules. On the river, mackinaw boats mounded with buffalo hides passed St. Louis steamers with cattle crowding the main deck and a parade of red-wheeled wagons on the roof.

From an Iowa farmer Kurz bought a badger for four dollars. He shared his bedroom with this pet, feeding him meat, bread and apples and enduring the animal's all-night scratching at the walls. After a month he had a whole sheaf of sketches of *Taxidea americana*, and a scarred and splintered room. So he had to shoot the animal, though he kept its pelt for a hunting bag.

Traveling with wagon trains into the great grasslands, visiting Indian camps, joining in hunts and migrations, Kurz roamed the central plains. In 1851 he was back in St. Joe, sketching Indians, trappers and restless men on the way to California gold camps. On a summer day a shout of "Steamboat!" drew him to the river in time to see the *St. Ange*, down from the mountains, splashing to the landing. Kurz looked at her with excitement—the famous little steamer, built by Captain Joseph La Barge, which in 1850 had run from St. Louis to the Yellowstone in twenty-eight days.

Kurz went aboard with romantic anticipation of the far Northwest, but the voyage turned somber. Cholera broke out and soon the vessel was full of dead and dying. As the tainted little steamer puffed upstream, Kurz helped dole out the remedy, cornmeal wetted with whiskey, while Father Van Hocken and Father De Smet, superintendent of Indian missions in the Northwest, consoled the sufferers. At the site of Chief Blackbird's grave on its windy bluff, the *St. Ange* stopped to sun the bedclothing and bury the dead. The next day Father Van Hocken died after two hours of retching illness. He was buried by torchlight under the bare Dakota hills.

When the steamer's clerk succumbed, Kurz inherited that job—waking the roustabouts, superintending the wood cutting, weighing out sugar, coffee, cornmeal and bacon for each day's mess. At Fort Berthold, after they had opened bales of goods from St. Louis, cholera broke out among the Indians. They died violently and quickly. Kurz had made portraits of the victims the day before; now he was blamed for the mysterious deaths. When Indians muttered about retaliation, the artist hid himself in the fort; he passed the time by drawing sketches of the busy courtyard from his narrow window and compiling a Mandan vocabulary with the help of a half-breed trader who was teaching him the language.

In September Kurz went on to Fort Union, the great trading post at the mouth of the Yellowstone. Under high autumn skies he ranged the tawny plains on buffalo hunts. As the Indians grew accustomed to his sketching, his portfolio filled up with studies of life at the fort and in their winter camps. When the snows went off he ranged the country with a tame wolf, named Schungtogetsche, sketching birds in the spring coulees. He left Fort Union in a long-oared keelboat and was back in St. Joseph after a year away.

After a steamboat trip to St. Louis, Kurz said farewell to the West. In New York he sold some paintings and Indian relics and sailed for Le Havre on the steamship *Sam Fox*. He went home penniless and shaking with malaria, but his mind held a panorama five thousand miles long of the great rivers of America.

8

~~~~~~

River Song

AT PITTSBURGH on a summer morning in 1846 a young man with melodies in his mind boarded the daily packet for Cincinnati. His older brother, Dunning Foster, after traveling the rivers as a cotton merchant, had settled in Cincinnati and formed a partnership with Archibald Irwin; in 1846 they had packets loading for Pittsburgh, Louisville, St. Louis, Memphis and New Orleans. That summer Stephen Collins Foster became a bookkeeper for the firm of Irwin & Foster, steamboat agents.

At No. 4 Cassilly's Row, East Front Street above the wharf, the new clerk sat at his desk with the life of the levee outside his window. In his big ledger each page was a packet—*Monongahela, Fairmount, Messenger, Clipper, De Witt Clinton, Oswego, Bolivar, Ohio Belle, Gladiator, Hibernia, Telegraph*. These were individually owned boats brought together into lines and companies providing scheduled service throughout the great valley.

In his neat, round, youthful hand the clerk recorded bills of lading—*100 brls Lime, 5 do Alcohol, 2 do Oil, 10 hhds Sugar, 13 sacks Wool, 7 hhds Bees Wax, 13 brls Potatoes, 25 do Whisky, 20 tons Sundries.* Outside, the merchandise rumbled on the pavement, passengers thronged the wharf boat, and big white packets made a mile-long festival on the riverside.

This was a high tide of inland commerce. In 1846 five hundred steamboats churned the rivers, nearly five thousand vessels passed Cairo between January and December, and ninety new packets were launched from Ohio River shipyards. In every valley town the newspapers carried long columns of RIVER COMMERCE. At the landings teamsters shouted, wagons clattered on the stones, bells and whistles clamored above the work songs of the roustabouts.

All humanity traveled up and down the rivers. Herman Melville, writing his extravaganza *The Confidence Man,* described the various species on the steamboat *Fidèle* en route to New Orleans. "Natives of all sorts, and foreigners; men of business and men of pleasure; parlor men and backwoodsmen; farm-hunters and fame-hunters; heiress-hunters, gold-hunters, buffalo-hunters, bee-hunters, happiness-hunters, truth-hunters, and still keener hunters after all these hunters. Fine ladies in slippers, and moccasined squaws; Northern speculators and Eastern philosophers; English, Irish, German, Scotch, Danes; Santa Fe traders in striped blankets, and Broadway bucks in cravats of cloth of gold; fine-looking Kentucky boatmen, and Japanese-looking Mississippi cotton-planters; Quakers in full drab, and United States soldiers in full regimentals; slaves, black, mulatto, quadroon; modish young Spanish Creoles, and old-fashioned French Jews; Mormons and Papists, Dives and Lazaruses; jesters and mourners, teetotallers and convivialists, deacons and blacklegs; hard-shell Baptists and clay-eaters; grinning Negroes, and Sioux chiefs solemn as high priests. In short, a piebald parliament, an Anarcharsis Gloots congress of all kinds of that multiform pilgrim species, man." In those years every steamboat was a microcosm. Melville portrayed the *Fidèle* as a Mississippi packet and a ship of fools.

Daydreaming at his desk above the riverfront, young Stephen Foster turned to a blank page and inked his feather quill.

> De smoke goes up and de ingine roars
> An de wheels go round and round.

Up from New Orleans came barreled molasses and baled cotton, merchants and planters, army men and Texas ranchers, and the soft-voiced women of the South. With them in the summer of 1847 came somber news: cholera was raging on the lower river. In New Orleans forty-three died in one day in the Charity Hospital, and thousands were fleeing the city. That season Cincinnati steamboat captains sailed shorthanded; they could not fill their crews for the trip to the Gulf. But winter checked the plague, and when January winds swept the Ohio landings there was lure again in a steamboat loading for the land of sugarcane and cotton. Early in 1848 Stephen Foster put words to a lilting tune in his head:

> I come from Alabama
> Wid my banjo on my knee.
> I'm gwan to Louisiana
> My true love for to see

The Ohio wind was chill and tatters of steamboat smoke smudged the pale sky. But the river led to the languid flowering Southland.

> O, Susanna! O, don't you cry for me,
> I've come from Alabama,
> Wid my banjo on my knee.

Outside his window a whistle rose, prolonged and calling. He dipped his quill again.

> I jumped aboard de *Telegraph*
> And trabbled down de ribber—

It was a handsome new steamboat that got into his song. In 1848 the *Telegraph* (No. 1) and the *Telegraph* (No. 2) were launched at Louisville, the venture of some rivermen who saw bright prospects in the Louisville-Cincinnati-Pittsburgh trade. *No. 1* was not successful and was dismantled after two seasons. The other *Telegraph* became famous. One of her early passengers was the twelfth President of the United States, then on his way to office in Washington. It happened to be a bad-luck run for the steamer.

In November, 1848, news of Zachary Taylor's election went by telegraph wire from Philadelphia to Memphis, then by the packet *Gen. Taylor* to Taylor himself at his Cypress Grove plantation near Baton Rouge; the captain carried the news ashore while his passengers cheered from the guardrails. In December the President-elect, a compact, ruddy, friendly man in rumpled clothing, started East by steamboat, stopping to visit Rough and Ready Clubs in the river cities. In mid-February he had a raucous welcome in Cincinnati. He was an established favorite of all the rivermen.

During the campaign the *Western Boatman* had recalled that while river trade had multiplied the old hazards remained. "Two hundred and fifteen boats lost in five years by snagging . . . Is it not perfectly easy to clear out and keep cleared out nine-tenths of the snags?" In the presidential campaign river work had been a political issue. The *Cincinnati Gazette* reminded its readers:

> General Cass holds it unconstitutional to appropriate the money of the
> General Government to improve our rivers and harbors. Remember it

was under Van Buren's administration that the work was stopped and the boats &c sold. If either of these men are elected President *not a snag or a sand bar in any of our rivers will be removed!*

Remember that the Whigs and Gen. Taylor are for improving the Rivers and Harbors, and if Taylor is elected the snags will be removed, the shoal places deepened, and the harbors made safe.

Stephen Foster's brother had served on a committee of "Steamboat Men and Owners for the support of Zachary Taylor and Millard Fillmore." Now they had their man in Cincinnati.

After a street parade and a crushing reception, Old Rough and Ready jumped aboard the *Telegraph* for Pittsburgh. While the wind blew cold down the river he had a quiet day beside the cabin stove, and his mind looked back upon the life he was leaving. Rivers ran through his memory. After a boyhood in frontier Louisville, where keelboats raced through the rapids, he had served at remote army stations—Fort Harrison on the Wabash, Fort Crawford and Fort Snelling on the upper Mississippi, Fort Jesup on the Red River, Fort Smith and Fort Gibson on the Arkansas. Living in these far places, he had never voted nor given a thought to political office. Politics had found him at Cypress Grove with its two thousand acres fronting the Mississippi. Now his old horse Whitey was in the pasture, and, from the gallery of his cottage, steamboats glimmered through the dusk.

The *Telegraph* was a fast boat. For a time she held a record, six and a half hours from Cincinnati to Louisville, and once she beat the *Brilliant* in a two-day race from Cincinnati to Pittsburgh. But this was a slow journey on low water through fields of drift ice. Five miles above Marietta she ran aground. They worked her free, only to jam again in the ice at Captina Island, seven miles below Moundsville. There General Taylor walked ashore, and he tramped nearly to Moundsville in the snow before a bobsled picked him up. He went on East by stagecoach over the icy Cumberland Pike. A February thaw released the *Telegraph* and she steamed back to Cincinnati.

That spring the firm of Irwin & Foster offered a new service, a steamboat passage to Independence, Missouri, where wagon trains were forming for the trek to California. As they trooped aboard at Cincinnati, the goldseekers sang their own version of "Susanna":

> Ho California! That's the land for me
> I'm bound for Sacramento
> With my washbowl on my knee.

With endless variations it became the marching song of the Argonauts. It crossed the plains and the mountains. It rounded Cape Horn in square-riggers and crossed the Isthmus of Panama on muleback. It rang in the streets of San Francisco, on the road to Hangtown and the trail to Grizzly Flats.

Meanwhile travelers had carried Foster's song across the Atlantic. On the sidewalks of Paris people sang

> Oui, j'arrive d'Alabam
> Mon banjo sur les genoux . . .

in the ports of Germany

> Ich kam von Alabama
> Mein banjo auf dem knie . . .

in Barcelona and Cadiz

> Vengo de Alabama
> Banjo en mano, es mi furor . . .

in Genoa, Naples and Palermo

> Son venuto dal Alabama
> Con la mia chitarra all braccio . . .

There were other versions in Greek, Latin, Chinese and Japanese.

That song made a Louisville packet the best-known steamboat in the world. Sailors were singing in *Marseilles* harbor

> J'ai sauté a bord le *Telegraph*
> Et j'ai descendu la fleuve,

and on the docks of Hamburg

> Ich sprang on bord des *Telegraph*
> Und fuhr den Fluss hinab.

Back on the Ohio the *Telegraph* was making records on the Cincinnati-Pittsburgh run. But when the Wheeling suspension bridge arched over the river in 1849 her 80-foot smokestacks could not clear the span at high water. Captain Mason hinged the chimneys and so passed under; his jackknife "Telegraph plan" would be used by other tall-stacked steamers in the years ahead. For the Wheeling bridge dedication the *Telegraph* brought Senator Thomas Hart Benton, but she ran aground and arrived too late for the ceremony. This record-breaker failed her two most noted travelers.

After six years the *Telegraph* (No. 2), no longer profitable, was beached and broken up. But she went on voyaging in Stephen Foster's song. In 1853 in Delhi, the old Mogul capital of India, Bayard Taylor heard a minstrel sing of jumping on the *Telegraph* and heading down the river. The singer knew no English but had picked up the words and music from British Army officers at Madras. In five years a river song had traveled around the world.

9

Voyage to Exile

FROM MUSCLE SHOALS it was three hundred miles to the bluffs of Knoxville, and until a steamboat got there Knoxville was a place in back of beyond. In Chisholm's Tavern travelers told about the steamboat trade on the lower Tennessee—by 1827 a dozen packets were running from Muscle Shoals to Paducah, occasionally making the long loop to Memphis, Natchez and New Orleans—and Knoxville men began to picture a steamboat service above the shoals. To hurry that prediction they made up a purse of money for the first captain to moor his steamer among the flats and keelboats at their landing.

Between the nearest steamboat and that money lay a series of barriers and perils. There were the great shoals, beginning at the mouth of Elk River, where the Tennessee fell 150 feet in 40 rock-strewn miles. Then came an open valley, smooth water for a hundred miles to Guntersville. From there the river led northeastward, through the wild Alabama hills, to the Narrows, a touchy 30-mile passage which contained four perils known to the keelboatmen as the Suck, the Skillet, the Boiling Pot and the Frying Pan; sometimes the whole strait was simply called the Suck. (In 1913 the Hales Bar Dam, the first navigation and power project on the Tennessee, buried the notorious Suck under a reach of deep water.) Then came the great loop of Moccasin Bend and the lift of Lookout Mountain. Here John Ross, a Cherokee chief, kept a store; Ross's Landing was the future site of Chattanooga. It was still a long way, past the mouth of the Hiwassee, up the twisting channel now lost in the TVA's giant chain of lakes, to hill-hemmed Knoxville on its bluff. Frontier

Knoxville had depended on six-horse wagon trade over the Blue Ridge to Richmond and Baltimore. But steamers had followed keelboats on other forbidding rivers, and they would come up this one.

Late in 1827 on a high stage of water a steamboat left Cincinnati to claim the prize money at Knoxville. The *Atlas*, a small side-wheeler with a mighty name, reached Florence at the foot of the shoals in January, 1828. There she took on a pair of pilots and waited for a freshet. The valley's newspapers had followed her progress, with doubt that she would ever reach her destination. In Huntsville, Alabama, an editor compared the rapids to no less a maelstrom than "Symmes Hole," the hypothetical whirlpool from which swirled the global ocean currents. But the *Atlas* fought through Little Muscle Shoals, past Poke-Stalk Island, Resting Island and Jackson Chute (all buried now beneath the wide waters of Wilson Dam). At the mouth of Elk River she tied up at Melton's Bluff to catch her breath, and to blow out her mud drum. The worst was over.

At Triana, where people flocked in from the woods and the cotton fields to see this wonder, the *Atlas* tackled the seething Narrows. At the Suck she tied up, refueled, and put a line ashore. Laboring with capstan and paddle wheels, she warped through a boiling passage. She surged on up to Knoxville, arriving on the 4th of March with a boom of her signal cannon.

Knoxville celebrated all that day, and at evening the steamboatmen were feted with a civic dinner. The thirteen official toasts were not enough; thirty more were drunk to the *Atlas* and all her men. With pleasure all around Captain Conner pocketed the purse of $640.

The first trip was the last trip for the *Atlas*. She ran downstream, traded for a few seasons on the lower river, and one day wrecked herself on the reef below Ditto's Landing. But the *Atlas* had shown the way, and other boats steamed up the river—about one a year in the 1830's—to establish an upper Tennessee trade. The biggest of them was the side-wheeler *Knoxville*, a hundred feet long, which inaugurated a service between Knoxville and Decatur, Georgia, near the head of the great shoals.

Except in seasons of high water the *Knoxville* was confined to one segment of river, between the shoals and the Suck. A canal was built around Muscle Shoals in the 1830's, but it was soon abandoned: its approaches were dry except at high water, which washed them away. When the massive Wilson Dam was completed in 1926, Big Muscle

Shoals became Wilson Lake, with the flinty riverbed buried and forgotten; now the spectacular Wilson Lock, a concrete canyon above the
rocky ribs of Jackson Island, lifts freight barges a hundred feet to the
lake level. But that was a long time away when the *Knoxville* shuttled
between the Suck and the shoals.

On the spring day in 1828 when the *Atlas* stood panting at the Knoxville Landing, one of the wonder-struck watchers was a 14-year-old
named George Washington Harris. His life was changed by her coming.
He built a miniature steamboat and ran it on a Knoxville pond. He
worked on flatboats and keelboats, learning the currents and channels
and seasonal changes of the upper river. At twenty he took command of
the steamer *Knoxville*. He would have later fame, as inventor, politician,
and writer of the racy yarns of "Sut Lovingood"; but in the 1830's he
was the best known steamboatman on the upper Tennessee. His chief
cargo was Indians, for these were the years of Indian Removal, when the
Five Civilized Tribes were taken from their own country to the windswept Territory beyond the Mississippi.

One of the recurrent themes in frontier folklore is the Indian's fear
of the white man's steamboat. On every river, from the Alleghenies to
the Ozarks, from the upper Mississippi to the upper Tennessee, savages
ran like rabbits from the presence of the "fire canoe." Their instinct was
right. Though scores of packets bore Indian names—*Tecumseh, Shaw-
nee, Pontiac, Dacotah, Cherokee, Red Cloud* and all the rest—the
steamboat was their mortal enemy. Wherever the smoking chimneys
came, the tribal fires went out.

Indian removal was always a sorry story, but nowhere was it so
pathetic and inglorious as in the land of the Five Civilized Nations—
the Choctaws, Chickasaws, Creeks, Cherokees and Seminoles. During
the 1830's sixty thousand tribesmen were driven from their lands,
crowded into flatboats or steamers or marched overland in desolate
companies, to the designated Indian Territory on the Arkansas. One-
fourth of them died on the way.

The great removal was ordered by Andrew Jackson and carried out
by army men under orders of President Van Buren. But history is more
responsible than any man. The idea began in the mind of Thomas
Jefferson; at the time of the Louisiana Purchase he proposed an eventual
exchange of Indian lands east of the Mississippi for wild lands in the
West. In the next thirty years army men and territorial governors met
the tribal chiefs at many council fires. In treaty after treaty Indian

country was ceded to the government in exchange for annuities and reservation lands. But the treaties, signed by bribed and conquered chiefs, were never the will of the people. No Indian willingly abandoned his ancestral country.

Of all the tribes those on the Tennessee were the most amenable to civilization. They took up farming and cattle raising; they welcomed missionaries and built their own schools and churches; many of them assumed white men's names. But the people of Georgia coveted the Cherokee farms, the people of Alabama wanted the lands of the Creeks, planters in Mississippi desired the pastures of the Choctaws and the Chickasaws. By bribery and pressure and promise of plenty in the West, one community after another was dispossessed. Some were transported in riverboats; some marched westward to Memphis and were taken in steamboats down the Mississippi and up the Arkansas; many walked all the way, leaving their dead at camping places on the long journey.

The Cherokee story was the saddest of all. This orderly and industrious nation of 16,000 was seeking American citizenship and appealing for statehood. They had earned it. They had developed a written language, a newspaper, and a representative from of government. Some of them, like solid Georgia citizens, owned Negro slaves. But the State of Georgia passed an act annexing Cherokee country along the Tennessee, and it was soon invaded by covetous white men and companies of militia. They drove Cherokee farmers off their land, plundered their houses, set fire to barns and granaries. Under this pressure bewildered Indians assembled on the Tennessee for removal to the West.

The first party consisted of 466 Cherokee, half of them children. They gathered at Ross's Landing—the future Chattanooga—on March 1, 1837. There they found floating "doggeries," flatboats loaded with pastries and whiskey, whose proprietors had come down the river for this last chance to cheat and debauch the tribesmen. A few days later the transport fleet was ready, eleven flatboats onto which the drunken Indians were herded. They huddled in the raw March wind while the boats swung downstream. At night they made camp on the shore, cooking their rations and rolling up in tattered blankets.

Three days' journey took them through the Narrows and down to Guntersville, where young Captain George W. Harris had steam up in the *Knoxville* to tow the flatboats over the clear reach of river to Muscle Shoals. While they were boarding, the *Knoxville* burst a steam pipe and the Indians fled ashore; it took all night to round them up and get them back again. Next morning the eleven flats were roped together and secured to the steamer for the run down to Decatur, Georgia.

With the Suck above and the shoals below, the *Knoxville* was confined to a hundred-mile stretch of river, past Fort Deposit, the old Creek Crossing Place, and the town of Triana. This was all the river that Captain Harris had, but he knew every foot of it. He piloted his own boat.

During the next two years Captain Harris shuttled thousands of Cherokees on this part of their journey—first the voluntary bands and later Indian companies prodded aboard by army bayonets. A short, wiry man dwarfed by the big-spoked pilot wheel, he ran his steamboat but he was not on the army's side. In 1838 when General Winfield Scott was on hand to expedite the removal, there came a clash of authority. Bringing his command aboard with him, as he supposed, the towering general overruled an order to the boatmen. Captain Harris bristled like a gamecock. Looking up at the six-foot, four-inch officer, he said,"I am captain here. My orders are going to be obeyed, and if you in any way attempt to interfere my next order will be to place you on shore." This detail did not get into General Scott's account of his "delicate duty of removing the Cherokee Indians."

In the first company transported to Decatur in the spring of 1837, Dr. C. Lillybridge traveled as attending physician. He went all the way to Oklahoma with the exiles and he kept a daily journal of the journey. No sooner had the *Knoxville* got the flatboats moving than Dr. Lillybridge found an Indian writhing with "whisky colic." The patient insisted he was not drunk; he had drunk "only two half pints of whisky and a few other times with his friends." Soon the doctor would have direr cases.

At Decatur the emigrants were transferred to railroad cars, another bewildering experience, for the trip past Muscle Shoals. At Tuscumbia, after two days in a wet and windy camp, they were put aboard keelboats in tow of the side-wheeler *Newark*. Now they were on the long voyage —down the Tennessee, the Ohio, and the Mississippi—to the Arkansas. The Indians were in two-story keelboats partitioned into rooms of fifty by twenty feet. On the roof were stone hearths for cooking. In March wind and rain the women nursed the fires and tried to keep their kettles boiling.

Each day Dr. Lillybridge made the rounds, treating colds, coughs, pleurisy, measles, diarrhea, fevers, and wounds from accidents and fighting. The Cherokees had lived in space, light and air; now they lived in pestilence. Back in his stateroom, smelling of quinine and camphor, the doctor wrote up his journal: "Henry Clay better than last night, got him a comfortable situation near the chimney of the steamboat and a breakfast of Coffee and Sea Bread, which appeared to afford him much satisfaction considering his case, consumption. Daughter of Young Squirrel sick with headache and fever; gave cathartic . . . James Williams taken very suddenly with inflammation of the spleen. Bled him and applied Blister." The first night below Cairo on the Mississippi the *Newark* struck a snag and damaged a paddle wheel. The thud and splintering and the clamor of midnight voices alarmed the Indians. They crowded onto the roof-decks where Dr. Lillybridge tried to explain the repairs going on in the leaping light of torch baskets. At last a sheet of rain drove the Cherokees back to their fetid quarters.

Down the big river they went, to Montgomery's Point at the mouth of the White River. Taking on a pilot at the woodyard there, they passed through the cutoff into the Arkansas. Snags and sandbars in that river did not permit night navigation; each evening the exiles made camp ashore. It was more wholesome than the floating barracks, but sickness persisted. Wrote the doctor: "Peggy Black Fox sick with influenza. Stand suffers much from his cough which is getting aggravated by change of weather. Found Henry Clay . . . laboring under much inflammation of the chest & difficulty of respiration. Ordered him to the Steamboat where he could be near the fire. Got Sally Rain Crow's [Negro] woman to cup him."

At Little Rock the river became too shallow for the steamer *Newark* and the boats were taken in tow by the *Revenue*. Even this light-draft steamer kept running aground. It was a tedious, toilsome journey— loosing the keelboats, working off bars, poling the keels alongside, lashing them fast, and churning up the river bottom. One evening, at the end of a strenuous day, the *Revenue* ran aground. In backing off, her guard passed over the guard of one of the keelboats, throwing some Indians into the river and all of them into consternation. At last, after four weeks on the way, they reached Fort Smith. Traders welcomed them with whiskey and the Indians were soon drunk. Some were debarked there; others were carried on to Fort Coffee, where the steamboat *Tecumseh* had been grounded for six months, and to Fort Gibson at the forks of the Arkansas. This was the end of the road, and the beginning of exile for the Cherokees.

Multiply this party by a hundred, see the tribes moving by river and land. Thousands followed the Creek and Chickasaw trails to Memphis and Vicksburg, where Mississippi packets moved them down that river and up the Arkansas, the Red River and the Ouachita. Into the steamers *Reindeer*, *Walter Scott*, *Talma*, and *Cleopatra* the Choctaws were crowded, five hundred to eleven hundred in a boatload, and taken to the short grass country. Long lines of Indian women were marched overland, with children beside them and on their backs. In two years ten thousand Choctaws made the weary journey.

The records of this exodus are full of desolation. Some companies, cheated by government contractors with short rations, had to sell their Oklahoma land claims for provisions. *The whole scene since I have been in this country has been nothing but a heartrending one. . . . If I could I would move every Indian tomorrow beyond the reach of the white men who like vultures are watching, ready to pounce upon their prey and strip them of everything they have or expect from the government of the United States.* Some fell off boats in the night and were drowned. *She had been to one of the cooking fires on the deck of the larboard keel and was returning below when her foot slipped & she fell over the stern of the boat . . . and the waters closed over her forever.* Some lost their possessions when the keelboats foundered. *It was a very dark night, the stove keelboat sinking fast, with about 250 Indians on board, causing great confusion and such a time to get them and their baggage on the Steam Boat.* On the way they burned with fever, coughed out their lungs with consumption, erupted with measles, writhed in the agonies of cholera. *At one time I saw stretched around me and within a few feet of each other eight of these afflicted creatures, dead or dying.* The rivers never carried a sadder freight than the Five Civilized Nations.

In their new lands, the surviving Cherokees received annual payments from the government, though the payment was late in 1846. That year Captain Armstrong was returning from New Orleans on the steamer *Cherokee* with the annuity money for payment at Fort Gibson. He had $100,000 in iron-hooped kegs, along with a small box of gold and a larger box of silver dimes that he had put in the clerk's office for safekeeping. Sixty miles above Little Rock the boat burst a boiler, killing twenty people and injuring twenty more. The captain was blown ashore, the mate and clerk were disabled, but the army paymaster escaped injury. His box of dimes went into the air and fell on the *Cherokee*'s bow where it went to pieces; Captain Armstrong, scrambling over the dead and injured, gathered up all but sixty-one dollars' worth. The box of gold landed onshore and broke apart; combing the brush the busy paymaster found all but ninety dollars. The kegs of specie withstood the explosion; they fell through the cabin floor to the deck below, where Armstrong recovered them. Reporting to the Superintendent of Indian Affairs a few days later, he concluded: "I saved the entire funds of the Government with the exception of $151 . . . altogether it was a miraculous escape."

Back on the Tennessee the steamer *Knoxville*, having struggled up past the shoals and the Suck, never returned to the lower river. For seven years she carried a local trade between Decatur and the Narrows, steadily losing money for her river-town owners. One of them proposed to end the loss by running her up to the deep water below Ramsey's Ferry, boring holes in the bottom planks and letting her sink from sight. But the Indian trade saved her. Ironically renamed *Indian Chief* she profitably shuttled between Guntersville and Decatur, towing strings of empty flatboats upstream for new loads of exiles. When the last Cherokee had gone down the river, the old steamer was retired. Her boilers and engines were loaded onto wagons and installed in a Georgia sawmill; her hull became a wharf boat at Chattanooga. But she would be remembered on the hazardous upper river. Years after she was gone, a valley man recalled how she had looked in his boyhood when he first saw her lying at the mouth of Suck Creek—"her great tall chimneys and her white-house-looking cabin, two or three stories high, her paddle boxes away above her decks, and another little house, a pilot-house, stuck above all."

With his steamboat gone, Captain George Washington Harris turned to politics (he became postmaster of Knoxville) and invention, devising a churn worked by a crank handle and a railway switch that led a train from one track to another. But his best creation was the lanky mountaineer whose racy yarns were "Spun by a Nat'ral Born Durned Fool, Warped and Wove for Public Use." For sardonic Sut Lovingood humor and politics mixed into each other "like two pints of bald face in a quart flask on a hard trotting horse." With his frontier tales George W. Harris left a mark on the mind and idiom of another young riverman, Sam Clemens, who would later sign himself Mark Twain.

10

~~~~~~

Horizon North

IN 1823 THE CZAR OF RUSSIA closed the Bering Strait to the shipping of
other nations, and John Quincy Adams, Secretary of State, informed the
Russian minister that the United States would contest the right of
Russia to *any* territorial establishment in North America. President
Monroe then proclaimed the doctrine that the American continents
could no longer be regarded as a field for colonization by European
powers. In the Indiana woods where Pigeon Creek flows toward the
Ohio, a frontier youth recorded his identity in a worn copybook:

> Abraham Lincoln, his hand and pen,
> He will be good but God knows when.

That winter in dense thickets where the Obion River joins the Mississippi Davy Crockett killed 105 bears and was then elected to the
Tennessee legislature.

In that year of events great and small, the first steamboat labored up
the diminishing Mississippi to the Falls of St. Anthony. Aboard the
little stern-wheeler *Virginia* was a romantic Italian "explorer," who
magnified the voyage into "an epoch in the history of transportation . . .
an enterprise of the boldest, of the most extraordinary nature." He went
on to an incredible statement (being unsure of certain English terms)—
"Never before did a steamboat ascend a river twenty-two thousand
miles above its mouth."

In 1823 the upper Mississippi was a wilderness river. For nearly a
thousand miles it flowed past unpeopled forest, bluff and prairie. It was

the country of the Sauks, Winnebagoes, Chippewas and Sioux, with Indian camps on the hills and Indian canoes on the water and occasionally a squatter's hut or a half-breed's shanty on the shore. The most populous place was a tableland above Rock Island where five hundred Sauk families lived on the edge of a big field of corn and pumpkins. Up the river crept an occasional keelboat freighting army stores to four lonely posts—Fort Edwards with its small garrison at Keokuk, Fort Armstrong at Rock Island, Fort Crawford at Prairie du Chien, and the newly planted Fort St. Anthony (soon to become Fort Snelling) at the mouth of the Minnesota River.

All the upper river cities were yet to come. At the site of Hannibal there was only the rustle of wind in the willows, though that fall John Miller would cross the river from Illinois, set up his forge and anvil and begin a clangor there. At present Quincy, John Woods, who in time would become governor of Illinois, was clearing bottomland. On an Iowa hilltop above a creek that fell into the Mississippi was the grave of Julien Dubuque among the shallow pits and slashes of his lead mines. On the Illinois side, a few miles up the Fever River, the dozen huts and cabins of Galena clustered around a crude smelting furnace. Fort Madison was an abandoned post with wolf tracks in the old compound. Near the mouth of the Wisconsin the settlement of Prairie du Chien spread over its bench of land. Except for the spring rendezvous, when hundreds of Indians brought their peltry to the trading station, it was a drowsy place between the dark woods and the shining water.

Past bold bluffs and headlands, past broad Lake Pepin and the pine-dark rivers of Wisconsin, the Mississippi led northward to the Falls of St. Anthony. A few miles below that barrier, on high ground overlooking the Minnesota and Mississippi rivers, rose the walls of Fort Snelling, the farthest army post on the frontier. Its loopholes commanded the great curve of the Mississippi with the trading settlements of Mendota ("Meeting of Waters") and St. Anthony on its shores. From the northern woods the Indians brought packs of peltry to the trading stations. From the Canadian prairies half-breed trappers came with caravans of creaking two-wheeled carts laden with furs, pemmican, and dried buffalo tongues. Up the Mississippi crept an occasional keelboat bringing trade goods and military stores. Now, in the spring of 1823, a steamboat was coming. Aboard her was handsome, dark-eyed Giacomo Constantine Beltrami, a former officer in the Italian Army, on his way to find the true source of the Mississippi.

It was the twenty-first of April when the *Virginia* left St. Louis for the lonely North. Not much larger than a keelboat, she had 118 feet of length and drew five feet of water. Though Giacomo Beltrami rated her at "2000 tons burden," she was registered as 110 tons. On this voyage she was loaded with pork, flour, beans, salt, soap, candles, vinegar and whiskey, in addition to powder and ammunition. A plain little packhorse, she had a boxy cabin and no pilothouse; her pilot worked a tiller at the stern.

The only record of this historic voyage was a travel diary kept by the romantic Beltrami; he made two copies, sending one to a countess in Italy and saving the other for publication. On the *Virginia* he was the guest of Major Taliaferro, Indian agent at Fort Snelling; the two shared a bunk in the cramped cabin. The other cabin passengers were a Sauk chief, Great Eagle, with his two nearly naked children, and a woman missionary whom the cavalier Beltrami put down as "one of those good women who devote themselves to God when they have lost all hope of pleasing men." On deck traveled a Kentucky family with their baggage, cats, dogs, hens and turkeys. Great Eagle was returning to his village near Keokuk after a visit to Governor Clark in St. Louis. The missionary and the Kentuckians were bound for the lead diggings on the Fever River.

Near the site of modern Quincy, while the crew were cutting fuel, Beltrami wandered after a flock of turkeys and got lost in the bottom thickets. When he found his way back to the river, the *Virginia* was gone. He set out to overtake her, scrambling through brush and timber. He was scratched, breathless, and beginning to feel desperate when he saw the steamer stranded on a bar. They sent a canoe for his rescue. As Beltrami climbed aboard the steamboat, Great Eagle and his children plunged into the river and swam ashore; the chief was disgusted with the pilot who had spurned advice about the river channel. The *Virginia* worked free and arrived at Fort Edwards the next day. Great Eagle was already there. He came aboard to claim his musket, his bow and arrows, and a uniform that had been given him by Governor Clark.

In the long Des Moines rapids the steamboat lost headway. After swinging against a ledge, she dropped back to slack water where the crew lightened cargo. On the next try they made the passage and pushed on past a Sauk camp on the eastern riverbank. Nine miles farther they passed the ruins of Fort Madison, abandoned ten years before.

Spring moved north with the little steamboat. Each day, under a fair blue sky, the meadows, groves and forests wore a richer green. Willows twinkled on the islands. When the hills opened, there stretched a vast wild prairie, washed by wind and sunlight. Beltrami, easily stirred by nature, exulted in that wilderness. "Never had I seen nature more beautiful, more majestic, than in this vast domain of silence and solitude."

At Fort Armstrong, on a height at the foot of Rock Island, the *Virginia* was saluted with four cannonades, and the Indians fired a ragged musket volley from their camp. The Sauk chiefs were puzzled by Beltrami since he was neither French, English, Spanish nor American. He told them he was from the moon. After an arduous ascent of the Rock Island rapids, with one glancing blow from a ledge of rock, the captain gave his exhausted men a rest, and Beltrami went exploring. In the bottoms he killed a rattlesnake, saving its skin for a trophy.

At the mouth of the Fever River the Kentucky family debarked and went prospecting for lead. The woman missionary went ashore to proselyte the Wisconsin Indians. Though the lead rush would not begin for three more years, there was a scattering of miners in the Galena valley. In the lead district on the western sides there was no settlement, only the lonely grave of Julien Dubuque in a lead casket on a hilltop. To see the mines here, Beltrami bribed the Indians with whiskey; they showed him lead outcrop which they melted down and carried across the river to white traders. Here the Italian made one of his more pointed observations; "The mines are so valuable and the Americans so enterprising that I much question whether the Indians will long retain possession of them." Dubuque would soon become a white man's town.

After 536 labored miles the *Virginia* reached Prairie du Chien, just above the mouth of the Wisconsin. Beltrami, impressed by the fierce mien of the Winnebagoes, refused to shake hands with their chief, who wore a string of American scalps, ears and noses around his neck. Above this point the river widened so that Beltrami speculated on underground channels that might carry a large part of the Mississippi to the sea. That night the sky was livid, and next day they steamed past miles of forest and prairie fire. Flames leaped from the hilltops and sparks

rained on the river; it reminded Beltrami of Vesuvius erupting. In that
leaping light they traveled all night, and ran aground at daybreak.

They were in Sioux country now. At a wooding stop a buffalo-robed
chief, blowing his nose with his fingers, came aboard to speak to Major
Taliaferro and to admire the hissing engine. To Beltrami the lofty shores
recalled the Rhine, between Bingen and Koblenz. On the wide waters
of Lake Pepin the *Virginia* rolled in a sudden squall. "Lake Pepin,"
wrote Beltrami in an abrupt incongruity, "is the headquarters for rattle-
snakes." At its upper end was a Sioux village whose headmen came to
greet Major Taliaferro and to ask for a handout. Beltrami wanted the
warriors' bows and arrows, promising to show them to his people on the
moon, but he had to part with some tobacco and gunpowder to get
those trophies. "Red men," he noted "give nothing for nothing, any
more than white ones."

Past the mouth of the St. Croix steamed the *Virginia*, past Little
Crow's village, and into the Minnesota River where she tied up at the
landing under the ramparts of Fort Snelling. They were three weeks out
of St. Louis, and Beltrami recorded the arrival in heroic terms. "I know
not what impression the first sight of the Phoenician vessels might
make on the inhabitants of the coast of Greece; or the Triremi of the
Romans on the wild natives of Iberia, Gaul or Britain; but I am sure it
could not be stronger than that which I saw on the countenances of
those savages at the arrival of our steam-boat."

For two months Beltrami enjoyed the hospitality of Fort Snelling and
of nearby Indian camps where he collected curios for museums in Italy.
Then he attached himself to an expedition under Major Stephen H.
Long which was assigned to survey the Minnesota-Canada boundary.
Somewhere near the border Beltrami left the Long party and struck out
with three Chippewa hunters through the wilderness, seeking the source
of the Mississippi. After exchanging bullets with a party of Sioux, his
Indian guides deserted and Beltrami was left alone in the swamps of the
Red Lake River. ("I bore all however with great philosophy.") Toiling
on toward Red Lake, scratched and torn and bitten, he met a party of
Indians and persuaded one of them to join his search for the springs of
the Mississippi.

Eighteen years earlier young Lieutenant Zebulon Pike had looked for
the true source, getting as far as big Leech Lake where his journey
ended. It was winter, the swamps were frozen, and he could not de-

113

termine which way the waters ran. In the summer of 1820 the Cass expedition had followed the dwindling stream to a sky-blue lake (they exchanged its ten-syllable Chippewa name for "Cass Lake") rimmed in cedar forest. The Indian guides said that the Mississippi had its source in Elk Lake, a small and shallow pond amid swamp forests to the west. General Cass took their word for it and headed his expedition back to Detroit.

Now an Italian wanderer, lured halfway around the world by the Mississippi, was taking up the quest. In his bark canoe, pushing through rice fields and tamarack swamps, he came to a heart-shaped lake a mile across in a circle of hills which he designated "the highest land of North America." Water bubbled mysteriously in the middle of the lake, and he conceived it to filtrate through the banks in two directions. Northward flowed the Bloody River, as he called it—the Red River of the North. Southward flowed the stripling Mississippi. THESE SOURCES, he exclaimed in his diary, ARE THE ACTUAL SOURCES OF THE MISSISSIPPI! (It would be a decade yet before Henry Rowe Schoolcraft with more scientific procedure would find the lake that he called Itasca.) Beltrami named his odd discovery Lake Julia for a past romance—he said the lady was no longer living. He made no map to locate it; in fact he had not even a sextant, and he excused that lack by saying that sextants were usually erroneous. But he had his great moment at Lake Julia, and he felt himself in immortal company. "The shades of Marco Polo, of Columbus, of Americus Vespucius, of the Cabots, of Verazani, of the Zenos, and various others appeared present and joyfully assisting at this high and solemn ceremony, and congratulating themselves on one of their countrymen having, by new and successful researches, brought back to the recollection of the world the inestimable services which they had themselves conferred on it by their own peculiar discoveries."

Through the northern wilderness, where his name now marks a Minnesota county, Beltrami groped back to Fort Snelling. There was no steamboat waiting there. The *Virginia*, after two trips up the long river, had been snagged and sunk in the Mississippi below St. Louis, on a run from Louisville. Beltrami went down to St. Louis in a keelboat with some army men. Beside his baggage he brought the Indian canoe that had carried him to Lake Julia. At St. Louis he took passage for New Orleans on the steamer *Dolphin*. His canoe was carelessly stowed on the cargo guard, and when the *Dolphin* ran aground just eight miles below St. Louis that keepsake was shattered. In his cabin Beltrami wrote a Latin epitaph to the craft that had taken him to his discovery.

At New Orleans Beltrami proposed a new journey "to Mexico and perhaps to countries still farther distant." There the Mississippi chronicle ends. It is a vainglorious account, full of references to Roman, Greek and Hebrew history and to the largeness of his accomplishment. But he was, in fact, the first man to travel the whole length of the Mississippi, and his mind rose to the greatness of the river. "Judge now whether another such river can be found on the globe . . . which combine so many wonders with such great utility, which surveys more than one hundred steamboats gliding over its waters, with an infinite number of other vessels freighted with the productions and manufacture of both worlds, and to which futurity promises such brilliant destinies. Judge whether the Mississippi be not the first river in the world!"

Galena is a Latin word meaning lead sulfide, the lustrous mineral which is the principal ore of lead. The existence of lead in the northwest corner of Illinois was long known to the Indians, but they had no use for it except in trade with the white men. For a hundred years soldiers and trappers on the upper Mississippi took lead from this district to mold their bullets. But a lead rush waited for the steamboat trade. In 1823 when the *Virginia* paddled up the Fever River (it was by right the *Febre* River, named by Frenchmen for the wild bean vines that softened the rocky slopes), the first real smelter in Galena began smoking in the hills. Twenty years later Galena produced four-fifths of the nation's lead, a city clung to the gulch of Fever River, and a fleet of packets shuttled between Galena and St. Louis.

The lead rush began in 1826. Soon Galena, jammed in its rocky hills, was the most boisterous and polyglot place in the West, a steep and staggered town with houses "like a flock of sheep going down to water." Brush, Prospect and High streets clung to the ledges above the wharf-lined river where steamers disgorged restless lines of immigrants. Men with picks and shovels scattered over the hills, and ore wagons rocked in from Hardscrabble, New Diggings and Scales Mound. The smelters smoked night and day. Lead wagons creaked down Franklin Street with drivers leaning on the brake poles. From the roof of granaries wheat poured into chutes that emptied at the river's edge. In the peak years of the 1840's Galena sent more than five hundred steam-boat cargoes—lead, grain, hides, beef, leather—down the river to St. Louis. It all began with the battered little *Virginia* in 1823.

In the spring of 1823 the keelboat *Colonel Bumford* labored up the Mississippi, bound for Galena. Taking his turn at the setting poles was rangy 15-year-old Smith Harris from Ohio. The *Bumford* had run from Cincinnati to Cairo in a few pleasant days; from Cairo to Galena took weeks of poling, warping and hauling. On the way north they were passed by the *Virginia*, puffing woodsmoke and threshing up the river. Young Smith Harris never forgot that. In the years ahead he became the leading steamboatman on the upper Mississippi.

At Galena there were 150 white people in the town and several hundred Indians camped on the hillsides. Smith Harris roamed the rough country with his father, looking for lead. When his father took up a farm in Jo Daviess County, the rest of the family came on from Ohio. The boys worked in the fields and drove into town with farm crops. On Sundays they went prospecting, digging under boulders and into gopher holes. One autumn afternoon in 1824, Smith Harris and his brother Scribe found an old weed-grown shaft in West Galena. They crawled in and hacked at the crumbling rock. It was a lucky strike. From that pocket they took nearly forty thousand pounds of lead, and their West Diggings Mine eventually produced four million pounds.

But mining was a sedentary business and the Harris boys were restless. In 1829 they went on the river, Smith Harris as a cub pilot and Scribe as a cub engineer. The Black Hawk War halted steamboat traffic for a year, but in 1832 it resumed with a rush. At St. Louis crowds of immigrants waited for passage to the lead mines, and the Galena ware-houses bulged with cargo for St. Louis, Louisville and Cincinnati.

For this clamorous trade the brothers built a steamboat of their own. While Smith Harris added a cabin to a keelboat at Galena, his brother went to Ohio to get machinery. On the Cincinnati levee he salvaged an old steamboat engine. He brought it up to the mouth of the Fever River and soon the Harris brothers had the first steamboat ever constructed north of Alton. Into their *Jo Daviess*, 90 feet long and 15 feet across, went a flywheel made of Galena lead. Her first run was up the Mississippi and the Wisconsin rivers, through country where Black Hawk's men had made their futile stand, carrying troops and military stores to Fort Winnebago on the site of present Portage, Wisconsin. All summer the little steamer served that run, rubbing over shoals and through the island chutes and clanging her bell at the fort landing. In the fall young Captain Harris took a load of lead down the Mississippi, swirling through the rapids on high water. At St. Louis he sold both boat and cargo; he had a bigger steamboat in his mind. In 1836 he brought the *Frontier* up the Mississippi and into the virgin waters of Rock River, abreast of the upper rapids. So delighted were settlers to see a steamboat at their door that they gave Captain Harris a waterfront lot in each townsite on Rock River. That was acceptable, but Smith Harris had the greatest satisfaction in the voyage itself. He liked to be first.

A year later the Harris brothers brought their brand-new *Smelter*, decorated with evergreens, up from Cincinnati. Despite snags, shoals, rocks and rapids, they made a record five-day run from Cincinnati to Dubuque. Quickly the *Smelter* became known on the upper river. With immigrants on the drafty main deck, and merchants, army officers and tourists in her staterooms, she ran all the way to Minnesota.

Year by year the upper Mississippi trade was growing. The far-ranging George Catlin had painted hundreds of scenes of Indian life and wilderness landscape above Galena; for travelers he outlined a "fashionable tour" up the river to the Falls of St. Anthony, returning to Prairie du Chien and crossing Wisconsin to Green Bay where a lake steamer journeyed eastward by way of the Straits of Mackinac, Detroit and Niagara. The tour attracted visitors from New York, Boston, Philadelphia and London, while the empty lands of the upper Mississippi drew immigrants from half the countries of Europe. In August of 1837 a startled word went up the river. On the *Dubuque*, under Captain Smoker, bound from St. Louis to Galena, a boiler exploded off Muscatine Bar, blowing freight into the water and killing twenty-two persons. It was the first disaster on the upper river. But tourists and immigrants still crowded the steamers, and cargo lined the landings. The upper valley hardly felt the panic of 1837.

Always seeking more speed and more power, Smith Harris brought the *War Eagle* up the river in 1845. She hustled between St. Louis and Galena in forty-eight hours a trip, but after three years the Harrises sold her and bought the *Senator*, a still faster boat. They built a second *War Eagle* in Cincinnati in 1854 and made her famous on the upper river. For sixteen years she carried the trade—tourists, sportsmen, merchants, miners, ministers, immigrants and harvest hands; cattle, horses, mules, hogs and sheep; geese, ducks, hens and turkeys; sawmills, gristmills, flour mills; plows, reapers, mowers, threshers; stoves, fire engines, pipe organs; cranberries, apples, potatoes. Once, landing a hundred barrels of flour at Winona, Captain Harris ordered his agents to sell it—or start a bakery. When she burned at La Crosse in 1870, the *War Eagle* left a storied name. Her legend began when she was spanking new, leading the great excursion up the river to St. Paul.

On February 22, 1854, groups of workmen laid the last span of railroad on the riverbank at Rock Island, and the Atlantic coast was linked to the Mississippi by rail. To celebrate the event a grand excursion was announced, by train and steamboat from Chicago to the Falls of St. Anthony. The Minnesota Packet Company, in which Captain Smith Harris had become a partner, was to furnish steamboats for the party. On the afternoon of June 5, 1854, two long trains decked in flags and bunting pulled into the new station at Rock Island. A busy port, with nineteen hundred steamboat arrivals every year, Rock Island was now a railroad town as well. From the trains, twelve hundred excursionists streamed aboard a fleet of steamboats. A gathering of eminence, the guests included President Millard Fillmore, the governors of Illinois and Missouri, the mayor of Chicago, statesmen, generals, scientists. Among a score of newspaper editors were Charles A. Dana of the *New York Tribune*, Epes Sargent of the *Boston Transcript*, and Thurlow Weed of the Albany *Evening Journal*. Writers included historian George Bancroft and Catharine M. Sedgwick, novelist.

That evening they banqueted aboard the steamboats and watched a display of fireworks from Fort Armstrong. At ten o'clock, to a chorus of bells, whistles and band music, the excursion fleet steamed up the dark river. At the head of the parade went the new *War Eagle* with Captain Smith Harris at the wheel. Then came the G. W. *Sparhawk*, *Lady Franklin*, *Galena*, *Jenny Lind*, *Black Hawk* and *Golden Era*. On the main deck were cows to provide fresh milk during the voyage, tubs of iced oysters, lobsters and clams, and crates of uneasy chickens and turkeys destined for the long cabin tables.

A midnight thunderstorm outdid the show of fireworks. Rivers of lightning ran through the sky. In a white instant the hills, the water and the tall-stacked packets were caught out of blackness. A ripple ran over the water, thunder crashed and rumbled, a rush of wind and rain drove the travelers into their cabins.

Next morning under a washed blue sky, Captain Harris led the parade up Fever River. With whistles blaring they tied up at the Galena Landing. Ashore, the visitors admired the colonnaded market house and straggled up Hill Street to the Old Fort on its rocky perch. They scattered over the high broken country pitted with lead mines and assembled around wagonloads of food and drink. Westward the hills unrolled to the Mississippi, and beyond lay the long horizons of Iowa and the future. The editors from New York and Boston, the scholars from Yale and Harvard, had long thoughts with their picnic dinner. After a lecture in Galena, Ralph Waldo Emerson had written to Thomas Carlyle in London: "There is prairie behind prairie, forest beyond forest, sites of nations, no nations." Now a haze of steamboat smoke hung over the river. The nations were coming.

On up the river went the fleet, stopping at settlements and clearings. While boatmen loaded wood, the visitors saw landmarks touched with the brief history of the Western country. They climbed in the sunset to the high lookout where Dubuque lay buried. They called at Battle Island where General Atkinson's troops had pushed Black Hawk's people into the river. They saw Indian trails webbing into La Crosse— three shanties in a woodlot; they climbed Trempealeau Mountain and watched the shadows fall on Chimney Rock. On the wide waters of Lake Pepin four boats were lashed together and the travelers danced to music from the *War Eagle's* orchestra.

Up the last reach of river they steamed in line. Passing sawmills, cattle yards and warehouses they came to St. Paul, a hilltop town with a row of steamboats already at the landing. Bands played, whistles blew, and five thousand people waved a greeting.

In the twenty-one years since the arrival of the *Virginia*, civilization had come to the northern wilderness. Now, in 1854, a British visitor, Lawrence Oliphant, was making notes for an article in *Blackwood's Magazine*. "St. Paul," he wrote, "is the best specimen to be found in the States, of a town still in its infancy with a great destiny before it. In 1847 a few trading huts, rejoicing under the sobriquet of Pig's Eye, marked the site of the present city. . . . There are now four daily, four weekly, and two tri-weekly papers, which is pretty well for a Far West town only five years old, and more than Manchester and Liverpool put together. There are four or five hotels, and at least half a dozen handsome churches, with tall spires pointing heavenward, and sundry meet-

1 1 9

inghouses, and a population of seven or eight thousand to go with them, and good streets with sidewalks, and lofty brick warehouses, and stores, and shops, as well supplied as any in the Union; and 'an academy of the highest grade for young ladies'; and wharves at which upwards of three hundred steamers arrive annually, bringing new settlers to this favored land and carrying away its produce."

In the streets of St. Paul the visitors jostled Indians, trappers, woodsmen and traders. They bought souvenir moccasins, painted tomahawks and Indian pipes. In carts and carriages they clattered out to the Falls of St. Anthony. They drove through the wooded glen past Minnehaha Falls and up the zigzag road to the stone walls of Fort Snelling. That evening they were received in the House Chamber of the white-columned capitol, and at midnight, aboard their vessels, they steamed down the starlit river. Three days later they were at Rock Island, boarding trains for the East and ready to tell the world about the future of the upper Mississippi valley.

The first railroads, running east and west, brought increased traffic to the upper river. In 1860 more than a thousand steamboats arrived at St. Paul before ice locked the river in December. Merchants, lawyers, land speculators and lumbermen mingled on the landings. German, Scandinavian, Irish and Welsh immigrants flocked to farms and town-sites on the Mississippi and the Minnesota. Eastern travelers, lured by Catlin's paintings and the Mississippi panoramas, made the fashionable tour.

One observant visitor came for his health. In the long June days of 1861 Henry David Thoreau, traveling with young Horace Mann, Jr., came up the Mississippi and at Mendota transferred to a smaller steamer for a trip up the winding Minnesota. He described that stream coiling through its fertile lands. "There was not a straight reach a mile in length as far as we went—generally you could not see a quarter of a mile of water & the boat was steadily turning this way or that. . . . Two or three times you could have thrown a stone across the neck of the isthmus while it was from one to three miles around it. . . . In making a short turn we repeatedly and designedly ran square into the steep and soft bank, taking a cart-load of earth, this being more effectual than the rudder to fetch us about again, so that we were obliged to run and break down at least 50 trees which overhung the water, when we did

Grand salon of the *Grand Republic* (Way Collection)

"The last of those old side-wheelers," wrote William Alexander Percy, "was the *Belle of the Bends,* which as a small boy I could never see steaming majestically through the sunset to the landing without a fine choky feeling" (Reproduced from the Collections of the Library of Congress)

not cut them off, repeatedly losing part of our outworks, though the most exposed had been taken in. I could pluck almost any plant on the bank from the boat. Very frequently we got aground and then drew ourselves along with a windlass & cable fastened to a tree, or we swung round in the current, and completely blocked up & blockaded the river, one end of the boat resting on each shore. . . . It was one consolation to know that in such a case we were all the while damming the river and so raising it." It was a strenuous navigation, but steamboats got through.

In 1856 young Grant Marsh, who would be a noted steamboatman on the Missouri, spent the winter at St. Louis as watchman on the *A. B. Chambers.* The river was lined with steamboats so that he could walk for twenty blocks, from Belcher's sugar refinery to the old Almond Street Landing, without stepping ashore. That same year the first railroad bridge crossed the river between Rock Island and Davenport—five spans on timbered piers at the foot of the rapids. The first train rumbled over in April, 1856. Two weeks later the packet *Effie Afton,* caught in swirling water, smashed into the central bridge pier. The jolt overturned the galley stove and the boat caught fire. While she lay there burning, her flames spread to the wooden bridge. Here was the new rivalry: a steamboat wrecked by the railroad, and the bridge destroyed by the packet. In the lawsuit that followed, with the railroad represented by Abraham Lincoln, the steamboatmen were beaten. Though the railroads were instructed not to impede navigation, there was no restraint of bridge-building. To the old river hazards of current, snags, bars, rocks and rapids, a new threat came wherever a railroad reached the riverbank. By 1886 fifteen railroads had bridged the upper Mississippi.

One of those bridges ended the career of stormy Captain Smith Harris. In 1856 for the Galena and Minnesota Packet Company he brought out the *Grey Eagle,* the finest and fastest boat on the upper river. In the fall of 1858, carrying the first Atlantic cable message, she beat the *Itasca* to St. Paul. She made records on every reach of the river until a spring evening in 1861 when she was surging downstream past Rock Island. A thousand times Captain Harris had made that run; he knew the rocks, the shoals, the ripples and eddies. But a new combination of wind and current caught his tall steamer, throwing her square amidships against the bridge pier. That was the end of the *Grey Eagle.* Years later a veteran pilot, Captain William Kelley, recalled her—"long, lean and graceful as a greyhound . . . the sweetest thing in the way of a steamboat that a man ever looked at."

Smith Harris had an emblem, as proud as himself. On every boat under his command he carried a gilded rooster perched on the jack staff, ready to crow in victory. After years of rivalry with the Galena and Minnesota Packet Company, he and his brother were persuaded to join that combination. But Captain Harris kept his emblem; in 1856 he moved it to his splendid new *Grey Eagle*. Near Hastings, Minnesota, the boat swung in a back current and rammed the bank. The jack staff snapped off and with it went the captain's "chicken cock." He recovered the emblem and set it on its perch again. Five years later the *Grey Eagle* slammed into the Rock Island railroad bridge and went to the bottom. Washed ashore in the wreckage was a battered rooster. Retiring from the river, Captain Harris returned to the dwindling town of Galena and watched the dwindling river trade, while the old chicken cock roosted in his barn. Years later it was dusted off, regilded, and placed over the entrance to Grant Park in Galena.

11

~~~~~

The Way to Future City

AT MILE 976 on the Ohio River, five miles from the Mississippi, pilots steer by a beacon flashing green at intervals of two seconds. It is the Future City Light on the empty riverbank just above Cairo. Future City was plotted in a swamp 120 years ago. Near it were Metropolis, Golconda and America, all founded in expectations which never materialized. Wrote Audubon in 1820, "We floated only about two miles and landed at America—to sell some more articles: people very sickly, a miserable place altogether." There was a chain of great names on the river—Memphis, Napoleon, New Madrid, London, Rome, Carthage, Warsaw, Moscow, Cairo. But the most alluring was Future City. For fifty years immigrants thronged the river landing, but they were not seeking the Old World capitals. Wherever they went, at whatever place they came ashore, they looked for Future City.

On a steamship from New York to New Orleans in 1855 Frederick Law Olmsted found a hundred Irish immigrants camped on the cargo deck. When the ship put in to Mobile, a hundred Negro slaves were marched aboard; they settled down on deck beside the Irish. Some of the slaves were to be sold at New Orleans; some were moving to Texas with their masters: the foredeck was filled with wagons, horses, mules and cattle. There were fiddlers among them, and for a few sunny days along the Gulf shore they were untouched by the future. They danced and sang in the sunset, and the Irish joined in, jigging to the Negro music and looking over the water for the land of opportunity.

New Orleans was a polyglot city where any immigrant could hear his own tongue in the babel. In the restless marketplace Olmsted found Indians, Spaniards, Frenchmen, Englishmen, Irishmen, Germans, Italians, Africans and "other breeds of mankind." In this rich mixture were Negroes of many grades—Sacrata, Griffe, Marabon, Mulatto, Quarteron, Metif, Sang-mele, Meamelouc, Quadroon. Some of them spoke French, English, Spanish and an Indian dialect; in the newspaper Olmsted found an advertisement offering for sale a Mulatto girl who had five languages. At the door of the cathedral he saw glittering coaches and ragged beggars; inside, kneeling in dimness and organ music, were white, black, brown and yellow women. On the Cabildo he met an Irish policeman with a Dublin brogue and a cabdriver who replied, "Oui, yer 'oner," and picked up the reins. They passed the levee mounded with bales of cotton and casks of sugar, with bags, barrels, crates and boxes, and saw an astonishing line of steamboats in the golden morning mist.

Penniless immigrants found work in New Orleans where labor bosses put them to work with Negro slaves. Irish wheelbarrowmen commonly hauled mortar for Negro masons. One morning in Canal Street Olmsted saw one Negro carrying mortar and another taunting him: "Hello, Lije! You is turned Irishman, is you?" On the levee were hundreds of Irish and German cartmen, draymen, coachmen and porters. Many would go North on the steamboats after a season in New Orleans.

Countless immigrants found their first jobs on the river. In the 1850's more than half of the steamboat deck crews were German and Irish. These "rousters," forty or more to a packet, turned out night and day to the mate's call. For twenty dollars a month they carried wood; unloaded horses, cattle, wagons, plows, bales and barrels; manned pumps and capstans; handled mooring lines and landing stages. They lived like cattle on the lower deck and ate leftovers—broken bread and meat along with boiled potatoes—from the cabin table. "Grub pile!" the steward cried, and they swarmed around the tubs and kettles. Putting his portion on a shingle, a man went off alone to eat it. The Irish and Germans fought each other, though once on the *Tishomingo* a German rouster tried to save an Irishman who slipped off the guard; together they went under the huge paddle wheel. Rousters lived close to boiler heat and steamboat hazards. They were burned by bursting steam pipes, crushed by falling cargo, drowned in the river. It was a young man's job, full of violence and change, of coming and going. After a few years they settled ashore in some growing city where they had wrestled cargo on the riverfront.

Sometimes at meal hours the roustabouts passed their own leftovers to immigrant families making a deck passage up the river. Watching them file aboard, Olmsted thought how the great valley was enriched by that migration. "Yonder is a steamboat load of bone and muscle—worth at slave evaluation two hundred and odd thousand dollars. Wisconsin or Iowa will get it, $200,000 worth, to saying nothing of the thalers and silver groschen in their strong chests—all for nothing." He saw them bringing the future to the upper valley. In a decade how many roads and bridges, how many shops, churches and schoolhouses would they have built. How many cargoes of wheat, corn, lead, timber, hides and leather would they send down the rivers. And what commerce they would create in the upper valleys. "How much cloth and fish would they want from Massachusetts, iron from Pennsylvania, hemp from Russia, tea from China, coffee from Brazil, silk from France, sugar from Louisiana, notions from Connecticut, machines from New Jersey, and intelligence from everywhere?" He saw the restless future traveling with the immigrants in the crowded main deck.

The guidebooks advised immigrants to the Mississippi valley to arrive in late fall or winter, after frost had checked the malarial fever. In January the boats at New Orleans were thronged with deck passengers. Cabin fare was a cent a mile, with a bed and three good meals a day. But deck passage cost a fraction of that. Down there, close to the hiss of boilers and the bang of furnace doors, immigrants could travel from New Orleans to Louisville, 1300 miles, for four dollars. Even that fare was reduced for a man who would work with the wood gang. "Woodpile! Woodpile! Let's see the wooders!" cried the mate—often at midnight—and the woodmen got up stiffly from the bare floor. By the light of fire baskets, a plank was thrown out to the riverbank. It pitched upward into darkness, and the wood gang scrambled up to the long dim ranks of cordwood in a clearing. Four, five or six logs were piled on a man's shoulders. He staggered across the swaying plank, threw the load into the furnace room, and went back for more. Where the bank was too steep and high to bridge, the wood gang threw logs down on the muddy riverside and wrestled them from there. After an hour of lugging mud-smeared logs, the bunkers were full, the paddles were turning, and the wood gang dried themselves by the boilers' heat. It was a strenuous way to save a few dollars but the immigrants were will-ing. One traveler told of German peasant women who gladly traded their labor for a cheap passage. A dozen of them, he said, could clear out a woodyard in a short time.

Down at the waterline swarmed the immigrant life—men, women and children amid bags and bales of cargo. They squatted on their little deck space, against barrels, boxes or a hay pile, near cattle and horses. They slept on bales, in wagon beds, on the woodpile or the bare deck. At a long sheet-iron stove they cooked their meal and porridge. From their baggage they doled out bologna sausage, dried herring, water crackers, cheese and whiskey. The main deck was open, like a roofed cattle pen. Immigrants crowded the guards in fine weather and huddled by the boilers when the river fog blew in. For fresh air and exercise, deck passengers could walk the guards—at their own risk. With the shaking of the engines and the jolting impact from logs in the channel, the unrailed guards made a hazardous promenade. On one packet an immigrant drowned when he was butted into the river by his ox, and another went into the river while dipping up a pail of water for his horse. Steamboat captains rarely stopped to rescue deck passengers.

While cabin passengers traveled in comfort and relative safety, deck passengers were never far from danger and the risk of death. Living close to the boilers and the waterline, they were the first victims of explosion and collision. When the *Helen McGregor* blew up near Memphis in 1830, the forty fatalities were all "on deck." In the ex-plosion of the *Majestic* in 1835, sixty German immigrants were killed. When the *Moselle* and the *Oronoko* exploded in the same week in April, 1838, more than two hundred Irish and German immigrants were lost. Forty deck passengers died in the wreck of the *Talisman* in 1848. When the *John Adams* was snagged in the Mississippi in 1851, eighty-two immigrants drowned. In the collision of the *Ben Coursin* and the *Key City* near La Crosse in 1857, a dozen immigrants were crushed. So careless were the records of deck passengers that no one knew the precise number of disaster victims.

The first attempted reform came in 1852. The Steamboat Act of that year called for escape stairways from the main deck to the upper levels, for bunks in the main deck, and for sufficient floor space for each pas-senger in a sheltered and ventilated common room. A boat's quota of deck passengers was specified, though the limit applied only to people traveling more than five hundred miles. These were reasonable provisions, but there was no machinery for their enforcement. Bunks and stairways could be required in new steamboat construction, but old boats still plied the rivers and the hazardous overcrowding went on.

The reform, such as it was, came late. The high tide of immigration by river was passing in the middle 1850's, when railroads reached from Atlantic seaports to the Mississippi. After that, deck passage was less crowded and more humane—at least humane enough that a boat would be stopped for a man overboard.

After the Civil War a Mississippi traveler told a story that could not have happened a generation before. "We left Memphis on a summer evening," he recalled, "and among the deck passengers I noticed a couple, man and wife, who gazed around as if they had never seen a steamboat before. They had an old coffee-sack with some clothing in it, but no other baggage. They moved about in a timid way, and both seemed very much afraid of the water.

"The boat had not gone five miles down the river, and the large number of passengers had not yet settled down, when there was an unearthly shriek, followed by the cry of 'Man overboard!' The boat was stopped and her wheels backed, and after two or three minutes it was learned that one of the couple I have mentioned—the husband—had fallen overboard. The woman 'took on' in the wildest manner, crying and moaning and wringing her hands, and when asked how it happened she replied:

" 'He just dun fell over—fell over—fell over!'

"By that time it was useless to think of lowering a boat. There was a swift current running, and as the man had not cried out there could be no doubt of his being drowned. Everyone pitied the woman, of course, and when somebody took off his hat and dropped a five-dollar bill into it, it was a 'go' all around. A hundred dollars was raised for her in fifteen minutes, and she went ashore at the first landing made by the boot, lugging the bag of clothes with her. I went down as far as Hernando, Mississippi, and stopped off there for two days, taking a second steamer down on the third night from the above occurrence. When I went down to the levee I saw a couple with an old sack between 'em who reminded me of the pair on the boat, and I also saw them come aboard. The resemblance astonished me, but it had to go for a coincidence.

"The steamer pulled out about 10 o'clock and had not been under way half an hour when there was a loud shriek, followed by the cry

'Man overboard!' It was a repetition of what I have related before, except that some of the passengers had gone to bed, and the shake purse didn't count up over $40. The hat was passed to me, but I declined to chip. The 'recent and grief-stricken widow' left the boat at the first landing and I went to bed with the curious feeling that coincidences were mighty thick on the Mississippi River. I left the boat at Helena, made a three days' stay, and was ready to take another boat on the down trip when I ran across the self-same couple at the levee, waiting for the same boat. After some minutes spent in solemn reflection I walked up to them and said to the man:

" 'Come now, this is a square deal and I give nothing away. I've seen you drowned twice, and I've seen this 'widow' go ashore with a breaking heart the same number of times. Tell me how you play it and I'll give you a five.'

" 'Let's see the money.'

"I handed it over and he stowed it away in his pocket and then replied:

" 'I've got on a rubber life-preserver under my clothes, as you see, and I generally make shore within a couple of miles. Stranger, don't give it away. We are poor but honest people.'

"I solemnly agreed that I wouldn't, but I think they rather mistrusted me, for they waited over to catch a boat next night."

In 1850 that appeal to charity would have gone unheeded. At the cry "Man overboard!" the mate would have a calming answer: "It's nothing but an Irishman." When chancy Huck Finn needed a story of his life to tell the Grangerford family, he invented a history of calamities ending in a deck passage on the river. He told how "pap and me and all the family was living in a little farm down at the bottom of Arkansas, and my sister Mary Ann run off and got married and never was heard of no more, and Bill went to hunt them and he weren't heard of no more, and Tom and Mort died, and then there warn't nobody but just me and pap left, and he was just trimmed down to nothing, on account of his troubles; so when he died I took what was left, because the farm didn't belong to us, and started up the river, deck passage, and fell overboard."

In the fall of 1832 John Wyeth of Cambridge, Massachusetts, walked the levee of St. Louis looking for a job. Though just eighteen, he had been to far places. After a year at sea, shipping out of Boston, he had joined his cousin's party bound for Oregon. In the spring of 1832 they went down the Ohio in the steamer *Freedom* and up to Independence, Missouri, in the *Otter*. From that jumping-off place they trekked overland. Four days' march beyond the ridge of the Rocky Mountains some of them turned back, reaching Independence at the end of summer. By canoe and skiff John Wyeth got to St. Louis, with one six-cent piece in his pocket. Ragged and dirty he asked for work and begged food from the steamboat cooks. After six days he got a job as fireman on the steamer *Constitution*, bound for New Orleans.

The *Constitution* made a smooth run down to Natchez, where she stopped overnight, allowing her passengers a visit ashore. A few hours after she left Natchez, cholera broke out. It went like fire through the steamer. "I saw men perishing every minute about me," wrote young Wyeth, "and thrown into the river like so many dead hogs." Eighty died before the steamer reached New Orleans. There Wyeth found everything closed—shops, taverns, schools, churches, even the gambling halls—and an epidemic sweeping the city. He joined a gang of grave-diggers, working for two dollars a day. At first they dug separate graves but the dead arrived too fast. In the damp New Orleans earth they carved a long trench and laid the bodies in—"filling up the vacant spaces with children." Said young John Wyeth, "It was an awful business."

So the somber epidemic of the 1830's began in America. It had come from central India, where travelers carried it by way of Teheran to Moscow. In the spring of 1831 it took thousands of lives in Warsaw; that fall it ravaged Hamburg. A trading ship brought it to Glasgow in October and from there it crossed the sea to America. In the spring of 1832 a British ship docked in Montreal with a list of 145 immigrants; forty-two had died of cholera during the passage. That same season it arrived in New Orleans. Before the year was over, cholera erupted in all the river cities between New Orleans and Pittsburgh and St. Louis.

After smoldering through the winter months, the plague flared up again. In 1833 three miles of shipping lay berthed at New Orleans—a mile of ocean vessels, a mile of solidly ranked steamboats, and a mile of huddled flatboats. That spring the New Orleans death lists numbered more than a thousand a week. Every vessel in the harbor was contaminated, and when the packets hurried away from the stricken city pestilence went with them.

On the 16th of May, 1833, Sol Smith, journeyman dramatist and actor, left New Orleans for Cincinnati on the steamer *Ohio*. On the evening of the second day, passengers lay on the cabin floor, gasping, writhing and dying of cholera, while men played "brag" and faro at card tables in the saloon. In the game of faro a Negro slave named Fred was staked and lost. At the next table a man fell from his chair and died, the cards still clenched in his hands. Another fell to the floor and was carried senseless to his cabin. Sol Smith helped to put him in a warm bath, which seemed to relieve him. The man looked up and asked, "What is your opinion, Mr. Smith? Will I get over this?"

Smith encouraged him. "You are already much better."

"I am glad to hear you say so," he said, and was seized by a final spasm.

While Smith helped the steamboat clerk measure out doses of calomel, opium and powdered rhubarb, the boat staggered and shook. It was not an explosion but a broken flywheel, hurled through the cabin and the hurricane decks. Most of the passengers transferred to another vessel but the Smith family stayed on the *Ohio*, plodding up the river with one wheel. It was slow progress but there was no more dying. The disease had gone ahead with the impatient travelers.

Like the dangers from explosion and collision, the toll of cholera was greatest on the main deck. Disease came aboard with the immigrants, and in their congested quarters, without proper food or sanitation, it consumed them; at night roustabouts wrapped them in blankets and dropped them in the river. Cabin passengers buoyed themselves with brandy flip and counted the days till the end of their journey. But at the northern river landings cholera was there before them.

In frontier Chicago Indians knew of the plague and sought the immunity of ardent spirits. A Potawatomi chief at the agency identified himself as a good man, a very good man, and a loyal friend of the Americans. Could he then have a dose of whiskey to protect him from the sickness? The agent replied that whiskey was a bad drink, for bad men only; good men never asked for it. Quickly the chief said, "Me damn rascal." When cholera reached the upper Mississippi a doctor at La Crosse said it was brought on by eating green apples and drinking milk and whiskey. Other supposed causes were exposure to the midday sun or to the midnight air. One prescription for its cure was a little nutmeg or essence of peppermint in a spoon of brandy. Another promised cure was offered by the makers of Wright's Indian Vegetable Pills. In Cincinnati where the eminent Daniel Drake had an enlightened germ theory of the disease, housewives barred their windows with mosquito netting to keep the germs out.

By 1835 the first epidemic had burned out, though cholera lurked along the rivers for decades. A second outbreak came in 1848 when the disease again flared up in New Orleans and again was spread through the upper valleys. One pestilential packet, carrying cholera like smoke, was the *General Lane*, named for a political leader in Indiana. Lane himself went to St. Louis on business, found an epidemic there and immediately returned to Indiana. Arriving home at night he went into convulsions and was dead at daybreak.

In 1849 it was said that every steamboat on the rivers was infected. This was a peak year of immigrant arrival, four thousand Europeans a week landing in New Orleans. With that stream of humanity, pestilence came to every landing in the great valley. In St. Louis an acrid pall hung over the city while coal, tar and sulfur were burned at street corners to purify the air. Schoolhouses were turned into hospitals and the gravediggers worked night and day in the new Bellefontaine Cemetery. Meanwhile the dead and dying arrived at the levee—thirty cases on the *Amaranth*; another thirty cases on the *St. Paul*; scores of infected immigrants on the *Sultana*; four hundred English Mormons on the *Iowa*, a third of them ill and dying. As summer wore on, the big packets poured more pestilence into the smoke-hung city.

During these years the rivers were routes of contagion and no valley escaped. Up the Arkansas, after months of low water, came the steamer *Reindeer*, with welcome provisions—and with cholera. On an upper Mississippi packet cholera burst out almost as suddenly as a boiler, killing all aboard except the mate and twelve roustabouts. To Nashville on the Cumberland, to Florence on the Tennessee, to Terre Haute on the Wabash, Pekin on the Illinois and St. Joe on the Missouri, cholera came with commerce.

But despite privation, disease and death the immigrant tide flowed on. Dickens told of Irish deck passengers, alternately singing hymns and firing pistols on the steamer *Messenger*; they remembered poverty and hunger and hoped for something better in America. In the winter of

1 3 1

1854 fourteen boats were ice-locked at Cairo, with two thousand German and Irish homeseekers on their exposed main decks. Some died of cold and sickness; the rest found a future in the broad central valleys. Up the upper Mississippi, the Wisconsin and the Minnesota went Germans, Swiss, Irish, Scots, Welsh and Scandinavians. They brought their songs—Irish jigs, Welsh lullabies and old hymns from Sweden and Norway—but with the Homestead Act of 1862 they learned a new song in a new language: "Uncle Sam is rich enough to give us all a farm." By that time immigrant Europeans made up more than half the population of Pittsburgh, Cincinnati, Louisville and St. Louis, and multitudes had found their way to Future City.

12

"Cotton Pile!"

On a bright December morning in 1853 a young man from Connecticut, Frederick Law Olmsted, wandered over the clamorous New Orleans levee looking for a steamboat bound for the Red River. From the market to the foot of Bienville Street, the river was lined with foreign shipping. Four, five, six deep, the barques, brigs and rigged steamships made a forest of masts and spars; voices in Spanish, French, English and German came through the creaking of cargo gear and the rumble of wagon wheels. At Bienville Street began a line of coasting vessels, rakish feluccas and schooners, up from Mexico, Texas, Cuba and Jamaica, with black and bronzed men on their decks and bright rags fluttering aloft. Then came the abrupt white wall of riverboats, head-on to the levee, with tall paired chimneys smoking. Over their landing aprons moved files of stevedores, black and busy as ants. Out of sight down the riverbank stretched the steamboats. From them came a clangor of bells, a hissing of steam and over their gangways came boxes, barrels, sacks and bales. Tiered blocks of cotton bales grew on the levee amidst a rattle of hoofs and wheels, the cries of mates and teamsters and the coonjine chanting of the stevedores. Two-thirds of America's cotton cleared through the port of New Orleans. On the levee it was transferred from riverboats to ocean vessels bound for Liverpool, Le Havre, Hamburg, Genoa, Göteborg, Copenhagen.

Out in the river an arriving steamer blew three sharp blasts and the captain stood at the break of the hurricane deck, looking for a slot. On the levee men shouted in French, Italian, Mexican, Choctaw, Cherokee;

but everyone understood the shout "Cotton Pile!" when the big packet nosed in with ten tiers of cotton on her guards.

Fred Olmsted was looking for the St. Charles and the Swamp Fox, both advertised to leave that day for the Red River. He moved on, through the roar, rush and rattle, past an old Negro woman with a kerchiefed head and a basket of cakes and pies, a Sicilian selling fruit, a one-legged man with a tin tamale oven; past vendors of newspapers and tobacco, pushcarts with steaming sausages and coffee, an old granny on a barrel with an umbrella shading a box stand of lemonade and whiskey. He found the Red River boats with steam up and chimneys smoking. The St. Charles was the newer packet; he went aboard to engage her last stateroom. Freight was coming aboard, and the mate was shouting at a line of stevedores. The boat would sail in half an hour.

That was on a Saturday afternoon. The big bell clanged at four o'clock, setting off an echoing clangor from the rival Swamp Fox. Two hours passed, and the bustle subsided. The clerk then said that the captain was not yet aboard, there was more freight to load and they would not likely get off until next morning. In fact, he thought now they probably would not leave before Monday. Monday, at noon—twelve o'clock sharp.

Fred Olmsted returned to his hotel and spent a lively New Orleans Sunday—another New Englander had noted that New Orleans people observed Sunday as Boston observed the Fourth of July. On Monday morning the newspaper said that the floating palace St. Charles with Captain Licking in command, would leave for Shreveport at five o'clock; it added that the low-draft favorite Swamp Fox, under veteran Captain Pitchup, would sail for the Red River at four. In an adjoining column both steamers were advertised for four o'clock departure. To be safe, the punctual Yankee went down to the St. Charles before noon and the clerk informed him that the newspaper was right, they had decided not to sail till four that evening. At four o'clock the St. Charles fired up and clanged her bell, as did the nearby Swamp Fox. A few passengers came aboard but nothing happened. By dark the fires had burned out, the stevedores were gone and the long levee was quiet, with a quantity of freight still waiting. Back to the hotel went Olmsted. The next day was a repeat performance—announcement, firing up, ringing of bells, and the boat never budging. On Wednesday the boat was again advertised to sail at four; at noon the clerk declared that all was aboard and ready but they would wait till the announced hour so as not to disappoint any travelers. At seven that evening both the St. Charles and the Swamp Fox were pouring smoke, blowing steam and ringing bells; both captains were pacing their hurricane decks and the mates were shouting at their crews. Last minute peddlers pushed through the passengers with fruit, newspapers, books—including a paperback edition of Uncle Tom's Cabin and a Bible defense of slavery by a clergyman in Kentucky.

At half-past seven, with a last look up and down the levee, the captain gave the word, "Throw off, Mr. Heady," and the mate barked at his men. As they backed out, one of the colored rousters on a pile of freight began a song. Waving hats and handkerchiefs the crew picked up the chorus:

> Ye see dem boat way dah ahead,
> Oa-ho-io-hieu!
> De San Charles is arter em, dey mus go behine,
> Oa-ho-io-hieu!
> So stir up fires dah, stir her up,
> Oa-ho-io-hieu!
> Oh we is gwine up de Red River, oh!
> Oa-ho-io-hieu!

The Swamp Fox still lay at the dark levee. She did not leave until the next Saturday.

The firemen on the St. Charles were Irish immigrants. They worked four-hour watches, with eight hours off, though all hands were called out for wooding or unloading freight. Behind the furnaces, in a chaos of cargo, dunnage and fuelwood, were two hundred deck passengers, white and Negro. They slept, like the crew, upon the freight, and they had a stove for frying pork and bacon.

At midnight a stir went through the St. Charles as a steamer came up from behind. The glare of furnace fires picked out the name KIMBALL on her paddle box. Down below the engineer shouted, "Shove her up, boys. Shove her!" and the Irishmen kept fires roaring in the flues. For a little while the two boats ran head and head, so close that the crews taunted each other. "You hear that whistlin'?" said a cabin passenger. "There an't any too much water in her bilers when ye hear that." Despite the rousters' song the heavily laden St. Charles fell behind. The Kimball crossed in front of her and the race was over.

After entering the Red River the *St. Charles* made slow progress. Every hour or so she swung in to a plantation landing to roll off a keg or a barrel or just to deliver a newspaper. Above the mouth of the Ouachita, fields of cotton stretched for miles beside the river. A Red River captain, wanting a big cotton trip when he returned downstream, would do anything to please the planters. A recurrent story tells of an old lady who waved her shawl at a packet and asked for the captain. "Well, cap'n," she said, holding out a small straw basket, "here's eleven eggs and I want you to trade 'em off for me and get me one spool of thread, one skein of silk, and the rest in beeswax. And, cap'n, would ye be kind enough to wait a little minute. That old hen is on the nest now, and I'll have another egg to make up the dozen." To pass the time on this slow journey, passengers fired pistols from the hurricane deck, trying their marksmanship on ducks floating in the river or turtles sunning on mats of driftwood. In the barroom the gambling tables were busy day and night.

At Natchitoches Olmsted left the steamer to begin a horseback trip through a country of pine flats and cotton fields to Texas. At a plantation on the way to Old Fort Jesup, he saw a slate hung on the piazza of the planter's office with a list of names and figures. Gorge 152, David 130, Polly 98, Hanna 96, Little Gorge 52. . . . These were the qantities of cotton picked, the day before, by each of the slaves. In the field thirty or forty Negroes worked together, moving slowly down the long white rows, dragging bulging bags behind them. With them went a "water-toter," a child with a bucket on her head. Cotton must be picked, Olmsted learned, the day it opened. At first gray daylight the Negroes went to the fields; dinner was brought at noon in a two-wheeled cart, and they did not leave the field till darkness. On wet days the cotton was ginned and baled in burlap. All winter the planters sent their cotton, a few wagonloads at a time, to the steamboat landings.

On the road Olmsted met cotton wagons, often two or three in tandem drawn by three or four pairs of mules or oxen. A wagonload was a ton of cotton—five 400-pound bales. Slowly over the rough back roads the wagons creaked, twenty, fifty, or a hundred miles to the river landing. Cotton depended on the rivers, and hundreds of steamboats depended on cotton. The river guidebooks thumbed by every clerk and captain listed all the plantation landings along the rivers of the South.

The first steamer that groped up the Red River to Natchitoches was the stubby little *Beaver* in the spring of 1820; she unloaded mixed cargo at the landing and splashed away with 350 bales of cotton on her foredeck. A man from Virginia, Major Ben Moore, had grown the first cotton in western Arkansas and had dredged a river channel through which the cotton packets came. When the great raft was finally removed in 1838, the Red River flowed through counties white with cotton; hundreds of thousands of bales were shipped from Towson Landing. By 1840, miles of cotton stretched above Little Rock. From all the back country roads, cotton wagons came into Little Rock; they creaked down Commercial Street to the landing where steamers unloaded plows, burlap and molasses and piled up lofty loads of cotton for New Orleans.

Every river valley—the Red, the Ouachita, the Arkansas, the White, the Yazoo, the Sunflower, the Wolf, the Obion, the Forked Deer—burst into snowy blossom in December. Through rich delta lands wound the Tallahatchie and the Yalobusha, joining in the slumberous Yazoo, with cotton packets loading at hundreds of plantation landings. Under Front Street in Memphis, where now the cotton brokers conduct the largest cotton market in the world, big Mississippi boats were piled to the pilothouse with cotton. Up the Cumberland and the Tennessee shallow-draft vessels loaded cotton along with mussel shells and peanuts.

The only cargo more bulky than cotton was peanuts. After autumn rains had ended a dry season in the 1840's, a captain took mixed merchandise to Nashville on a rising river. There he looked for return cargo and agreed to carry two hundred tons of sacked peanuts to Pittsburgh; he would load the peanuts first and then fill up with cotton. When the peanut cargo arrived, it covered the entire wharf and overflowed up the street. Peanuts, the captain saw, were something like unbaled cotton. He loaded peanuts on the hull, deck room, boiler deck, right up to the roof and on top of that. Still a hundred tons remained on the wharf. The captain was wrathful all the way to Pittsburgh where a crowd came down to see the huge cargo; they could not believe it all came on one boat. Congratulated on his big trip, the captain called his boat the champion peanut carrier on the Cumberland. But he never returned to Nashville in peanut season.

Back on the Yazoo, the Sunflower and the Ouachita, the cotton boats woke up the landings with their arrival blasts. The long stages bridged the bank, and cargo came aboard—baled cotton, sacked cotton-seed and barreled cottonseed oil. Rousters spun the barrels, rolled the bales, and jogged under bagged cottonseed while the mate roared from the hurricane deck: *Roll, roll, roll! Where are ye? Where are ye? Where are ye? Grab a sack! Grab a sack! Grab a sack!*—all in one pitch and cadence. The rousters kept up their own rhythm, and their own chorus:

> De coonjine, jine de coonjine
> Roll dat cotton down de hill
> De coonjine, jine de coonjine

When the departing whistle sounded, bales were mounting on the wide cotton guards. More came aboard at lower landings; while the clerk kept tally in his ledger new tiers rose on the cotton pile. Past Baton Rouge went huge blocks of cotton, only pilothouse and smokestacks jutting above the bulky load. Like the rivers themselves, a many-branched commerce of cotton streamed down to the Gulf.

When Sir Charles Lyell went up the "coast"—the broad deep river just above New Orleans—in the steamer *Rainbow* early in 1846, he passed a parade of cotton. Within a few hours he saw a hundred thousand bales, each bale worth forty dollars, going down to market. That season eighty million dollars worth of cotton passed through the port of New Orleans. On the *Rainbow* men were talking of new cotton boats and new records of cotton cargo.

Cotton boats were ordered by capacity—2500-bale packets for the side rivers, 5000 or bigger for the main stream. All the packets had high stacks so that sparks could burn out before lighting on the cargo; in the side rivers the chimneys brushed overhanging cottonwoods and syca-mores. Cotton steamers carried flaring guards, an extension of the main deck, and narrow cabins. An empty cotton boat looked pinched and small; laden with cargo it stood big as a river bluff. The bales were piled six, eight, ten, even twelve tiers high, up to the hurricane roof. A fully loaded packet looked like an enormous bale of cotton with a landing stage tilted out ahead and a pilothouse peering over. "If our passengers get a peep of daylight" wrote the captain of the *Thompson Dean*, "they have to go up on the hurricane deck or in the pilothouse."

The cotton trade moved through many waters on big boats and little ones, through many chutes and channels, with many stops at lonely land-ings. It was profitable and, in side rivers with limited visibility in the pilothouse and a cargo like tinder, it was often risky. Follow a cotton boat and find a story.

La Belle—"the Dirty Belle" her rousters called her—rained soot and sparks on her cargo but she did not burn. She carried cotton down the Arkansas, the Red and the Mississippi rivers till a February day in 1878 when she snagged and sank at Orleans Landing on the Red River with 2700 bales of cotton. The little *Shark* carried sixty bales a trip to Shreveport; she was fueled with "meat, bread and whisky," having no engines but a stern wheel operated by two men with cranks. The *Tensas*, named for Tennessee and Arkansas, carted cotton out of the Ouachita, where the farmers admired her emblem—a circular saw enclosing a figure 10 between her slender stacks. The fine big *Magnolia* was deliberately destroyed in 1862 to keep her from enemy capture, but the *Natchez* (No. 5) ran up the Yazoo River to Fort Pemberton impervious in her armor, four bales deep, of cotton. In 1863 when the Mississippi was reopened after the fall of Vicksburg, the first northbound cargoes were cotton. Cotton brought a fantastic two dollars a pound in the North, and bales were pulled apart by deckhands and dock thieves whenever a boat stopped on the Ohio.

The steamer *Dacotah*—the *h* was added because a six-letter name was considered unlucky—made the longest maiden voyage of all time; she carried 550 tons of mixed cargo from Pittsburgh to Fort Benton, Montana. After setting records on the Missouri, she came down to the Red River and made records there. In 1889 she whistled into New Orleans with twelve thousand bags of cottonseed. The *h* in her name served well. After fourteen prosperous years, the *Dacotah* was dismantled at Jeffersonville and still she was not finished. Half of her hull went into a wharf boat at the old town of Manchester, Ohio; the other half became a Pittsburgh excursion barge. Her engines, having churned past more than half the states in the Union, went into a new cotton boat, the *Imperial*, which ran the Southern rivers and bayous for eighteen years until she sank on a summer midnight in 1912.

The early *Autocrat* carried a big cotton pile for her time, but it was hard to keep her seven boilers fueled; she was a notorious wood-consumer. While she was lying at a woodyard in Tennessee, taking on a lot of flimsy cottonwood, a passenger asked the captain how much wood his boat consumed in twenty-four hours. "Of good hard oak wood," said the captain, "say seventy cords. This kind of wood," he spat toward the woodpile, "it's just like throwing shavings into hell."

The *Silver Moon* of Cincinnati was the last boat up from Memphis when the river was blockaded in 1861. She had a calliope, one of the earliest, and came into the Cincinnati levee playing "There's no place like home"—generally a bad-luck tune on a steamboat. After the war, resuming the cotton trade, she brought a big cotton pile under the new Cincinnati-Covington suspension bridge in the midst of the dedication ceremony. She made a touchy trip through ice early in 1869 and ran on the rocks at Louisville eight months later. For nearly seventy years more, her name survived on a Cincinnati riverfront saloon.

The *Corona*, owned at Wheeling, had eleven good years in the cotton trade, until the spring of 1889. Then, steaming past Prophet's Island in the Mississippi, she met the Anchor Line packet *City of St. Louis* whose captain came from Steubenville. Captain Blanks of the *Corona* gave him a long whistle, which ended in a blast like thunder. Her boilers had exploded. The captain sailed 150 feet and came down in the river. With a few other survivors he was picked up by the *City of St. Louis* and hurried back to New Orleans.

One of the great cotton packets in postwar years was the *Belle Lee*. She was brought out by Captain Tom Leathers who had a bristling rivalry with Captain John Cannon—a rivalry that eventually was climaxed in the famous race, on three exciting days in July of 1870, of the *Natchez* and the *Rob't E. Lee*. In 1874 the *Belle Lee* made all the river columns, coming in to New Orleans on New Year's Eve with 6000 bales of cotton on her guards and towing one barge with a big cotton pile and another with 7600 sacks of cottonseed. The next year she steamed south with a crowd of passengers for Mardi Gras and 5000 bales for the cotton market. During a stop at Vicksburg she caught fire and burned to the water.

A better memory was left by the *Pargoud*, a cotton packet that had a long life on the Greenville-New Orleans run. During William Alexander Percy's boyhood, the *Pargoud* arrived at the landing on Sunday mornings. Often her whistle sounded in the midst of morning worship, and to a man the male members of the congregation rose and left the church with an air of important business just recalled. With the *Pargoud*, Will Percy remembered, came the week's mail and gossip of the river from St. Louis to New Orleans and rumors from the distant world outside.

In 1882 the first *Kate Adams* came out of Pittsburgh, one of the finest of the long line of steamboats from the yards of James Rees & Sons—a firm that sent steamboats to Alaska, Africa, Russia and South America. On a May day in 1883 the *Kate Adams* raced down the Mississippi from Helena to Memphis, 90 miles, in a record 5 hours and 18 minutes. She was still wearing her deer horn trophy five years later when she burned like a bonfire on a gray Sunday morning two days before Christmas. She was loaded with baled cotton and bagged cottonseed. Perhaps that wall of cargo kept some people from escaping. Thirty-three died in her fire. A few days later word of the *Kate's* disaster reached the cotton packet *John M. Hanna* at the landing in Plaquemine, Louisiana. While the *Hanna's* people were exclaiming over that disaster, smoke and fire poured through their cabin. The *Hanna* burned so fast that twenty-one were trapped within her tiers of cotton.

A storied steamer, more than once called "the pride and wonder of the western waters," met her end while waiting for the winter cotton trade in 1877. For three months she had lain at the foot of Lesperance Street in New Orleans; there on a moonlit September midnight a man ran over the rutted road past the dog pound and told a policeman that the *Grand Republic* was burning. Thousands streamed onto the levee where flames leaped up to a lurid sky. The *Grand Republic* had once delivered 8210 bales of cotton, and her owners claimed a capacity of 15,000 bales. During her launching just below Pittsburgh, a workman had been crushed; with that omen it did not surprise old rivermen that she came to a violent end.

Cotton records grew like the steamboats themselves. In 1819 the first steamboat load of cotton went to New Orleans on the fuming little *Vesuvius,* 830 bales piled up on her foredeck and her roof. Thirty years later the *Autocrat* carried 4000 bales and forty years later the *Magnolia* loaded 6000. That record held until 1875, when the *James Howard*—"Oil Cake Jim" to her roustabouts—the boast of the Anchor Line, unloaded 7701 bales at New Orleans. Her people were prouder of that cotton pile than of carrying Grand Duke Alexis of Russia. On the 13th of March, 1881, just in from New Orleans with a big cargo of sugar, she took fire and burned herself out. The famous *Thompson Dean,* carrying twelve tiers of cotton on her guards, replaced the "Oil Cake Jim" in the Anchor fleet.

In 1877 St. Louis people flocked to the levee to see their first electric lights—in the big iron-hulled steamer *Charles P. Chouteau*. A year later the *Chouteau* had another fame, when she loaded 8841 bales of cotton. In 1881 she set a season record of 76,950 bales, but lost her title to the biggest cotton trip when the Cincinnati stern-wheeler *Henry Frank* carried 9226 bales and a cabin full of passengers—in the dark. Three years after this all-time record the *Frank* burned at Davis Creek Bend a couple of hours' run above St. Louis.

On a December night at the St. Maurice Plantation Landing, six miles above Bayou Sara, was moored the grandest steamboat that ever graced the Mississippi. The *J. M. White*, the greatest of the hundreds of vessels built at the Howard shipyards in Jeffersonville, had an octagonal domed barroom, stained glass, statuary, and gilt chandeliers; ornamental iron leaves, taller than a man, crowned her tall twin chimneys. For the cotton trade she carried guards extending 22½ feet beyond the hull line. She was only waiting for good times to load 10,000 bales of cotton.

On the night of December 13, Captain J. F. Muse, feeling under the weather, had gone to bed while the crew was stacking cotton. A clangor from the roof bell roused him; he donned some clothes and hurried outside. The texas was in flames. He slid down a guard chain to the half load of cotton and found a fiery forward deck. Through the cabin he ran, pounding on stateroom doors and sending people aft where the crew was manning skiffs and yawls. Now smoke poured through the chimney breeching and the stairways were aflame. With the last survivors he leaped into the water. From shore they watched the boat go up, with 3500 bales of cotton, 8000 sacks of cottonseed and 200 pounds of oil. In a fiery eruption, bagged gunpowder blew out of the hold. By daylight nothing was left but a smoldering hull with twisted hog chains and blackened boilers. For years the hulk lay against the riverbank, slowly mounding over with silt and sand.

The glamorous *J. M. White* symbolized the last great decade of steamboating, and her end was timed like a fable. In 1886 the river trade from Memphis to New Orleans was almost over. The first railroads to reach the lower Mississippi were short stub lines ending at Memphis, Vicksburg and Bayou Sara. These local lines fed the river trade; the first railroad in the State of Mississippi connected Woodville and Bayou Sara, bringing cotton to the river. But in the 1880's a rush of railroad building laid tracks along the Mississippi, the Red River, the Arkansas and the Yazoo; and by 1886 every sizable town in the lower valley had rail connections with New Orleans, Memphis and St. Louis. As the railroads grew, the steamboat trade diminished. By 1886 Memphis was shipping four times as much cotton by rail as by river. Steamboats would hold on to a token trade for two more generations, but there would be no cotton queens to replace the *Grand Republic* and the *J. M. White*.

13

~~~~~~

Jim Bludso's Ghost

IN THE SUMMER of 1837 Count Francesco Arese of Milan traveling past the poplar-lined shores of the Mississippi was reminded of his native River Po. But he forgot the peaceful Po when he saw the hulks of wrecked vessels in the river. Between Cairo and St. Louis he counted twenty-five derelict steamers, and he was told that every year twice that many were wrecked, burned or blown to pieces—"an awful ten percent of the 400 or 500 boats in the West."

One afternoon while reading in his stateroom in the *Tempest*, Arese heard excited voices. He ran up to the hurricane deck to see two steamboats sinking; one had burst her bottom timbers while trying to float another vessel already half submerged. That spectacle lost interest for him when flames broke out on the deck where he was standing. Someone cried "Fire on board!" and passengers, crew and officers streamed up the stairways. Arese helped put out the fire—sparks from the smokestacks had ignited mattresses spread on the roof for open-air sleeping— and went down to his stateroom to record the incident. "Five minutes later," he wrote, "and it would have been the end of the *Tempest*."

Next day the Count was in St. Louis, visiting the office of the American Fur Company on the levee. At a thunderous explosion from the river he ran out and saw "an immense mass of white smoke—or rather steam—human bodies, boxes, bales of merchandise, floating planks," where a moment before there had been a steamboat. When the startled Italian asked about safety laws he was told, "If there was a law, either it would be a dead letter, or no one would wish to be captain."

Within twelve months there was a law, the Steamboat Act of 1838. It required inspection of hull, boilers and machinery, the replacing of tiller ropes with iron rods or chains, and the use of running lights at night. But it was a vague, loose law and it promptly became a dead letter. The later Act of 1852, including mandatory examination and licensing of engineers, was more realistic and effective. By that time 420 steamboats had been lost on the Western rivers, half of them by explosion and the rest by snagging, collision and fire. The Act of 1852 reduced accidents but it did not end them. Racing was as needful as food and drink to rivermen, and when two boats locked horns no one consulted the safety regulations. Casks of bacon were broken up and thrown into the roaring fires. Limber boats ran faster; sometimes crews sawed half through the framing timbers to loosen a rigid hull and gain on a rival. Engineers crammed their furnaces and tied down the safety valve.

In one of the river counties of Illinois lived a youth who would become President Lincoln's private secretary, an Ambassador to Great Britain and Secretary of State under Presidents McKinley and Theodore Roosevelt. John Hay went a long way from Pike County, but he is remembered for a dozen frontier poems, *Pike County Ballads*, that perpetuated the folklore of his boyhood. One of the ballads gave America a new hero.

He was Jim Bludso, engineer of the *Prairie Belle*—

> And this was all the religion he had—
>   To treat his engine well,
> Never be passed on the river,
>   And mind the pilot's bell.

Jim knew the hazards of the engine room and he vowed if ever the boat caught fire he would get her people off. One night a light came up behind and Jim crowded his engines. With resin and pine in the furnace and a rouster squatting on the safety valve, he raced the fast new *Movastar*. It was too much for the old *Prairie Belle*.

> The fire burst out as she cleared the bar,
>   And burned a hole in the night.
> And quick as a flash she turned and made
>   For that willer-bank on the right.
> There was running and cursing but Jim yelled out
>   Over all the infernal roar,

"I'll hold her nozzle agin the bank
Till the last galoot's ashore."

. . . .

And sure's you're born they all got off
Afore the smokestack fell,
And Jim Bludso's ghost went up alone
In the smoke of the *Prairie Belle*.

Though Jim Bludso was legendary, the town of Louisiana, Missouri, claims him as a native and a visitor can see the very willow where he held his boat against the bank till the last soul got ashore. Some engineers got their people off, some didn't, but many of them went out like Jim Bludso. The engineer was close to the flues and the boilers; he had a risky calling.

The Act of 1852 followed a series of disasters; each season between 1847 and 1852 saw an increasing number of explosions, collisions and fires. In 1851 more than six hundred lives were lost, and in seven months of 1852 seven startling accidents took nearly as many. The Act of 1852 fixed a limit to allowable steam pressure, it defined rules for passing in the channels, it required fire hose and fire pumps, it regulated the stowing of fuel and cargo and called for escape routes for all passengers. It also required examination and licensing of both pilots and engineers, and to enforce the regulations, it provided inspection service in the major river districts.

The new Act showed some results. In the five previous years fifty steamboat explosions took nearly twelve hundred lives; in the next five years explosions dropped to twenty, with 224 casualties. Then in 1858–59 three big packets, the *Pennsylvania, Princess* and *St. Nicholas*, exploded in the lower Mississippi with frightful loss of life. There still remained the hazards of the river and the failings of men.

Living amid chance and violence, the riverman was inveterately and ingeniously superstitious. A white cat was a bad omen, though black cats were harmless. A coffin containing a corpse made a convenient lunch or card table for the crew, with no bad luck involved. But, as mentioned earlier, six-letter names were considered risky for steamboats, and names beginning with *M*—the thirteenth letter of the alphabet— were suspect for a century. (Twenty-seven vessels have flown the flag of the Greene Line since 1890; many of them bore family names, but none was named for Captain Mary Greene, the only woman captain on the rivers.) A white horse or a white mule brought bad luck to a steamboat. Rats were good luck, but a preacher aboard made some captains uneasy. Several superstitions came together on a voyage up the Missouri—when a preacher's white mule jumped off the *Marsella* at Jackass Bend, and in trying to save the mule the mate was drowned.

The worst disaster on the Missouri was the wreck of the *Saluda* in the spring of 1852. A side-wheeler with two large boilers, the *Saluda* was bound upstream, crowded with cargo and Mormon passengers. The river was in April flood and a heavy current kept the steamer laboring and gasping. When Captain Belt called for more steam to get around the bend above Lexington, both boilers flew apart. Among two hundred killed were Charles La Barge and Louis Guerette, pilots and brothers-in-law. The steamer's bell was blown onto the bank, salvaged by a Lexington man and presented to the Christian Church in Savannah. There for many years it rang for Sunday worship.

Disasters were much alike—a snagged bow and the river gushing in, fire racing up from the main deck and sheathing a boat in flames, a burst boiler hurling timber and metal to the sky. Yet each one had a separate horror and some accidents had bizarre features of their own. One night a traveler on a Southern river was awakened by shouts of alarm. When he got dressed and out on deck, the crew had abandoned the boat and he was alone. Fire was spreading toward a barrel of turpentine but he snatched a bucket and drowned the flames. When the smoke cleared the crew came back aboard. They made some small repairs, got steam up and went on down the river. Then the traveler saw three hundred kegs of dynamite under the charred deck.

The Diamond Jo boats served the upper Mississippi for fifteen years; they carried a diamond emblem on all four sides of the pilothouse and a JO between the chimney braces. In 1867 Diamond Jo Reynolds sold his first vessel, the *Lansing,* to the Rambo's, father and son, for the trade between Davenport and Le Claire. When the emblem was erased from the pilothouse, the *Lansing's* life was ending. On the 13th of May, 1867, toiling through the Rock Island rapids, she burst her twin boilers, hurling half the steamboat at the sky. The clerk and the pilot were old friends but at that instant they parted company. The clerk's body, it was reported, landed in Iowa, and the pilot was found in a field in Illinois.

Late on a November afternoon in 1849 the big packet *Louisiana,* lying between the *Bostona* and the *Storm* at the foot of Gravier Street in New Orleans, blew her departing whistle. She had a big trip of cargo and passengers. The engines turned, the paddles revolved, she began backing out. While the rousters fended her guards from the *Bostona* and the *Storm*, her boilers let go and things flew in all directions. An iron bar cut a mule in two and hurtled on to kill a horse and driver on the levee. A piece of engine landed at Canal and Front streets where it collapsed the roof of a coffeehouse. In the excitement on the levee, a pickpocket lifted a watch from the New Orleans mayor. The blast wrecked the upper works of the *Bostona* and the *Storm*, where fifteen passengers were killed. The *Louisiana* sank in ten minutes. Trapped in her main deck were scores of Irish immigrants. One of the dead cabin passengers was the son of the Italian consul. His body was never found, but his marble monument in a St. Louis Cemetery shows a winged angel lifting Joseph A. Barelli, Jr., from a flaming steamboat.

On a May midnight in 1837 the *Ben Sharrod* on her way from New Orleans to Louisville, overtook the *Prairie*, which did not want to be passed. Forcing her fires with resin, the *Sharrod* crept ahead. But the furnace heat set fire to sixty cords of wood stacked against the boilers. While the pilot steered for the riverbank, a series of explosions—from kegs of whiskey, brandy and gunpowder—threw two hundred crew and passengers into the river. When the *Columbus* came along, half of the *Sharrod's* people were drowned. One survivor was rescued by the steamer *Statesman* after floating fifteen miles down the Mississippi.

The Christmas number of *Harper's Weekly*, dated December 26, 1868, began with a Christmas song:

> And all the mellow Christmas bells
>   Clash their wild tunes upon the air,
> And gathering in melodious swells
>   Wake the white echoes everywhere.

The next item was "Steamboat Disaster on the Ohio River"; it told of alarm bells clanging at midnight and shipwrecked people in the water.

In the windy night of December 4, the two big boats of the U.S. Mail Line were approaching each other near Warsaw, Kentucky. The *United States* was barreling downstream at twenty miles an hour; the *America* was making ten miles an hour, upbound. In the bright cabin of the *United States* passengers were serenading two bridal parties, while up in her dark wheelhouse, the pilot saw a blur of lights ahead. The sister packets regularly met in this part of the river, with the up-bound boat holding to the Kentucky shore. But on this run the *America*'s customary pilot was replaced by an "extra," the elderly Napoleon B. Jenkins, who decided to take the Indiana side. In the gusty darkness he blew two whistles and spoked his wheel over; he heard one whistle in reply. He blew again, but the wind was the only answer. Minutes later the two big vessels collided in midstream.

On the *United States* the shock threw some barrels of petroleum from the guards onto the furnaces, and the boat burst into flame. She backed away, toward the Indiana shore, but her fire had already spread to the *America*, which also carried a combustible cargo—bacon, cotton, brooms and whiskey. In five minutes both vessels were destroyed and seventy-four lives were lost. One of the survivors from the *America* waded ashore holding a violin case over his head; he was the great Norwegian artist, Ole Bull. The hull of the *United States* was towed to Cincinnati where a new *United States* was built upon it. The wreck of the *America* stayed on the river bottom near Bryant's Creek, Indiana. For thirty years its gaunt bones were bared in seasons of low water.

On the night of November 5, 1885, Holland and McMahon's circus was loaded onto the steamer *Mountain Girl* after a performance at Lawrenceburg, Indiana. An hour after midnight, rounding Split Rock two miles below Aurora, a vessel's lights appeared. The captain of the *Mountain Girl* was feeling ill, but he sat on the bench in the pilothouse directing the mate at the wheel. The two boats exchanged signals, agreeing to pass to starboard. Then the mate unaccountably spun the wheel over and swung into the path of the *James W. Goff*. That steamer struck the *Girl* amidships, cutting her in two. In torchlit darkness, the *Goff* stood alongside and picked up sixty-five show people. Seven circus men were lost along with the trick stallion Comet, the performing mare Silver and some other show horses, a cage of monkeys and a collection of snakes.

In 1856 James T. Lloyd of Cincinnati compiled a grisly list of steam-boat disasters. Stamped in gold on the cover of his book was the *Moselle* bursting apart (the *Moselle* was a fast new boat beginning her second trip to St. Louis on April 25, 1838, when she exploded at Cincinnati, killing eighty-five people); inside were graphic drawings and accounts of a hundred collisions, collapses, sinkings, capsizings, burnings and explosions. But his catalog of calamity was compiled nine years too soon to include the greatest disaster of all.

On April 21, 1865, just twelve days after Lee's surrender at Appomattox, the side-wheeler *Sultana* left New Orleans on her regular run to Cincinnati. She carried about a hundred cabin passengers, a cargo of sugar, a hundred horses and cattle, and a ten-foot alligator in a wooden cage. Her legal capacity was 376 persons, including her crew. Three days out of New Orleans she stopped at Vicksburg where her leaky boilers were repaired. Vicksburg was swarming with Union Soldiers just released from Andersonville and Catawba prisons and there being embarked on riverboats for passage to the Ohio. While engineers hammered on the *Sultana's* boilers, the *Henry Ames* cleared Vicksburg with 1300 troops and the *Olive Branch* shoved off with 700 more. Two other boats were waiting at the landing, but for some reason Federal officers ordered all the remaining men to the *Sultana*. They streamed aboard, 2000 worn and restless men with their own rations in their knapsacks. They crossed the stages shouting and singing, eager for home. Most of them were from Ohio, Indiana and Michigan regiments.

When the steamer left Vicksburg, men were jammed in every space from the main deck to the roof of the texas; no Mississippi vessel had ever carried so many. On the night of April 26 she docked at Memphis. While a hundred hogsheads of sugar were discharged, hundreds of soldiers went ashore. Many of them visited "Whiskey Chute," a riverfront alley lined with fourteen saloons, and some lucky ones did not get back in time to sail at midnight. The steamer crossed the river, took on bunker coal from a barge, made some new repairs to her boilers and headed upstream for Cairo where the troops would disembark. Two hours later the overloaded steamer with a strong current against her was toiling past a string of islands called the Hen and Chickens, their cottonwood saplings half drowned in high spring water.

At two o'clock that morning the new side-wheeler *Bostona*, steaming down to Memphis to go into the White River trade, approached Island No. 40, just above Redmond's Point. Loftus Keating of Newport, Kentucky, was in the dark pilothouse along with Captain John Watson and Keating's son Charles, a cub pilot. A flash of light puffed up beyond the point and the sky turned lurid. Keating said, "That must be some man's cotton gin going up, Captain."

But when they rounded the point they saw a steamboat burning, just

151

opposite Old Hen Island on the Arkansas line. The *Bostona* bore down quickly in the fast current. Keating said, "Why, just look at the cattle jumping into the water." But the captain said, "My God, them ain't cattle. They're people! Holler down to the engineer, Lof. We must get there as soon as we can. Why, just look at them jumping!"

Soon, with checked engines, they were coasting into lurid water dotted with people. The chimneys fell and a cloud of sparks and embers erupted from the burning boat. From the *Bostona* they threw out boards, boxes, barrels, anything that would float. Up to Loftus Keating came shrill and pleading voices. He had to back in the strong current, and he feared for men who might be clinging to the paddle wheels. After two hours, with a hundred dripping survivors on her deck, the *Bostona* went on to Memphis. Scores of skiffs and canoes were landing the rescued at the wharf boat and going back for more. By daylight they picked up men clinging to cottonwood branches and floating on broken cargo. Four hundred were saved before the terrible morning was over.

On the *Sultana* a few hours earlier, Captain W. S. Friesner of the 58th Ohio Volunteer Infantry watched the roustabouts roll out the sugar cargo at Memphis. Then he went to sleep in his stateroom. He was wakened by a thumping like a hogshead of sugar dropped on deck. He turned over to sleep again but a new commotion broke out. This time he thought it was a fight among the soldiers and he got up to quiet them. The cabin was full of smoke and steam, fire was eating at the forward end of the boat and men were jumping from the guards. Captain Friesner could not swim, but he pulled a cabin door from its hinges and jumped in. He clung to that raft amid hundreds of floundering men. After a while he saw a steamer hauling people from the water. It drew near, a man reached down and drew him aboard the *Bostona*.

At midnight Private Perry Summerville, Company K, 41st Regiment, Indiana Cavalry, stood at the guardrail watching the lights of Memphis dwindle in the distance. The *Sultana* worked alongside a coal barge and began to load fuel. Then Private Summerville lay down on the crowded larboard guard of the cabin deck. The next thing he knew he was in the water. His first thought was that the steamer had been running close inshore and he had been dragged off by the branches of a tree; then he saw steam and fire gushing up from the steamer. Quickly it was a mass of flame. Grasping a rail he swam downstream, away from the heat and the cries on the burning vessel. He found a plank which

Towboat *J. W. Van Sant II* shoving ten acres of logs, with bowboat *Lydia Van Sant* maneuvering the head of the raft (Audio-Visual Service)

Opening of Davis Island Dam, Ohio River, 1885 (Way Collection)

he added to his rail, holding one with his feet and the other in his hands. By now he was shuddering with cold. He heard a horse coughing and snorting; the head drew near and he saw a dozen men clinging to the animal's mane and tail. A man came along, splashing his feet to keep astride a barrel; it was Jerry Parker of the Second Michigan Cavalry. They met others clinging to wreckage, drifting on the current toward Memphis. A Negro pulled them into a skiff and rowed them to a rescue boat. When Private Summerville got out of the water he found that his back was scalded and half his ribs were broken.

The flaming *Sultana* drifted onto a wooded island, half drowned in the high water, where it burned out. Before daylight, with a last hiss of steam and smoke, it sank into the river. Next day the rescued were counted in Memphis. Of 2300 aboard the steamer some 600 were brought to shore, but a third of them died in Memphis hospitals. The official report listed 1547 dead. For weeks afterward bodies were found in thickets and sandbars along the falling river. Every day a search barge from Memphis brought back a load of dead.

The survivors found their separate ways back to farms, towns and cities in the Midwest. They had a bond of terrible memory and mysterious mercy. On New Year's Day, 1886, some of them met at Fostoria, Ohio, and formed the Sultana Survivors' Society, proposing to hold annual reunions. On the 27th of April, twenty-one years after the fateful night, they met in Columbus, Ohio. The next year they met in Toledo. Out of the past they called up startling memories: When the explosion came three men were blown off the boat on a piece of her hurricane deck; they landed with that ragged raft still under them and so they floated down to Memphis. In the pandemonium of the burning boat a soldier remembered the big alligator in a bulkhead corner under the cabin stairway; he stabbed the reptile, dragged out the crate and pushed it into the river. He rode that floating cage until a rescue boat picked him up. One man had lain down on deck beside a comrade; when they pulled him out of the water a forage cap was clutched in his hand—that was all that was left of his comrade.

The Survivors' Society planned to compile their reminiscences, but that project died and after a few meetings the society disbanded. Once they had exchanged their haunting memories there was nothing left to do, except for each man to wonder again, silently, why he had survived that night of disaster.

In the 1870's steamboat accidents decreased and the life of the packets lengthened. But in those years a slow disaster overtook the river commerce. James T. Lloyd's long list of shipwrecks ends with a historical summary of the "Principal Railroads of the United States." In unconscious irony he ended his book with the greatest blow of all.

The steamboats collaborated in this calamity. In 1881 the *Cherokee* delivered iron rails for railway lines on the west side of the Mississippi. The *Ashland, Henry Frank* and *Maria Louise* brought locomotives and freight and passenger cars—to carry the cotton and cattle, the soldiers and immigrants, the boxed, baled and barreled cargo that for half a century had moved on the Mississippi.

Already railroads had strangled the trade on the upper river. In 1881 veteran Captain George Merrick (who had become a railway agent in Wisconsin) went down the empty Mississippi on the *Mary Morton*. At Prairie du Chien, where he remembered a dozen boats loading grain and cattle, long trains of freight cars rumbled over the bridge on the way to Milwaukee and Chicago. In St. Louis he looked at the silent river. Along three miles of levee there were three boats—an Anchor Line packet, a single side-wheeler from New Orleans, and the little *Mary Morton*. That was all, where twenty years before there had been boats from Pittsburgh, Cincinnati, Louisville; from New Orleans, Shreveport, Helena, Memphis; from St. Paul, Winona and Prairie du Chien; from Peoria, Terre Haute and Nashville; from St. Joe, Sioux City and the Yellowstone. Now he saw trains passing over the Eads Bridge that spanned the empty river.

14

Mark Twain, Pilot

ONE AUTUMN DAY a few years ago on the Twin Cities Zephyr rolling west from Chicago, I found a group of German tourists in the observation dome watching the woods and fields wheel past. After crossing the Rock River the train raced through the pine forest of Ogle County, and I heard some laughing comments on *"der kleine Schwartzwald."* It was a gray November morning with bright streaks in the sky. The train leaned into a long curve, leading northward. Suddenly the woods opened and there, beyond a golden frieze of bottom timber, lay the mile-wide Mississippi.

"Ah! Der Fluss! Der Mississippi!" cried the visitors, reaching for their cameras. The sun broke through, lighting the great river. *"Wunderbahr! Ganz wunderbahr!"*

Around the bend came a steam towboat with twin plumes of smoke above it and a wheel of water at the stern. "Mark Twain!" the voices chorused, "Mark Twain!"

No other river in the world is so identified with one man. Mark Twain made the Mississippi known to the world, and the river made him immortal. It gave him a name that crossed all borders, and he gave America's river to a universal folklore.

As a boy in the dusty town of Hannibal, Sam Clemens discovered the river's endless wonder and delight. It ran in grandeur between the bluffs of Missouri and the prairies of Illinois. It enclosed wilderness islands where boys could land their skiffs, go swimming, play Indians and pirates, and cook catfish on a driftwood fire. In Hannibal the main street faced the river. A few piles of freight stood on the levee and a couple of barges, tiered with fuelwood, lay at the landing. On summer evenings men sat there watching the silent river, telling river stories.

To Hannibal came the steamboat—up from St. Louis and down from Keokuk. The first sign of it, a cloud of smoke beyond the point, brought the town to life. When it came in, hissing and splashing, the mate shouting down to the rousters and the pilot's bell clanging signals to the engineer, half the town was gathered on the levee. While freight went aboard and a few passengers crossed the landing stage, the town was linked with unseen places—St. Louis, Quincy, Muscatine, Galena, St. Paul. When the boat was gone the world went with it, leaving a lost town until the next whistle sounded at the bend. In 1846 Hannibal was not included in Banvard's panorama. Sam Clemens was there, aged eleven, but as yet there was no Mark Twain.

The river had moods, mysterious in fog, majestic in moonlight, radiant in sunrise and gemmed with midnight stars. It changed by seasons, high water and low water, full of drift ice in January and drifting timber in June. The June rise brought cordwood down the river, pieces of timber, fence rails, runaway skiffs and dugouts that might catch in thickets where the current ran close to shore. Out in the broad stream passed big log rafts, acres of pine logs from the rivers of Wisconsin. On a summer night a boy could swim to a raft, climb aboard and steal up close to the cookshed where the men lay smoking their pipes and talking. "All boys steal rides on rafts," said Huck Finn. It was a frontier hitchhiking.

Steamboat traffic from Hannibal was hemp, hides, tobacco, pork and lard. It was also dreams and wonder. Past the town went boats to St. Louis, Galena, Prairie du Chien, St. Paul. Woods and prairie hemmed Hannibal on three sides, but there was another horizon, always moving and alive with light. No boy could be enclosed by the local life while the river tugged at his imagination.

One day barefoot Sam Clemens stole a ride on a steamboat bound for St. Louis. He stowed away, hiding under a yawl on the upper deck. After an hour he crept out and watched the strange shores going by. They put him ashore at the next town, nine miles below; he had an uncle there who took him back to Hannibal. But Sam Clemens had made his first trip on the river.

Ten years later he was living with his brother Orion at Keokuk, working as a typesetter in his brother's printshop. One night he read the diary of an American naval officer who had traveled up the Amazon. Twenty years old and restless—for two years he had worked in the East as a journeyman printer—Sam Clemens saw himself on a cocoa plantation in Brazil. But he had no money and Orion could not pay his back wages. He waited until, by a chance stranger than fiction, some money came his way. On a gusty October morning he saw a piece of paper blowing across the street; it was a fifty-dollar banknote. That sent him on his way—first to St. Louis, then to Cincinnati, working as a printer and writing travel letters for the *Keokuk Post* at five dollars each. These rustic letters, detailing the misadventures of "Thomas Jefferson Snodgrass," added modestly to his printer's pay, but a fondness for cigars was a drain on his savings. When spring came to Cincinnati he was restless again and thinking of the Amazon. He paid sixteen dollars for a passage to New Orleans on the old steamer *Paul Jones*.

It was a slow trip, including four days aground at Louisville. He watched the river towns come up and drop behind. He sat in the warming sun, a slender youth with blue eyes under a shock of curly sandy hair, and saw the shores go by. He watched the steamboats passing, bound for Pittsburgh, Charleston, Nashville, Terre Haute, Peoria, St. Joseph, Little Rock, Shreveport and a hundred other places. This was the vital mainstream of America.

In the pilothouse was a peppery, sharp-tongued little man whose back grew lame during his long wheel watches. When Sam Clemens steered for him, his future swung in a new direction. But for that pilot's pain, he later said, "I would have drifted into the ministry, the penitentiary or a graveyard somewhere." Instead, Horace Bixby agreed to teach him the twelve hundred winding miles of river channel between New Orleans and St. Louis.

For $500, on credit, Sam Clemens began his apprenticeship. After the first trip up the river he borrowed $100 from his brother-in-law in St. Louis. The rest would be paid from his wages after Bixby had made a pilot of him. But $500 was a big fee, and it caused some friction. Eventually Horace Bixby knocked off $100 of it and Sam paid the rest. Later, after Sam Clemens was a professional pilot, Bixby borrowed $200 from him and grew angry when he was asked for payment. He was a lightning pilot but a waspish man.

The apprenticeship took seventeen months, journeying up and down the river, learning every bend, bar, and crossing, every island, shoal and towhead. The cub pilot learned the river by sunlight and starlight, even in fog and blackness. He learned the changing channel depths, the landmarks of bluff, point and bend, the currents and eddies. When his mind was a jumble of names and numbers and the task seemed hopeless, Bixby stopped shouting at him. "My boy," he said, "you must get a little memorandum book, and every time I tell you a thing put it down, right away. There's only one way to be a pilot and that is to get this entire river by heart. You have to know it just like A B C." The next landing place was Cairo and he must have got his notebook there; its first entry concerns the channel just above the mouth of the Ohio. Now, a century later, in the Mark Twain estate are two worn, bound river logs, with blue pencil headings and black pencil notations—

> Delta to head 62. Coming up when all the Bar is covered there is ¼ less 2 in chute of Montezuma. Shape bar till head of towhead & main point open—then hold open to right of high trees on towhead till get close enough to go upshore of towhead. Channel out past head of towhead. . . .
> Outside of Montezuma—use 6 or 8 feet more water. Shape bar till high timber on towhead gets nearly even with the low willows do. do. then hold a little open on right of low willow—run 'em close if you want to, but come out 100 yards when you get nearly to head of T.H. . . .
> Heave lead at head of 55—no bottom—ran no channel in it. 8 ft. bank on point opp. Densford's—or rather up shore at head of timber.

Sam Clemens was a dreamy, drawling, easygoing youth. Here he found his first demanding discipline. In those years a pilot had only knowledge and instinct to steer by; there was not a single navigation mark to help him. Steamboats ran day and night, in high water and low water, calling at scores of cities, towns and rural landings; and the only map was in the pilot's mind.

Sam Clemens cubbed on the battered old *John J. Roe*, a big packet for her time and a dismally slow one. "The only races on the *Roe*," Mark Twain recalled, "were with rafts and islands, and her fastest trip took 16 days up the river to St. Louis." Old rivermen said she could run all day in the shade of a big tree. She had three boilers, a lot of cargo room and little cabin space; she was in the freight business and she had an easygoing captain. If a cub pilot ran her aground, it would not fret a throng of impatient travelers.

But Sam Clemens was glad to go from the *Roe* to a faster and fancier vessel. The *Aleck Scott* had a row of gleaming furnaces building steam in eight big boilers. She had a long mahogany cabin and a mirrored barroom. She carried planters, merchants, army officers, journalists, scientists, actors, drovers, missionaries, gamblers and fancy women. In this glittering packet the cub went on with his lessons. When he came down from observing the river he observed humanity. All the world traveled in the packets, and the landings were clamorous with as many tongues as Babel. Years later Mark Twain said of every character he found in fiction or biography, "I have known him before—met him on the river."

After a year Sam Clemens was steering on the big *Pennsylvania* under pilot Tom Brown, a friend of Bixby's. Sam's younger brother Henry, having caught the river fever, was aboard as "mud clerk," learning to be a purser. At night, in St. Louis or New Orleans, the brothers shared Sam's job of watchman, patrolling the freight piles on the levee and talking about their future. When the big packet steamed away, Henry sorted bills of lading in the clerk's office while Sam stood wheel watch under the eyes of Pilot Brown—"a snarling, fault-finding, mate-magnifying tyrant."

One spring day in 1858 while Pilot Brown was at the wheel, Henry came up to the pilothouse with word from the captain: they were to stop at an unscheduled landing. Brown, who habitually ignored underlings, swept right on in midstream. As they were passing the landing Captain Klinefelter called from the hurricane deck, "Let her come round, Mr. Brown. Didn't Henry tell you to land here?"

No, the pilot said, but Sam Clemens spoke up—Henry had delivered the message and had been ignored. When Henry appeared on another errand, the fuming pilot ordered him out of sight and took a lump of coal from the stove bin to throw after him. Sam Clemens flew at the pilot with both fists. When Brown refused to stay on the boat with Clemens, the captain gave Sam an order for passage to St. Louis on the *A. T. Lacey*. From the New Orleans levee Sam Clemens waved to his brother as the *Pennsylvania* started up the river.

Two days later Sam followed on the *Lacey*. When they touched at Greenville, two days out, he heard startling news: the *Pennsylvania* had exploded at a woodyard sixty miles below Memphis. A few hours later, at Helena, Arkansas, there was further word: four of the *Pennsylvania's* boilers had burst, blowing away the forward end of the boat. A rescue steamer had taken survivors to Memphis.

The next day at Memphis Sam found his brother, badly burned, lying amid dying men in a public hall. For a week Sam watched over him while Henry grew stronger. Then, on medical rounds at midnight, a young doctor gave him an overdose of morphine. He died a few hours later.

It was a heavyhearted Sam Clemens who went back to the river, but he buried himself in the task of piloting. Under mellow George Ealer, who quoted Shakespeare and Goldsmith between orders, he learned to read the riffles and eddies, the sheen and the shadows, to judge from the surface the hidden depths and currents. The river was growing as familiar to him as the remembered streets of Hannibal.

An unlicensed steersman could pilot a cargo boat, and Sam Clemens finished his training with a monthly salary on a freight carrier. When winter closed the Missouri to navigation, some of the Missouri River craft ran down to New Orleans, carrying barreled flour and livestock. Late in 1858 the A. B. Chambers (No. 2) loaded flour at St. Louis and hired two Mississippi River pilots. One of them was Sam Clemens, and on the Chambers he found a young mate named Grant Marsh. That winter two immortal rivermen traveled together.

On their second trip deep winter had come to St. Louis and the river was clogged with ice. When they got down to the "graveyard" at Commerce, Missouri, mid-channel was massed with a grinding ice pack. Hugging the shore of Powers Island, the Chambers ran aground. The firemen fed the furnaces, the paddles labored, but the boat would not budge. While she lay there the fuel ran out. Captain Bowman ordered a crew into the yawl; they were to pull back to Commerce and float a woodflat down to the stranded steamer. Grant Marsh took Sam Clemens along as his navigator. This was a new kind of piloting, but Sam figured out a course. Avoiding the ice-choked channel he had the men cross over and pull upstream through a backwater inside of Burnham's Island. This brought them to the town of Thebes, Illinois, opposite from Commerce, at a narrow place where swift current left an open crossing below a gorge of pack ice. But the gorge might break at any minute. It was touch and go.

When Sam gave the word, the men pulled for the Missouri shore. They were nearing midstream when the gorge gave way. The mate wanted to turn back, but as the ice swept toward them Sam kept his rudder square. Pulling grimly, the oarsmen raced the ice. They made the Missouri shore a moment before the avalanche swept past. With a woodflat in tow they returned to the *Chambers*, and when the engineer had a full head of steam the paddles worked free. Years later the biographer of Grant Marsh exchanged letters with Mark Twain about that icy crossing.

With spring the *Chambers* loaded St. Louis cargo for the Missouri (she was sunk by a snag just above the Missouri mouth in 1860), and Sam Clemens went to the office of the District Steamboat Inspector. He came away with a document more precious than money.

> The inspectors for the district of St. Louis certify that Samuel Clemens, having been duly examined, touching his qualifications as a PILOT of a Steam Boat, is a suitable and safe person to be entrusted with the powers and duties of Pilot of Steam Boats and do license him to act as such for one year from this date on the following rivers, to wit on the Mississippi River to and from St. Louis and New Orleans.
>
> 9 April 1859

Now he was in authority in the pilothouse. He loved its splendors, its aloof elegance, its pomp and glory. That roomy glass-walled observation tower held a polished stove, shining cuspidors, brass-knobbed bell signals, a big wheel of inlaid wood, a sofa, a high leather-cushioned bench for visiting pilots, red and gold curtains at the windows. A tap on a bell would bring a steward's boy with tarts, ices and coffee. A signal on the pull cord would reverse the huge paddle wheels. A turn of the wheel would swing the big vessel into a crossing, swerve it through it a chute, or point it toward a landing.

When the pilot wanted a sounding, a deckhand at the bow heaved the line and up came the melodious cry: *Kee-you—warter le-ess thy-hy-hyy-yree!* The leadsman's call combined the many voices of Kentuckians, Frenchmen, Irishmen, Negroes who had traveled the greatest of rivers. The weighted hemp rope showed its first marking at six feet—mark one. After that each call marked another 18 inches up to 24 feet, which was *Mark Four—De-e-ep Four, Ocean Deep!* Tabs of leather and colored lanyards in the lead line showed the depths. At nine feet there was a red stripe from some tattered old steamboat flag. It gave the line good luck —*Le-itt-le Re-eud Fla-ag!* At nine feet a big packet would rub bottom.

The boat staggered, paddles threshing, and if the luck was working it lurched free. Once a leadsman told a pilot confidentially, "I laks you better dan de other pilot, an' I always gives you mo' water."

A pilot's life . . . Midnight silence in the dark wheelhouse, the solitude of the great river, the thoughts of a man alone with the river and the stars. Midday in the bustling cabin, a clink of glasses in the barroom, the clash of voices on states' rights, total immersion, fugitive slaves and wildcat banknotes. At the end of the run, flashing his hundred-dollar bill, Sam Clemens strolled down Dauphine and Bourbon streets, ate a lavish dinner in a French restaurant, smoked a cigar under the palm fronds and church spires in the Place d'Armes. Then coffee with brandy in the French market and back to the levee where miles of steamboats made the most exciting facade in America.

While piloting the *Edward J. Gray*, Sam Clemens read the pontifical river news of the oracular Captain Isaiah Sellers: "My opinion for the benefit of the citizens of New Orleans: The water is higher this far up [Vicksburg] than it has been since 1815. My opinion is that the water will be four feet deep in Canal Street before the first of next June." The brash young pilot wrote a burlesque under the name of "Sergeant Fathom," predicting water on the roof of the St. Charles Hotel before the middle of January, and concluded with a reference to the time when "me and De Soto discovered the Mississippi." His travesty was passed around among other pilots who relished it enough to get it into the New Orleans *Daily Crescent*. Several years later Sam Clemens mistakenly stated that Captain Sellers signed his articles "Mark Twain" and that his burlesque crushed the old captain; the confusion of memory might have resulted from the similarity of his "Fathom" and the river term "Mark Twain" which signified two fathoms.

One of the young pilot's assignments was the *City of Memphis*, a big, fast packet with visiting pilots always on the bench. Their talk was all river talk, endless memories and lore, talk about floods and droughts, about caving banks, vanished islands and bygone channels. They recalled the landslips near Port Hudson, when three acres of forest slid into the river while acorns and beechnuts showered down like hail. A herd of pigs feeding on that windfall were carried down fifty feet, still eating. Some fell into the river and swam back to the feast. . . . There was talk of new boats and old boats and the old record that no new boat could match, when in 1844 the *J. M. White* ran up the March river from

New Orleans to St. Louis in two hours less than four days. For some veterans there was a more somber reason to remember the year 1844. On the middle river a long winter was followed by a rainy spring, and every stream and creek ran brimful toward the Mississippi. By the end of May water was in the lower streets of St. Louis. In early June the river fell, but the Missouri flood was yet to come. For a week in June the upper Mississippi had a downpour of rain. Again the tributary streams were flooding. Past St. Louis floated dead horses and cattle, wrecked boats and bridges, battered sheds and cabins. By the third week of June the Mississippi was nine miles wide. The steamer *Indiana* traveled over the submerged road to Kaskaskia in time to remove the Sisters of Charity from their convent; she brought them to the door of the Female Academy in St. Louis. Hundreds of farmers left their homes in the American Bottom, while others climbed to the lofts of barns and gin houses. . . . At Plum Point, a hundred miles below the mouth of the Ohio, a wrecked steamboat near the Arkansas shore caught enough brush and silt to form an island. The island grew; willows and sycamores sprouted in the soft rich soil. A few more years and the wreck had become a farm and a woodyard, selling fuel to passing steamboats. Then the current edged westward and the island, in mid-channel now, began to wear away. After floodwaters the river fell, exposing the decks of the long buried steamer. An island had come and gone in the changing Mississippi. . . . There was endless talk on the high bench while the river shores swung past.

No one knew it then, and least of all Sam Clemens, but this was the end of an age. Only a little longer would the river be the mainstream of the nation's life. Now it was at full tide, carrying the motley traffic of democracy, rafts and scows and shantyboats, medicine shows and minstrel troupes, dramshops and gospel missions and the big white packets. Past spreading towns and drowsy landings and the occasional smoke of woodcutters, river pirates, squatters, fishermen and fugitives, Sam Clemens rode the full crest of the river. But the tide was soon to turn. He got there just in time.

In the last months of 1860 there was talk about political troubles, the bitterness of the presidential campaign and the secession of South Carolina. In the last week of January, 1861, when Louisiana seceded, Sam Clemens was in New Orleans, and his boat was held there. He took passage for St. Louis on the *Uncle Sam*, traveling in the pilothouse though he had paid a cabin fare; one of her pilots was his old friend John Leavenworth, once captain of the *John J. Roe*. They steamed up an almost empty river and were halted at Jefferson Barracks. After Union troops had searched the boat for contraband, they passed on to St. Louis. It was the last regular trip up the river until the war was won.

For Sam Clemens the river years had ended. He would go to Nevada and California, to Europe and the Holy Land, to Buffalo and Hartford and New York, but the river would run through his memory. As a newspaper writer in Western mining camps he began to use his river name, and when his wanderings were done the river flowed again in his books.

The first part of *Life on the Mississippi* was written for the *Atlantic Monthly* in 1874. One summer day at Hartford, walking in the woods with his friend Joseph Twichell, Mark began talking about old steamboating memories on the Mississippi. In the midst of his recollections Twichell exclaimed, "What a virgin subject to hurl into a magazine!" Mark hadn't thought of that. A few months later, in January, 1875, the first of seven chapters appeared in the *Atlantic*.

In 1882, preparing to write the second part of his river memories, Mark Twain returned to the scene, making a voyage on various vessels from St. Louis to New Orleans and back. He found it all changed after twenty-one years away.

On the St. Louis riverfront were half a dozen lifeless steamers, where he remembered a solid mile of them and the levee alive with their commerce. "Mississippi steamboating," he reflected, "was born about 1812, at the end of thirty years it had grown to mighty proportions; and in less than thirty more it was dead!" He traveled on the *Gold Dust* down to Memphis, looking for old landmarks that had disappeared. Hat Island was gone, completely carried away. A man living above Jessup Timber behind the vanished island had seen twenty-nine steamboats wrecked within sight of his house; the perilous "graveyard" through which the packets used to grope was far out of the channel now. Of menacing Goose Island below Commerce, Missouri, nothing remained but a scrap of sand and willow. It was the opposite of a towhead, which Mark Twain, now more interested in language than river soundings, explained as a word for a fair-haired child applied to an infant island with a healthy growth ahead. At New Madrid he saw two steamboats—two at once! After that it was a river of solitude, as empty as when

La Salle had found it, vast, voiceless, lonely, without a sign of life. But as they passed the mouth of the Obion River in Tennessee there was a steamer, lying at the bank half canopied in a bower of forest. Through the telescope they made out fading letters on the nameboard—MARK TWAIN.

So many changes, and yet it was changeless too, the river in the glare of noon and the mystery of midnight. The summer sunrise was the same—first the deep before-daybreak hush and stars paling in the stealthy light, the black shores softening to gray, the river emerging from darkness with white wreaths of mist dissolving. From the breathless forest the first bird called, in growing light the river mirrored the green-gold sky and the deep green shores. A stir of air brought the morning smell and all at once it was full day with rosy sunlight burnishing the great unruffled river. Said Mark Twain, one cannot see too many summer sunrises on the Mississippi. In Chapter 19 of *Huckleberry Finn* he arrested that sunrise, caught it and held it forever.

Despite all the changes, he found the same river, and it stirred him so that he took up the story of Huck Finn, that he had put aside six years before. In a rush of recollection he wrote the great tale, harsh and idyllic, simple and inexhaustible, of a ragged boy and a runaway slave drifting down the Mississippi.

On the street in New Orleans Mark Twain met the man he most wanted to see—Horace Bixby, just as wiry, brisk and testy as he had been twenty-five years before. He was Captain Bixby now, master of the *City of Baton Rouge*. Traveling up the river with him, Mark Twain saw pilots using the river chart that Bixby had devised and the powerful new headlight that searched the midnight shore. Piloting had changed more than the river in Mark Twain's years away.

Mark Twain met his old mentor with spontaneous warmth, but Bixby had not forgot the past strain between them over a financial question. This may account for his later statement that Mark Twain was not a good pilot, that he lacked the forthrightness and nerve that piloting required. His appraisal was accepted by rivermen generally, who felt that Mark Twain had preempted their profession and who resented the Mark Twain legend. Though Sam Clemens never had any serious mishaps at piloting, rivermen were more willing to let him have fame as a writer than as a pilot. One of them made a remark in Mark Twain's own vein—"He was a droll fellow and was always getting off something—sometimes it was a sandbar."

From St. Louis Mark Twain headed north on an upper Mississippi packet, getting off the next morning at Hannibal. You can't go home again; he found a railroad bridge spanning the river and trains rumbling past the Bear Creek swimming hole of his boyhood. Hannibal, with a stern-wheel steamboat on its city seal, had become a railroad town of fifteen thousand people. The river was forgotten. But it still flowed with all its motley commerce in the memory of Mark Twain.

Now, nearly a century later, a hundred thousand visitors a year come to the old river town to see the scenes of Mark Twain's boyhood. At the foot of Cardiff Hill they find two bronze figures, barefoot boys in tattered clothes, Tom Sawyer and Huck Finn, walking toward the river. A path leads up to Riverview Park and there is the bronze figure of Mark Twain, looking across the river. This is the central figure in a memorial that eventually will show Joan of Arc and Becky Thatcher, the Prince and the Pauper, Colonel Sellers and Captain Stormfield, Tom Sawyer, Huck Finn, and Injun Joe—all the people, in rags and splendor, of his imagination. They belong to the world but they came from the mind of a riverman. Late in his life, on a warm night in India when his thoughts went back to the Mississippi, Mark Twain wrote: "All that goes to make the *me* in me was in a Missouri village on the other side of the globe."

III

~~~

The Chained River

Now the river of our greatness is free, as God made it.

WILLIAM TECUMSEH SHERMAN

15

The Fleet

at

Pittsburg Landing

JEFFERSON DAVIS knew the Mississippi, lower and upper, as well as any steamboat man. As a boy in New Orleans he saw the pioneer packets of the 1820's; as a young army officer at Fort Crawford, Wisconsin, he saw the first steamboats smoking under the northern bluffs; his Brierfield Plantation overlooked the Mississippi and his slaves hauled cotton to his own landing. But in the fateful months of 1861 in the Confederate capital of Richmond, he lost sight of the Mississippi. Having closed the river with a row of batteries below New Orleans and a barrier chain at Columbus, Kentucky, the Confederates left it almost undefended. While the South won battles in Virginia, the North was massing troops, transports and gunboats for the great Mississippi campaign.

The river blockade was the first Southern strategy on the Mississippi; its destruction was the first Northern objective. Upon the fall of Fort Sumter, General Leonidas Polk, C.S.A., a nephew of President Polk, was entrusted with defense of the Mississippi. He knew the importance of navigation; as a missionary bishop he had traveled all the winding rivers of the Southwest. A fellow cadet with Jefferson Davis at West Point, he had left the army for the church. Now, erect and stalwart, he was an Episcopal bishop on leave, giving army orders instead of benedictions. In the summer of 1861 he seized the high ground at Columbus, Kentucky, known locally as the Iron Banks, and pointed cannon at the Mississippi. Into the bluff he imbedded a six-ton anchor and attached a massive iron chain. When it was stretched across to Belmont, Missouri—a makeshift, marshy town that denied its name—the chain was armed with torpedoes. The gate was closed. On the hill General Polk enlarged his batteries: 140 guns in tiered rows studded the rust-colored bluff. Across the river he had a garrison of troops at Belmont.

That fall the drowsy port of Cairo became a strategic place, with fleets of steamboats massing Northern men and material on the muddy river-front. In November, 1861, Grant moved south from Cairo in a long line of transports, landing his men on the Missouri shore near Belmont. He overran the Confederate garrison and burned their camp. But General Polk sent troops across the river and drove the invaders back to their boats. The river was still chained.

But there were other rivers leading into the South; and Grant, having already seized Paducah and Smithfield, commanded the entrance to the Cumberland and the Tennessee. That winter, when the inland roads were deep in mud, he prepared an invasion by water. His staging point was Cairo, and Cairo was an uneasy place. Southern settlement pre-dominated in lower Illinois and Southern ties were strong. Rumors reached Springfield and Chicago: secessionists were about to proclaim a separate State of Egypt and to join the Confederacy; at Cairo "river rats and mud-wallopers" were plotting to cut the levee and turn the river into the town. Troops were rushed by railroad from Chicago, and when artillery ringed Cairo the rumors ended. Said a local farmer, "Ten brass missionaries has converted a heap of folks that was on the anxious seat."

Then came a new rumor—Confederate General Gideon Pillow was marching north toward Cairo with an army of ten to thirty thousand. In Washington it was acknowledged that Cairo was second in importance only to the capital itself, and a Memphis newspaper announced that Cairo would be the scene of the first great battle between the North and the South. More troops poured into Cairo and military cargoes piled up on the levee. From Washington, General Winfield Scott ordered fortification of "the heights of Cairo" so as to command Bird's Point on the Missouri shore. (A St. Louis reporter noted that the most elevated point in Cairo was just sixteen inches above high water and could no more command Bird's Point than it could command the moon.) But a distillery at Cairo Point was converted to a fort, and batteries bristled along both rivers while troops jammed into Camp Defiance. Saloons and brothels lined the muddy levee, vendors peddled catfish and jelly rolls, the wind brought mosquitoes from the swamp and the din of gunboats building in the Naval Station at Mound City. On the bare riverbank were rows of cannon barrels and pyramids of cannonballs. In his headquarters in a Cairo hotel full of heat and flies, a silent stocky man was planning the attack on two half-built strongholds, Fort Henry on the Tennessee and Fort Donelson on the Cumberland.

In January the wooden gunboat *Conestoga*, a converted Cincinnati packet, her sides walled with oak "armor plating," made a reconnaissance run up the Tennessee; at Paducah, General Lew Wallace came aboard, saluting Commander Phelps who showed him to his quarters. Up the river passed the squat black gunboat, anchoring at nightfall in midstream. As they came to rest one evening, engines falling quiet and steam sighing away in the escape pipe, they heard the baying of hounds. From the gunboat they watched a tattered Negro throw himself over a rail fence and stagger across a cornfield. Over the fence swarmed the frantic hounds. Behind them three horsemen took the fence and came crashing through the corn.

Commander Phelps of the *Conestoga* ordered a yawl to shore. "Faster lads!" he called across the water. "Faster!" The slave plunged into the willows along the river. He jumped into the branches of a half-submerged tree as the dogs snapped at his heels. A moment later the yawl ran in and took him off.

As they pulled back to the gunboat General Wallace at the guardrail put down his glasses. "It was a close call," he said.

Said the commander, "It may be our turn tomorrow."

Next morning they steamed up to Fort Henry. The big bow gun was uncovered; beside it stood a red flannel bag of powder and a shell like a nail keg. But there was no gunfire that day. The *Conestoga* crept through the torpedo zone and found three heavy guns pointing at the river. Beyond were depots, barracks, and other guns trained landward. After that glimpse the gunboat dropped behind the screen of Panther Island. That night she hurried down the river to report.

Two weeks later a long line of steamboats nosed in to Paducah. As word went from camp to camp, tents came down and wagons were loaded; soon all the roads were black with troops marching toward the river. By sundown the second division of the Army of the Tennessee was afloat. Next day a string of seven gunboats filed past Paducah and into the Tennessee. Behind them came a mile-long line of transports from Cairo and St. Louis. It was mild bright blue-sky weather, with a false spring in the air. Bands played and cheers rang across the water as the flotilla steamed toward Fort Henry. The Tennessee had freighted cotton, corn, cattle and a hundred other kinds of cargo. Now it was carrying 17,000 troops to warfare. For miles the smoke rolled up to a cloudless sky.

Next day, with a thundering barrage from the gunboats, the troops poured ashore three miles below Fort Henry. While the gunboats went on up to pound the fort, the soldiers trudged through muddy roads and flooded fields. On the river Grant had fifty-four guns to the twelve guns at Fort Henry. It was mostly a duel of cannon, while rain poured down and men sloshed through the bottoms. One gunboat was put out of action; another took thirty hits. But the fleet closed range and pounded harder. After an hour's slugging, the fort had but four guns left. The troops moved onto the road toward Fort Donelson, a dozen miles away, while a flag of truce glimmered through the cannon smoke. The river fleet had won its first victory.

The next contest would be at Fort Donelson on the Cumberland, twelve miles east by land and a long way round by water. While three wooden gunboats went on up the Tennessee to seize Southern shipping, the four ironclads hurried down the flooded Tennessee, amid floating trees, sheds and fences. Passing Paducah they turned into the Cumberland. Meanwhile Grant was marching through an ocean of mud. It took five days to cover the twelve miles to the Cumberland, and when he arrived the ironclads were throwing shells from the river. The weather had turned bleak. Through a curtain of snow the Union troops closed in on Fort Donelson. One Confederate colonel got his cavalry out, slogging over the freezing back roads; he was Nathan Bedford Forrest and he would be heard from again. The rest surrendered. With his fleet and his army Grant had won two strongholds in a single week.

Now the Union forces could move on up the Tennessee, but General Halleck at St. Louis found fault with Grant and relieved him of command. By the time Lincoln had intervened, raising Grant to the rank of major general, the scattered Confederates had gathered at Corinth, Mississippi. When Grant took charge again, the splendid Army of Tennessee awaited the approach of his Army of the Tennessee. They would meet at Shiloh.

To bring new troops from St. Louis and to provide transport on the Tennessee, a fleet of eighty-two steamboats waited at the St. Louis levee.

One of them was the *John J. Roe*, the big slow packet Mark Twain had steered around the bends of the Mississippi. Aboard her as mate was Grant Marsh, at the beginning of his long career on the rivers. Loaded with army supplies the *Roe* steamed up the Tennessee to Fort Henry where she embarked two regiments, one from Indiana and one from Missouri; with them came their commander General Lew Wallace and his big horse John. They jammed the packet, as solid as a load of cotton, and went on up the river to Crump's Landing, four miles below the river hamlet of Pittsburg. At Savanna, on the east bank of the river, opposite Pittsburg Landing, scores of steamboats were tied to roots, stumps and tree trunks, and a huge commissary camp stretched over the hill. In the dusk hundreds of fires gleamed along the shore. The river-borne troops had lived on hardtack and river water; now they were feasting on salt pork, ham and corn bread. General Wallace moved his men ashore and took up his headquarters on the steamer *Jesse K. Bell*, moored to the western shore. The *Roe* pushed on, past miles of flickering campfires, to Pittsburg Landing. There Captain Baxter, commissary officer, brought his staff aboard and set up his command. Scuttlebutt said that the Confederate Army, under Johnston and Beauregard, were digging in at Corinth, twenty miles away.

For a week the Union buildup continued, steamboats pushing in with bargeloads of wagons, horses, ammunition and crates of Enfield rifles. In fine spring weather the river kept falling, and a barge loaded with new army wagons went aground at Savanna. Captain Baxter sent Grant Marsh with a detail of soldiers to work the barge free. They toiled for several days, in a falling river, in sight of Grant's headquarters in the Cherry mansion on the shore. Each day Grant rode his buckskin horse aboard the side-wheeler *Tigress* for an inspection of the troops at Pittsburg Landing. Most of the outfits had diarrhea—"Tennessee quickstep" —from drinking river water; otherwise there were no complaints. The weather held fine, birds sang in the thickets, the willows turned golden in the sun. But one day Grant's horse fell on the muddy riverbank, injuring the general's leg.

On Saturday, April 5, Marsh and his men got their barge half floated; a few more hours would finish the job. Across the river a rash of campfires spread—Buell's army was arriving. Next morning was Easter, a bright sunrise and vireos and catbirds singing. Then came a rumble, from over the hill toward Shiloh Meetinghouse. Thunder grew in the cloudless sky. From the riverbank Marsh saw General Grant hobble onto the *Tigress*, an orderly bringing his horse. Marsh followed them aboard as the crew cast off. Hissing and rumbling, the *Tigress* charged up the river. On the way she met the steamer *John Warner* with a message from a desperate division on Owl Creek near the Shiloh churchyard. At Crump's Landing the *Tigress* swung into the bank beside the *Jesse K. Bell*, and speaking across the guardrails Grant instructed General Wallace to hold his division in readiness until Grant could assess the situation and send orders. Backing into the stream the *Tigress* plunged on to Pittsburg Landing where cannon shells were crashing through treetops and the roar of musketry rose like a wall. When the landing stage touched down, Grant was helped onto his horse. He rode up the smoky hill toward Shiloh churchyard.

That Easter day was hellish. Down the riverbank streamed wounded soldiers, stragglers, commissary guards, driverless horses dragging broken wagons and gun carriages. Through the chaos Marsh made his way to the *John J. Roe*. He went aboard just ahead of a messenger with orders for Buell's army at Savanna. Some of the troops could use the road along the east bank of the river; it would be late in the day when they arrived. Meanwhile transports were churning the river white.

Back and forth the *Roe* shuttled, bringing up troops to the trampled landing, pouring them onto the gashed riverbank. Each time they returned, the din of battle sounded nearer. Just over the hill rose the wild Confederate yells and the crash of musketry; shells erupted in the river and hurtled into the woods beyond. Shaking with the rockers driving her big paddle buckets, the *Roe* hurried up and down the river till the smoky night closed in.

Then the roar of battle rolled away and the Shiloh woods were silent, but the Union gunboats began to boom from the river. All night they threw shells over the dark ridge where Northern and Southern men huddled under the shattered trees. When a cold rain began Grant hobbled into a log house. Army surgeons were working there by lantern light. The general limped back to the dripping woods.

The next day, with Buell's fresh regiments and Wallace's division coming in through Stony Lonesome, Grant had superior power. Slowly, absorbing fearful punishment, the whole Union Army got into motion. They pushed on, through cannonade and musket fire, around stubborn hillocks and through gashed ravines, past the scarred log Shiloh church and beyond it, retaking the field they had lost. That afternoon the din died away. The Confederates, covered by Forrest's cavalry, drew back toward Corinth, and the Union men streamed toward Pittsburg Landing. Behind them they left 13,000 dead, one-fourth of their number, in the trampled fields and thickets.

The next morning long lines of bandaged men filed out of the tent hospitals and boarded the transports. These were the walking wounded. Others would wait for the hospital boats with their elevators and amputating rooms, their surgeons and wound-dressers. That night the *John J. Roe* backed off the landing and headed down the river. On her decks lay six hundred wounded Indiana soldiers. Her engines throbbed and the big paddles lifted a pale wheel of water in the darkness.

The Army of the Tennessee had hard campaigns ahead, but gunboats and transports had made Union rivers of the Cumberland and the Tennessee. Supplied by barges and transports, the army would push on through the long, winding valley to Perryville, Stones River, Chickamauga and Chattanooga. Beyond Lookout Mountain lay Sherman's route to Atlanta and the sea, and his final march up the coast for the finish. When the valley was at peace and the memories had lengthened, riverboats again brought army men, with fifes and bugles and marching songs, up the Tennessee. For many years the Grand Army of the Republic held its annual encampment on the peaceful riverbank at Pittsburg Landing.

16

<del>~~~~~</del>

Eads's Ironclads

ON APRIL 17, 1861, four days after the surrender of Fort Sumter in Charleston Harbor, James Buchanan Eads in St. Louis received a letter from Edward Bates, Attorney General in Lincoln's Cabinet. Bates was a Missouri man and a good friend of Eads, but this was a business letter. "Be not surprised if you are called here suddenly by telegram. In a certain contingency it will be necessary to have the aid of the most thorough knowledge of the Western Rivers and the use of steam on them, and in that event I have advised that you should be consulted."

A few days later the telegram arrived and Eads was on his way to Washington. At stake was control of the Mississippi River system. Eads knew the river from the Head of Passes in the Gulf of Mexico to the Falls of St. Anthony. To the problems of war he brought twenty years of strenuous experience on the Mississippi.

James Eads first saw the Mississippi on a September day in 1833. A restless, curious boy of thirteen he was on his first steamboat, traveling with his mother and his sisters from Louisville to their new home in St. Louis. When the packet neared the mouth of the Ohio, passengers looked ahead expectantly. On the low Illinois shore stood three green mounds, silent as death; thirty years later, in a deafening din, James Eads's ironclads would be taking shape at Mound City. Past the brushy site of Cairo, the river curved and widened. Beyond a big towhead fringed with willow thickets, the boy saw a new water flowing. Around him the travelers were repeating "Mississippi . . . Mississippi."

It was nearly daylight when the boy woke to a clangor of bells and a clamor of voices. Outside the cabin rose a swirling cloud of smoke. Down on the main deck men were pushing burning cargo into the river. For a moment the smoke blew clear, and in the first long light of sunrise the streets of St. Louis showed on the sloping riverbank. The boat swung in, racing the fire to the landing. In a surge of people young James Eads was swept ashore. On the levee in the sunrise he watched the steamboat burn.

James Eads began his career as a peddler, selling fruit on the swarming riverfront, carrying his basket aboard the ferryboats that shuttled across to Illinoistown; forty years later his massive three-span bridge would put the ferries out of business. From apple boy he moved up to errand and stock boy in a dry-goods store. Outside the shop he heard steamboat bells and the clatter of commerce on the levee. At home he was building a model packet, powered by a rat on a treadmill. He dreamed of steamboats in the night.

In 1839 a tall, slender, level-eyed youth of nineteen went aboard the steamer *Knickerbocker* and began his job as mud clerk. He signed "James Eads" to manifests and checked freight and baggage for Galena. From noon till night and from midnight until morning he collected freight bills, bargained for fuel at the muddy woodyards, and sorted lists of lading. By the end of this summer he knew every landing between St. Louis and Galena. He knew the island chutes and narrows, the points and crossings, the turbulence of the rapids and the clear river reaches between them.

On a clear and quiet night late in the season, the *Knickerbocker*, loaded with cattle and Galena lead, ran upon a submerged snag. In a hiss and rumble of steam the fires went out and the cattle swam for shore. Passing flatboats took the people off before the heavy boat went under.

It was low-water season and nearly every day the St. Louis papers reported steamboats snagged and sunk. On a new packet Eads kept wondering about wrecks on the river bottom. He had tallied many kinds of cargo—pork, beef, flour, sugar, lead, iron, plows, axles, bars, flanges, mandrels. To some of it, river water was no threat. There were thousands of pigs of lead on the river bottom, and thousands of tons of implements, tools and machinery. On the back of old freight bills James Eads began drawing designs for a diving bell. After three years he had his invention ready. He persuaded a St. Louis firm to build a twin-hulled boat with suction pumps and steam-powered derricks.

His first salvage job was at Keokuk where a bargeload of lead had sunk in the rapids. In a diving bell made from a whiskey barrel Eads made his first descent to the river bottom, and for the first time in history the river gave up its wreckage. From Keokuk, Captain Eads took his salvage boat down the Mississippi, learning the river bottom at scores of dangerous places and reclaiming lost cargoes. He worked in side rivers, the Ohio, the Tennessee, the Illinois, exploring drowned steamboats and their lading. Between underwater jobs he designed a new boat powerful enough to lift a derelict out of the mud. His *Submarine (No. 2)* was ready when disaster struck the St. Louis riverfront.

On the night of May 17, 1849, scores of packets lined the levee, bright in their new season's paint and polish. On the steamer *White Cloud* the steward had been airing bedding on the hurricane deck. Sparks from a passing vessel set fire to a mattress and the boat was soon burning. Wind carried flames to the *Eudora* and the *Edward Bates*, lying alongside. The *Bates* burned loose from her moorings and drifted free. She was flaming then, spreading fire to every boat she touched. The midnight sky rained sparks and embers over a whole riverfront. Fire raced through the upper Mississippi packets *American Eagle, Montauk, Red Wing, St. Peters*; the Missouri boats *Alice, Alexander Hamilton, Boreas (No. 3), Eliza Stuart, Kit Carson, Mandan, Martha, Alice, Timour*; the New Orleans packets *Belle Isle, Sarah, Mameluke*; the Illinois River boats *Acadia* and *Prairie State*; the Pittsburgh packet *Taglioni*; and the towboats *Frolic* and *General Brooks*. When the sun came up in the smoky sky, twenty-eight charred wrecks strewed the St. Louis Harbor.

With his diving bell Eads got chains and cables under the drowned hulls; his powerful derricks hauled them away. Soon the noise of commerce returned to the long St. Louis levee.

In 1855 when the government had lost interest in the waterways, Eads bought five discarded snag boats, converting them to salvage and wrecking craft. The next year he proposed to clear the neglected river channels, but Congress was preoccupied with sectional issues. Then came another disaster. In the winter of 1857, when steamboats were lined for twenty blocks along the St. Louis levee, the river froze from shore to shore. A sudden thaw loosed the current above the city and a gorge of ice moved down. In a grinding destruction it carried forty steamboats away and left a mountain of wreckage on the Lower Dike. One of Eads's salvage boats was crushed in the ice. But he had ten wreckers left and soon they were clearing the harbor. When the task was done, he retired to a country home on the southern edge of St. Louis. His health was failing and he thought his work was finished.

In Washington in May of 1861 James Eads proposed construction of an armored fleet to break the blockade of the lower Mississippi. But he was a civilian and a riverman, talking to salt water admirals. The Mississippi seemed far from Washington, and Eads's logic and passion could not bring it nearer. The Navy Department ordered three wooden gunboats for the Ohio and turned back to salt water.

In July the three gunboats with their "oaken armor" grounded in the Ohio, en route to Cairo, and the rivers were undefended. Then someone in Washington woke up, and the Navy Department advertised for bids to build seven ironclads for the Western rivers. Eads himself made the contract bid, proposing to complete the seven vessels in sixty-five days.

The contract freed his pent-up energies. Soon he had timber coming down from the upper Mississippi, armor plate from the Ohio, and thousands of workmen hammering day and night. Four boats were building at his Union Ironworks on the edge of St. Louis at Carondelet, three others were taking shape at Mound City near Cairo. In five weeks the *St. Louis*, the world's first ironclad gunboat, was launched at Carondelet. In November four squat powerful vessels were afloat. They were soon followed by the massive *Benton*, converted from Eads's biggest twin-bowed wrecker; the twin bows were planked together and sheathed in armor plate which enclosed the entire hull and the big paddle wheel. With Eads aboard, the *Benton* steamed toward Cairo. She was invulnerable to cannonballs, but forty miles out of St. Louis she grounded on a shoal. The naval officers did not know how to get her off, but with hawsers stretched to trees onshore and her paddles backing, Eads inched the big boat free. She pushed on to Cairo, where Grant was waiting. Crews of inland boys, training in a boot camp at Mound City, came aboard for the invasion of Tennessee. It was Eads's ironclads that won Fort Henry and Fort Donelson—Eads's ironclads in fact; he had spent his own fortune on them and his government contract was still unpaid.

With the fall of forts Henry and Donelson, General Leonidas Polk on the Iron Banks was outflanked; he could not hold his position on the

Mississippi. Late in February the gunboats came down from Cairo and shelled the Iron Banks. Polk withdrew, moving 130 pieces of artillery down the river for a new stand at Island No. 10. The Northern gunboats followed. While they were shelling the island batteries, Eads boarded a tugboat at Cairo and hurried down the river. Before he saw the low, crouching ironclads he heard the boom of their cannon and smelled their powder smoke. He went aboard the burly *Benton*, wanting to stay for the showdown, but Flag Officer Foote urged him back to Cairo to spur the work on four more gunboats. He was not there to see his monitors run the gantlet of Island No. 10.

At the corner of four states, Kentucky, Tennessee, Missouri and Arkansas, the river makes a huge double loop, and the narrow channel passes under the wooded shores of Island No. 10. Miles of swamps and sloughs protected the island from approach by land. Just one passable road led inland to Tiptonville between the river and Reelfoot Lake— the big cypress-studded backwater created by the earthquake half a century before. In the high water of March the bottoms were drowned, and General Pope's Union Army cut a channel through the forest to bypass the island. Working from rafts Pope's engineers cut off the trees which were hauled away by tugboats. Then another barge gang with a sawing machine cut off the trunks underwater. In nineteen days of cold and brutal labor, a six-mile canal was opened. By this route bargeloads of Union troops passed through the drowned woods to New Madrid where Pope planned his march south. But he needed cannon to knock out Confederate batteries at Point Pleasant, and Foote's gunboats, drawing six feet of water, could not pass through the canal. To support the army they must run the gantlet of massed artillery on Island No. 10.

Time was short for the Union advance. In Memphis two big Confederate ironclads were nearing completion; very soon they would be ready to drive the Union troops from their foothold on the Missouri shore at New Madrid. A Union gunboat was needed below Island No. 10. It looked like long odds—passing under rows of Confederate cannon in a narrow channel in strong current. A grounded boat would be a sitting duck, and any craft would draw the fire of massed artillery. But Henry Walke, black-bearded, bushy-browed commander of the *Carondelet*, wanted to try.

To prepare her for the run, some bizarre armor was added. Her deck was covered with planks from a wrecked barge, cordwood was stacked against her boilers and an 11-inch hawser was wound around her pilot house, leaving a slit to steer by. At dusk twenty-four sharpshooters from the 42nd Illinois Infantry came aboard, and a barge piled with baled hay was lashed alongside—toward the island batteries. Said the captain, "She looks like a farmer's wagon," and he ordered the lines cast off. It was ten o'clock on the night of April 4.

On the gunboat were two news correspondents, one from the St. Louis *Democrat*, the other from *The New York Times*; the *Carondelet's* run is one of the best-reported events in the long history of the Mississippi. Weather was on the Union side. In the moonlight the monitor lay dark as an island, but at ten o'clock storm clouds blotted out the moon, a sheet of rain swept the river and thunder shook the sky. Amid flashes of lightning, the gunboat slipped into the stream. Black and silent she pushed ahead, "through checkers of darkness and flame," wrote the New York reporter, toward the enemy works. Lightning picked her out —a black low form with sloping sides, portholes sheathed, black smoke pouring from her twin funnels and a flag tugging at her jack staff—and dropped her back into darkness. In the torn black night she moved like a shadow past the first Confederate batteries, and Captain Walke wondered if he might get by unseen. Then the darkness lifted. To relieve the puffing of steam pipes, escape steam had been led through the wheelhouse; now the accumulated soot in her smokestacks took fire. Twin flames leaped up, brighter than torches, just as the gunboat was passing the head of the island. Muskets banged, rockets arched over from the shore batteries, and cannonballs came whistling. (At that hour, a hundred miles away, 103,000 men were huddled in the rain at Shiloh, with shells screaming over.)

With engines pounding, the gunboat surged through the narrow channel. At the bow leadsmen took soundings, but the roar of cannon drowned their cries. The storm crashed down again, lightning, thunder, and a rush of rain that quenched the soot fire in the chimneys. By the intermittent light a steersman kept the gunboat close inshore, shells bursting over and around her. A current caught the hay barge and swung the vessel toward a bar, but in a new burst of lightning the wheel went hard over and the gunboat answered. From the forecastle came a reassuring cry, "No bottom!"

Thirty minutes carried the *Carondelet* to safety. Behind her the cannon faded and the storm rolled away. Shouting and laughing, the crew fired the minute guns, telling the fleet, and Pope's army, that they had made it to New Madrid. While the answer from Foote's flagship echoed up the river, Commander Walke made shore. A bonfire leaped up at the fort where General Pope ordered a barrel of grog for the crew. The *Carondelet* was undamaged, though one cannonball was found in her coal barge and another embedded in a bale of hay.

Two nights later, in another thunderstorm, the ironclad *Pittsburgh* ran the forty-nine guns of Island No. 10. With two gunboats on hand, General Pope shuttled troops across the river and blocked the road to Tiptonville, sealing the defenders in. On April 7, while the Confederate Army was streaming south from Shiloh, Island No. 10—with 7,000 men, ten boats, hundreds of horses, and mounds of ammunition and supplies —was surrendered. It was all won by the midnight run of the ironclads.

Augmented by their captured vessels, the Union fleet pushed down the river, to the next fortified point on the Chickasaw Bluffs. This was Fort Pillow, halfway between Island No. 10 and Memphis. At Memphis the Confederates hastily formed a new squadron to check the Union advance. Without shipyards and foundries they did what they could, converting barges into mortar boats and steamers into rams and "cottonclads." Massed timbers and a pair of cannon at the bows were their offensive weapons; a corps of sharpshooters manned firing stations behind timber barricades. The heavy bows were their chief threat. With engineers throwing oil and resin into the furnaces, and bales of cotton absorbing enemy fire, they would use brute strength to block and batter the Union vessels. Eight of these cottonclads gathered at Fort Pillow, while seven federal ironclads lay at anchor a few miles upstream, with the *Cincinnati* on lookout ahead of the flotilla.

On the hazy morning of May 10 the cottonclads came charging up the river. The *General Bragg*, at the head of the column, took a broadside from the Union gunboat *Cincinnati* and crashed into her. It was a glancing blow but it tore a hole as big as a barn door in the *Cincinnati*'s side, and, while she was reeling, the *Sumter* rammed her stern, demolishing the steering gear. Right behind the *Sumter* came the cotton-armored *Colonel Lovell*. She buffeted the *Cincinnati* amidships and a rebel sharpshooter caught her captain giving an order; he put a bullet through his open mouth. With water pouring in, the *Cincinnati* lurched over and sank. Only her pilothouse remained above-water.

The racket brought the rest of the Union fleet boiling through the hazy sunlight. Around Plum Point came the *Mound City*, and the *General Van Dorn* charged her, head on. The crash opened up her bottom and the ironclad ran, sinking, onto shore. Then came the massive *Benton* and the *Carondelet*. Soon two of the rebel rams were drifting out of control. The rest turned back downstream.

The Confederates had won a victory, but they could not drive off Eads's ironclads which kept a rain of shells bursting around Fort Pillow. Meanwhile Union forces pushing south from Shiloh forced the Confederate Army to abandon Corinth, and Fort Pillow was outflanked from the east. The cottonclads had no choice but to drop back to Memphis; Fort Pillow was abandoned, and the Union ironclads took over another segment of the Mississippi.

On the morning of June 6, thousands of people crowded the bluffs of Memphis to watch a battle for their city. Remembering the Plum Point victory they were in sanguine spirits; the women brought basket lunches and parasols against the summer sun. The two fleets approached with cannon firing; soon the river was wreathed in smoke, with only the steamboat chimneys showing. It was a blurred battle for the onlookers, and even for the dueling vessels. The Union fleet had some reinforcements, squat, fast, unarmed battering rams, trussed and cross-braced, solid as pile drivers. The leading ram, *Queen of the West*, raced through the smoke, piled into the *Colonel Lovell* and sent her to the bottom. In the smoky welter of infighting, the fast Union rams dealt deadly blows, and with a jarring collision two Confederate vessels disabled each other.

It all happened in twenty minutes. When the smoke lifted, one cottonclad was on her side on the Arkansas shore, another was burning. Two more were disabled, their colors lowered in surrender. Just one Confederate vessel got away, scrambling down the river with Union shells splashing around her.

From the bluffs, their lunches uneaten, the Memphis people went home in a daze of shock and dismay. The Federal crews swarmed ashore and whooped through the empty streets. Soon a smoke-stained Union ensign flew over the Memphis post office.

While Eads's ironclads had fought their way down 230 winding miles of Mississippi, Admiral Farragut, with a fleet of ocean gunboats, had come in from the Gulf of Mexico. He slugged past forts Jackson and St. Philip, and in a pitched battle destroyed a Confederate flotilla at

A busy day at Vicksburg, Mississippi, 1883 (Way Collection)

Steamboats crushed in the ice at Cincinnati, 1918 (Way Collection)

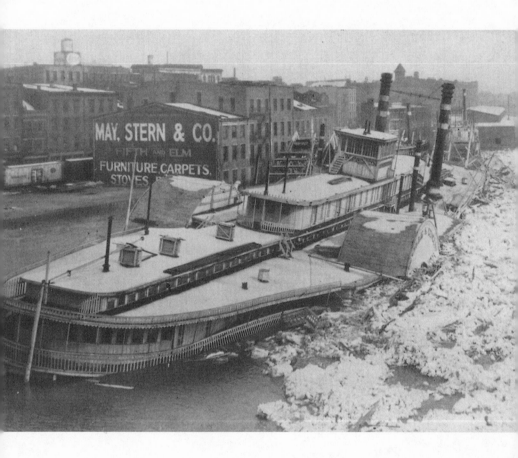

New Orleans. On April 25 that great port fell to the Union Navy. On up the river Farragut came. With little trouble he took Baton Rouge and Natchez. Now the Confederate West—Louisiana, Texas, Arkansas with their great resources of men and material—was cut off from the beleaguered South. With Farragut below and Eads's ironclads pushing past Memphis, the Confederates clung to one point on the Mississippi— the stubborn, strategic, hill-girt riverport of Vicksburg.

17

~~~~~

Guns at Vicksburg

BETWEEN TALL STACKS the side-wheel steamer *Ruth* carried her ancient and gentle name, meaning "Friend," and her paddle boxes showed a white-robed maiden gleaning in a field of golden grain. She did not look like an army boat, but she spent her short life carrying troops, ordnance, ammunition and supplies into the disputed South. On her first voyage, in January, 1863, she ran down to Helena, Arkansas, with a cargo "billed to the United States." Stamping in the main deck were 21 cattle, 18 mules, 11 horses. The army was billed $3.20 a head for the horses, $2.76 for the mules, and a mere $1.10 for the teamsters who went along. Three officers, including a general, were carried at $2.10 each. The officers had beds in the cabin; the teamsters could stretch out on 12 boxes of small arms, 15 cases of muskets, or 3 army wagons and an ambulance. Each of the vehicles was billed at $3.20.

This was a routine run, but seven months later the *Ruth* carried a more important cargo. On the first of August she loaded military stores along with nearly three million dollars in Federal currency. That fortune was stowed on the cabin deck directly above the fuel bunkers. In the cabin, among some Union soldiers on the way to their outfit in Arkansas, traveled a Confederate saboteur. On August 4, a few miles out of Cairo, fire raged through the bunkers and the *Ruth* went up in smoke. Then there was one less transport supplying Union forces for the campaign against Vicksburg.

Just below Mile 440 and the old mouth of the Yazoo River, the Mississippi bends eastward toward the Vicksburg bluffs. Since 1876 the

Centennial Cut-off has eliminated the final loop, but in 1863 the big stream made a narrow inverted *U* with the second reach paralleling the first; between them lay a low tongue of land barely a mile across. On terraced bluffs rising 260 feet above the shore, the town of Vicksburg overlooked the looping river. It was the highest and strongest point in the whole valley. On shelving slopes and jutting ridges Confederate guns commanded the parallel river courses. Water batteries were planted in deep woods below the town. For three miles the shores were guarded by smoothbore cannon and rifled guns. At the head of the river's loop, screened rifle pits could pour a short-range fire.

This was the key to the rich Yazoo valley with its cornucopia of cattle, grain and cotton and its Confederate navy yard at Yazoo City; and when Farragut's fleet pushed up from the south and the Northern fleet under Captain Charles H. Davis moved down from Memphis, it was the last Southern stronghold on the Mississippi. Confederate batteries at Port Hudson and Grand Bluff, below Vicksburg, could not stand without the Vicksburg anchor.

It was clear enough that Vicksburg could only be taken by a land army, but at the War Department's urging Farragut tried an attack by river in June of 1862. Some of his vessels got through but they did no damage to the Confederate emplacements. It was the first of several fruitless dashes while the Vicksburg batteries still controlled the river.

In that hot tense summer up the Yazoo's tunnel of vine-twined cottonwoods, the Confederates were armoring their powerful ram *Arkansas*. Within sloping casements of dovetailed railroad iron, backed with heavy timber and braced cotton bales, she carried a firepower of shell guns along with smoothbore and rifled cannon. On a hazy July morning a Union flotilla steamed up the Yazoo to find and destroy her, but the *Arkansas* got out. With her smokestack pierced like a sieve and smoke pouring from her ignited cotton armor, she fought past the Union ironclads. In a furious half hour she gave more damage than she took, and ran down to refuge under the Vicksburg cannon. Rankled by this daring feat Farragut braved the Vicksburg batteries, hoping to demolish the *Arkansas* as he dashed by. In a running fusillade the *Arkansas* suffered a few killed and wounded while land batteries pounded the Union vessels.

A week later Captain Davis sent a squadron past the shore defenses to attack the *Arkansas*. Though they inflicted damage they did not disable her. While she remained a taunt and a threat, parties of Confederate riflemen on the riverbank peppered Union transports, and new rebel batteries were planted on the shore. Vicksburg was growing stronger. The hot summer nights rumbled with cannon fire and the racket of rifles. In a last bold fight, charging the Union ironclads, the *Arkansas* went dead with an engine breakdown. Helpless, her commander got his men ashore and set fire to the vessel. She blew up with a roar that shook the heights of Vicksburg.

When low water idled the Union fleet, silence settled over the river except for guerrilla bands firing on unarmed transports and plundering their cargo. As the year ebbed, Union ironclads patrolled between Helena and Vicksburg. Again and again they steamed past the pretty town of Lake Providence where green lawns came down to the river. On November 28, 1862, pilot Charlie Ross of the *Marmora* noted in his diary that the beautiful plantation ladies gathered on the bank and screamed at the passing gunboat, "Oh you dirty, mean Yankee abolitionists! Hurrah for Jeff Davis!"

At Cairo that winter Commander David Porter enlarged his squadron with light-armored "tinclads" and heavy rams. To man the ram fleet, a recruiting letter was circulated in the Ohio valley: in the Mississippi Marine Brigade, it said, there was no marching, no carrying knapsacks, no trench digging, no picket duty, no camping in the mud—but good cooks, bedding and a roof overhead. It did not add that there would be a rain of shot and shell, gun duels and collisions, boats riddled, burned and sinking in mid-river.

Meanwhile Captain Walke was taking gunboats up the Yazoo to clear an approach for Union troops from that direction. In the sodden winter Grant's army trudged in to the west bank of the looped river and began digging a canal across the tongue of land toward a point two miles below Vicksburg. (They never made that wet ditch deep enough for navigation, but fourteen years later the Centennial Cut-off led the river through the low peninsula.)

Confederate vessels were doing a brisk trade in produce and supplies between the Red River and Vicksburg, and to disturb this commerce a Union task force prepared to run past the strengthened Vicksburg batteries. In command of the lead vessel, *Queen of the West*, armored with a double wall of cotton bales, was 19-year-old Charles R. Ellet. He had orders to creep down in darkness, then to open up full speed and

189

ram the Confederate steamer *Vicksburg* at the wharf, to fire turpentine balls into her and dash for dear life. In the predawn blackness of February 3, 1863, the *Queen of the West* moved out, but steering trouble developed, and daylight found her at the head of the bend. Rebel cannonballs chased her down the river. She rammed the *Vicksburg*, as ordered, and fired her with turpentine, but Confederate shells pierced the *Queen's* cotton armor and set it afire. Cutting the burning bales adrift, young Colonel Ellet ran on to safety. After eighteen hours of repairs he took his vessel to the mouth of the Red River where he found three Confederate steamers loaded with military cargo. He burned them along with a lot of skiffs and flatboats. In pursuit of other craft up the Red River, the *Queen*, accompanied by the *De Soto*, ran aground in plain view of a Confederate cannon on a low bluff. A direct hit put her engines out of business and left her helpless. The crew climbed onto cotton bales and were picked up by the *De Soto*.

Ellet could not burn his vessel because he left on board an engineer with a shattered leg. So the *Queen of the West* was taken by the rebels, for whom she fought as sturdily as before. With another Confederate ram she steamed up the Mississippi, meeting the Union ironclad *Indianola* at Palmyra Island, twelve miles below Vicksburg. In black night, with the *Indianola* unable to sight her target, the Confederates disabled her and captured her crew. To get the vessel beyond the reach of Union salvage they towed her down the river and across, leaving her to sink in ten feet of water in front of Jefferson Davis' plantation.

Heading back upriver, the *Queen* met a deadly looking gunboat moving slowly downstream under a cloud of smoke. At this threat the rebel rams swung around and dashed away. A Confederate captain attempting to salvage the *Indianola* quickly dismantled that vessel, pushed her cannon into the river, set fire to the hull and fled ashore with his crew.

It was a grotesque alarm—the feared gunboat was a dummy made of an old coal barge with pork barrels piled up for chimneys and smoke pouring from smudge pots of tar and oakum. It had drifted down, unmanned, through a barrage from the Vicksburg batteries. Daubed black with pitch, it was menacing with rows of timbers tilted like cannon barrels. Two leaky yawls hung at the davits, a privy was set up for a pilothouse, a Union ensign fluttered aft and a skull and crossbones forward. It bore no nameboards but a small sign, readable at close range:

DELUDED PEOPLE, CAVE IN! There were some clumsy craft in the Mississippi squadron, but none to equal this.

At daylight the dummy had beached below Vicksburg in sight of Grant's soldiers. Glad to get in on this joke they shoved her back into the stream, but they did not have the satisfaction of knowing how she put to rout two rebel rams and the salvage crew on the *Indianola*.

Two months later the end came for the *Queen of the West*, when the once-Union vessel was sunk by Union gunboats of the Gulf Squadron.

In mid-March Farragut brought up a flotilla to blockade the mouth of the Red River. Three of his vessels were disabled by the Confederate batteries at Port Hudson and only Farragut himself got through with his flagship *Hartford*. To maintain the blockade and to patrol the Mississippi, he called for reinforcements from the fleet above Vicksburg. Down came the rams *Switzerland*, in command of young Charles Ellet, late of the *Queen of the West*, and *Lancaster*, under his brother John A. Ellet. The *Lancaster* took a shell in her boilers and sank, but her men escaped, on cotton bales, to the *Switzerland*. The *Switzerland* got through, though damaged, to join the patrol fleet.

Meanwhile Grant, with his army mired in the marshes and retreating from the flooded bottoms, asked for enough transport below Vicksburg to get his troops across to the east shore of the river. He meant to gather them on high ground below Vicksburg and fight up to the rear of the river-trained batteries. In April falling water left roads on the west bank passable, and the troops began moving toward the crossing place at New Carthage.

At the same time Admiral Porter prepared to send his fleet past Vicksburg. For fueling, each vessel lashed a coal barge on the off side, leaving the port guns clear to return the Confederate fire; their vulnerable sterns were shielded with logs and wet bales of hay. Seven gunboats, a ram and a line of cotton-swathed transports moved into line, advancing slowly at fifty-yard intervals with no lights showing in the river darkness. Just before midnight as they rounded the point Confederate sharpshooters gave the alarm. They set fire to tar barrels and some riverfront houses, and in that light the Vicksburg guns began to fire.

In a sudden din and glare the Union gunboats fired back at the smoky hills and splashed through the erupting river. Some lost their barges; several grounded and struggled back into the stream with shells raining down; one caught fire, burned and sank. By two hours after midnight all but the *Henry Clay* were at Hard Times, Grant's staging point. A few nights later Porter brought down another line of transports.

Grant crossed the river below Grand Gulf which he took from the rear. Then he marched on firm ground toward Vicksburg. Three times he assaulted the town and three times he was beaten back. So began the siege, with Grant's big army arced around the southeast heights of Vicksburg, Sherman entrenched on the bluffs to the northeast, and Porter pounding from the river. During the siege the Mississippi Squadron kept open Union lines of supply. Though no Confederate vessels were left on the river, guerrillas infested the shores and harried the transport fleet; if a vessel escaped one ambush they cut across a neck of land and attacked it again. While Vicksburg held out they took a steady toll.

But the Union had possession of the river and the port was doomed. On the 4th of July, 1863, after forty-seven days of siege, Vicksburg surrendered. Amid rejoicing in the Union camps and in the Union fleet came word of a Union victory at Gettysburg. Five days later Port Gibson surrendered and the Mississippi was a Union river. Soon cotton would go north to the great mills, and a hundred kinds of manufacture would come south from the Ohio valley. In Washington, President Lincoln announced that the Father of Waters once more went unvexed to the sea.

Thirty years later historian John Fiske toured the country from Maine to Oregon, giving lectures on the war on the Mississippi. With a stereopticon lantern he showed the river defenses and traced the movement of the river squadrons. By then the rams and ironclads were gone, but for an hour in the darkened lecture hall they fought again, the *Carondelet* running Island No. 10, the *Arkansas* butting past the Union monitors, the dummy gunboat winning a bizarre bloodless victory, the *Switzerland* and the *Queen of the West* firing from an armor of baled hay and cotton. The struggle for the great river could not be forgotten.

But while John Fiske gave his lecture he was giving an elegy. Between 1861 and 1863 a tide had turned forever and the Mississippi ceased to be the main road of America. Though the river flowed south, railroads had reached and crossed it from the East, and the trade routes of the future would link the midland cities to the Eastern seaports. The river songs would linger; in memory white packets would whistle at the landings and glimmer in the dusk, legends would haunt the Father of Waters. But the war had tied the West to the East with iron bands and a new industrialism would reach to the far corners of the nation. The mile-wide Mississippi rolled on, unchanging, to the sea. For another generation it would carry new steamboats, more splendid than before, but the great commerce would not flow again.

IV

~~~~

Indian Summer

As the word Abraham means the father of a great multitude of men, so the word Mississippi means the father of a great multitude of waters. His tribes stream in from east and west, exceedingly fruitful the lands they enrich. In this granary of a continent, this basin of the Mississippi, will not the nations be greatly multiplied and blest?

HERMAN MELVILLE

18

~~~

The Splendid Packets

At St. Louis the morning of September 8, 1866, began with dense fog on the river. Along the dim levee sounded the bang of fire doors, the throb of engines, a clamor of bells and voices. Gradually a row of pilot-houses lifted through the shroud. Then the fog burned off and a fleet of packets lay shining in the sun. Bells clanged above the swish and rumble of paddle wheels. With a chorus of whistles they moved upstream, thirty-six white and gleaming steamboats, each with a banner for one of the thirty-six states in the Union, and a thirty-seventh representing the District of Columbia. They were going to Alton to meet President Andrew Johnson, Admiral David G. Farragut and General U. S. Grant.

At noon the flotilla lay under the hills of Alton and escorted by an honor guard the dignitaries boarded the steamer *Andy Johnson*. With a band playing martial music the *Johnson* backed into the stream. Beside her were the packets *Ruth* and *Olive Branch*, flying the banners of New York and Pennsylvania; they were lashed alongside. The three abreast steamed down the river with thirty-four packets in line behind them.

Andrew Johnson had few triumphs in his troubled life, but there was a radiant September day when he came down to St. Louis in the most stately procession ever seen on the Mississippi.

For President Johnson, the farmer and tailor from Tennessee, this was his first acquaintance with the upper Mississippi. For General Grant it was a homecoming. Six long years he had lived on Hardscrabble Farm in St. Louis County, in debt and self-doubt, hauling loads of mine props to sell on the St. Louis levee. Now he smoked his cigar on the gallery at the head of a river parade with thousands cheering from the shore. The parade ended at Jefferson Barracks where welcoming salutes echoed over the river. Then the fleet swung round and steamed back to the St. Louis Landing.

The parade of 1866 was celebrating more than a presidential visit. It signified a hopeful new rush of river commerce, and it displayed the splendid new packets that replaced the wartime ironclads on the Mississippi. With these stately steamboats the railroad had a rival. In their block-long cabins thick carpets drank the tread of travelers, and deep chairs invited relaxation. There were oil paintings on every door, orchestra music for dinner, a brass band saluting every landing. For a decade great glimmering packets, massive yet lacy, backed off the landings plumed in steam and swung into the current while the whistle roared departure. It was a last flourish on the river. In 1882 Mark Twain found an empty Mississippi and below New Orleans a line of lifeless and decaying steamboats, all of them built, put into service, and abandoned in the twenty years since he had been away. But there was excitement in the valley in 1866.

A new queen of the rivers was the *Ruth*, replacing the short-lived *Ruth* of 1863. Launched from the Howard shipyards at Jeffersonville in 1865, she was powered by engines from the *H. R. W. Hill*, a big cotton carrier and Confederate transport that had been captured in the Battle of Memphis. Described in a New Orleans paper as "The Wonder of the West," the new *Ruth* was a stately four-decker. Her main deck carried 2500 tons of bulk freight—livestock, cotton, hay and tobacco. Her second deck could house "very comfortably" a thousand deck passengers. The main cabin contained a 268-foot drawing and dining room lined by staterooms with landscapes painted on their panels. The staterooms were described as "two long rows of cosy white cottages with marble steps and rosewood doors." When all her space was taken, the *Ruth* carried 1600 persons.

For her cabin passengers this splendid steamer provided rooms for servants, a nursery, a laundry, a barbershop and a spacious bar. To handle cargo she had a steam freight hoister working an endless chain which moved boxes, bales and barrels to and from the hold. Between her lofty chimneys six-foot gilt letters spelled RUTH, and a reporter predicted that she would "undoubtedly prove to be the greatest gleaner that ever harvested along the Mississippi." She was a fast boat, making the run in 4½ days and triumphantly blowing her three long blasts of arrival at St. Louis and New Orleans. But her gleaning came to an early end. On the 13th of March, 1869, she caught fire at Pawpaw Island above Vicksburg and burned to the water's edge.

Already the *Ruth* had been eclipsed by the *Great Republic,* the largest and most lavish steamboat to that time. Built near Pittsburgh in 1867 she steamed down the Ohio with a glittering passenger list to her home port of St. Louis. (She could never return to the upper Ohio as the top sections of her chimneys, added at Jeffersonville, would not clear the railroad bridges.) At Wheeling, Cincinnati and Louisville, crowds stood in the raw March winds to see the river queen come down. There was jealousy in the lower Ohio valley; to a Cincinnati reporter she looked dull and dingy, and a Louisville editor found her abrupt and boxy without the graceful lines that were the mark of local shipwrights. March weather kept the passengers indoors but they had enough to look at there—fluted columns and scrolled cornices, floral carpets and frescoed walls, glittering glass chandeliers, carved and inlaid furniture.

With gaudy grandeur the *Great Republic* swept into St. Louis and the Mississippi trade. Legends quickly grew around her. She was given calendar dimensions—365 feet long, for the days in the year, 52 feet wide for the weeks, 12 feet deep for the months, 7 decks high for the days in the week; and it was said she cost $365,000, a thousand dollars a foot. What her admirers did not know was that she dragged a hundred-thousand-dollar mortgage up and down the river and burned five thousand dollars worth of fuel on every trip. Her crew called her "Workhouse," and they had stronger names for her mate and captain.

In two years the owners went bankrupt. For $48,000 the palatial packet was eventually bought by a plunging river captain and ex-gambler named William Thorwegan. He made her still larger, lengthening the hull to 350 feet—still 15 feet short of her legendary dimension—and adding a seventh boiler to her big engine room. In 1876 he changed her name to *Grand Republic* and decorated her paddle boxes with a picture of the new Eads Bridge spanning the river at St. Louis. She had carried her new name just a year when she burned at the New Orleans levee, lighting up the midnight sky on September 19, 1877.

In the 1860's the canal around the Falls of the Ohio was too small for the biggest packets, which could only pass Louisville on a high stage of water. Just below the falls were the New Albany shipyards whose builders launched the handsome *Richmond* and the legendary *Rob't E. Lee*. Rivaling anything on the rivers, the *Richmond* carried a string orchestra and a brass band. A daily newspaper, *The Richmond Headlight*, was printed for her passengers who were described as "rich and titled people from all over the world." The roustabouts called her the "Rebel Home."

When the artist painted ROB'T E. LEE on the huge paddle box of a new vessel, some New Albany Hoosiers made vague threats against the "rebel" steamboat. Though her captain, John W. Cannon, was a Northern man, the boat was hauled over to the Kentucky side for the final paintwork. When she steamed down the Ohio, people on both shores admired the powerful sound of her steam valves and the deep dingdong of her bell. The *Lee* was a handsome boat inside and out— one of her landscape doors, showing the Natural Bridge of Virginia, is now in the Howard Steamboat Museum in Jeffersonville. She was also a speedster, as that roar of steam from her escape pipes promised. "Hoppin' Bob," the rousters called her; when the throttles were open she had a jerky pace. Her famous race with the *Natchez* was more than a steamboat contest. It was a personal rivalry as well, a rivalry that began with a disagreement about freight rates on the lower Mississippi.

Among the bearded captains who met in St. Louis offices and New Orleans cafés were two longtime associates and friends, John W. Cannon and Thomas P. Leathers. Captain Cannon was a composed soft-spoken man; Captain Leathers was positive, aggressive and headstrong. (His final packet the *T. P. Leathers* was known by her crew as "T. P. Mule.") Tom Leathers began steamboating as a youth in the *Sunflower* on the Yazoo. By 1870 he was a huge and powerful man known on all the rivers as a racing captain and an unreconstructed rebel. He wore ruffled shirts with a diamond pin and suits of Confederate gray. For twenty-four years he refused to fly the Stars and Stripes on his packets. Finally, on March 4, 1885, when a Democratic President took office in Washington, he had his own celebration. At Vicksburg he fired his signal cannon, declared the war ended, and ran up the flag of the United States.

Beginning in 1845 Tom Leathers built and commanded a succession of *Natchez* steamers, running them with a dash and flair no other captain could equal. On the *Natchez,* (No. 5) for Christmas dinner in 1859 his passengers were given a lavish bill of fare offering four kinds of fish, six broiled meats, six oven roasts, eight entrees, nine cold dishes, five choices of game, and thirty-six desserts. All his *Natchez* packets had red stacks which stood out from the black forest of chimneys at the terminals, and their departure was a ceremony. For years, running in the Bends trade between Vicksburg and New Orleans, he left the Crescent City on Saturday afternoon. As the cathedral clock struck five, huge Captain Leathers came out of the texas and clanged the departing bell. With a roar of steam and a rumble of paddles the *Natchez* backed off from the levee and swung downstream as far as the New Orleans mint. There she came around. With steam pluming her escape pipes and black smoke pouring from her tall red stacks, she breasted the current. At Canal Street the skipper fired his signal cannon and dipped the Stars and Bars on his jack staff. The band burst into music and a multitude waved from the levee.

In 1869 Captain Leathers brought a brand-new *Natchez,* the sixth of that name, down from Cincinnati. In 1870 he ran a famous trip on the Mississippi, beating the 26-year-old record of the *J. M. White.* At the New Orleans levee he berthed his boat beside the speedy *Rob't E. Lee.* While the two packets loaded cargo for St. Louis, the rival captains prepared to race and the word went out to the world. Bets were placed up and down the valley and as far away as London and Paris. In the river cities Northern men favored the *Lee* because Captain Cannon had supported the Union; Southerners sided with the *Natchez* and her Confederate skipper. While telegraph operators prepared to report the progress of the race, spectators went ahead in the *Great Republic, Grand Era* and *Mary Houston* to watch the rivals pass.

They took off from New Orleans on June 30, 1870, in the long shadows of evening. They never raced side by side, as the lithographers pictured them; the *Lee* kept ahead from the start, but the *Natchez* hung on. They were an hour apart at Helena. They passed Memphis at night, one hour and three minutes apart, furnaces agleam and chimneys pouring fiery cinders, while cannon and fireworks saluted them from the crowded bluffs. At Cairo the *Lee* led by seventy minutes, and in the "graveyard" stretch the *Natchez* was slowed by fog and engine trouble. On July 4, to the roars of thousands, the *Lee* panted in to the St. Louis levee. She was three days, eighteen hours and fourteen minutes out of

New Orleans, a record that has never been equaled. Six and a half hours later the *Natchez* churned in. Both captains attended a banquet that evening—though the partisans claimed that the *Lee* had unfairly taken fuel on the run in midstream—and a pair of wide-spreading antlers, the blue ribbon of the Mississippi, was given to the *Lee*.

Six years later the *Lee* was broken up. The hull of the famous packet was towed down to Memphis and made into a wharf boat. The crystal chandeliers from her long cabin were hung in a church at Port Gibson, Mississippi.

Railroads webbed the country in the 1870's, and from the riverbanks locomotive engineers tooted derisively at the steamboatmen. But in that expanding decade, with trade enough for both, the steamboat builders turned out their finest vessels.

In 1872 the *Thompson Dean* was launched in Cincinnati. For ten years her graceful silhouette was familiar on the lower Mississippi where she ran the winter cotton trade between Memphis and New Orleans. It was a leisurely run with many stops and always a burst of band music from the big steamer and shouts of welcome at the landing. Captain William B. Miller left a nostalgic account in a long letter to his children in Cincinnati, a letter now preserved in the River Museum at Marietta, Ohio. The *Thompson Dean* always left Memphis on Wednesday evening with the brass band playing in the sunset. Aboard were perhaps fifty passengers and a thousand bales of cotton. That night she stopped at four landings—Bennett's, Mhoons, O.K., and Trotter's—picking up a hundred bales of cotton at each stop. By morning she was at Helena where a big cotton pile waited on the levee. It would take all day to load —1500 or 2000 bales—and when the *Dean* backed off she was swathed in cotton halfway to her texas. Next day she called at a string of places with names like a bouquet—Delta, Friars Point, Sunflower, Australia, Laconia, Carson's, Waxhaw, White River, Terrence, Floryville, Riverton, Napoleon, Prentiss, Niblett's, Storms, Bolivar, Kentucky and Chicora. At every landing there were the chants of the rousters and a harangue from the mate while thirty, fifty or a hundred bales of cotton came aboard and mounds of bagged cottonseed grew up in the dim main deck. Passengers came and left at every stop.

On Friday morning the *Dean*'s whistle woke up drowsy Chicot City. From there she crossed Choctaw Bar which had formed in a single season over the wreck of the steamer *Indiana* in 1875. Beyond Choctaw

Bend the *Dean* landed at Eutaw, Stops, Mound Place, Glencoe, Welcome and Wilkinson's, backing down from one to the other past big white fields of cotton. Here the band had a constant audience, as darkies ran through the fields to watch "de big Dean" go by. After a dozen more stops it was Saturday night, the passengers lounging on the hurricane deck in the languid Southern dusk. All night the roustabouts were up, adding a few more tons of cargo at Leland, Sunnyside, Refuge, Eggs Point, Auburn, Longwood, Bernards, Leota, Maryland, Carolina, Pilcher's Point, Skipworth's, Duncan's, Homachitta and Lake Providence. On Sunday the band played an endless medley, and for a hundred miles darkies waved and shouted from the shore.

When she took on fuel at Vicksburg, halfway to New Orleans, the boat was loaded with 10,000 sacks of cottonseed and bales ten tiers high. Next morning she was at Natchez where armloads of flowers came aboard. From there on the only stops were for fuel, as the cotton plantations gave way to miles of sugarcane along the riverbanks and bayous. On Tuesday afternoon the church spires of New Orleans lifted beyond the level fields. Soon the *Dean* was steaming around the river crescent amid boats from all the rivers and ships from half the world. With a long blast of her whistle she crept in to a berth at the foot of Canal Street where hundreds of stevedores, shouting a dozen languages, were ready to roll away the cotton and shoulder the seed. "Here," wrote Captain Miller, "we put out our cargo and receive on board hundreds of hogsheads and barrels of sugar and molasses, boxes and barrels of oranges and coconuts, bunches of bananas, etc., and on Thursday evening we drop out into the stream and commence our upward journey."

Of the hundreds of side-wheelers that came from the Howard shipyards at Jeffersonville, the finest, by common consent, was the *J. M. White*. With her launching in 1878 the name, already famous, gained a new luster. The first *J. M. White* was built in 1842 by three St. Louis men including a merchant of Herculaneum whose name the packet carried. She made just four trips before being snagged and sunk in the "graveyard" stretch above Cairo in 1843. Her successor, built by the same three men in 1844, had a life of just four years but an enduring fame. With a shallow draft, a long, slightly curved hull and huge paddle wheels set two-thirds of the way astern, she was the culmination of thirty years of steamboat design. Swift, powerful, graceful, she made a record on her first run: leaving Pittsburgh at noon on March 6, 1844, she eased into the Cincinnati Landing as the clocks were striking noon the next day. After setting records all the way to New Orleans and back, her captain placed marks along the Mississippi indicating his 24-, 48-, and 72-hour runs; the posts rotted away while a generation of packets raced against them. Not till the race of the *Natchez* and the *Rob't E. Lee,* in 1870, were her records beaten.

Merchant White of Herculaneum died in 1846 while young J. M. White in Cloverport, Kentucky, was watching the big Ohio boats go by. Twenty years later he was Captain White, master of the handsome *Glendy Burke,* and Stephen Foster put both the packet and the captain into a roustabout song:

> De *Glendy Burke* is a mighty fast boat,
> Wid a mighty fast captain too;
> He sits up da on de hurricane roof
> And he keeps his eye on de crew.

After the *Burke,* White commanded the steady *Governor Allen,* the speedy headstrong *Katie,* the great cotton carrier *Belle Lee* and the gold mine *Frank Pargoud.* The *Pargoud* made a fortune for her owners, who kept their money on the river; they put $300,000 into a palatial steamer which was named for the Cloverport captain. This final *J. M. White,* built in the Howard yards at Jeffersonville, was the finest river-boat in the world. Wrote the Louisville river reporter Will S. Hays:

> Aladdin built a palace,
> He built it in a night;
> And Captain Tobin bought it
> And named it *J. M. White.*

From her heart of oak keel to her 2880-pound roof bell, her five-tone whistle and the seven-foot ornamental leaves on her eighty-foot chimneys, she was the queen of the rivers. All her china showed her own handsome picture. Her Irish linen was monogramed J M W, and her silver was engraved with her twin-stacked silhouette. Turning the spokes of her eleven-foot wheel her pilots were lordly men, until a December day in 1886 at Blue Store Landing, in Pointe Coupee Parish, Louisana, when the stately packet caught fire. As flames reached a cargo of gunpowder in the hold, she went out with a bang. Slowly the river silt buried her under the rustling cottonwoods of St. Maurice Plantation.

The *White* never carried her full capacity of people—thanks to railroad competition—though her roustabouts had a ten-tier cotton song:

> Oh, roll, Nancy gal, roll, gal,
> I'll meet you by and by;
> We gwine to roll de cotton
> Way up ten tiers high.
>
> . . . .
>
> Oh shovel up de furnace
> Till smoke put out de stars;
> We's gwine along de river
> Like we's bound to beat de cars.

But of course they couldn't beat the cars. "In this fast age," said a St. Louis writer, "everybody takes the quickest route and our steamers have to look almost entirely to their freight list for their profit." It was reported in 1876 that nearly all the passenger travel between St. Louis and the South had been diverted from the river to rail. With a backward look, sixty years later, William Faulkner wrote, "There were railroads in the wilderness now. People who used to go overland by carriage or on horseback to the river landings for the Memphis and New Orleans steamboats could take the train from almost anywhere now. And presently Pullmans too, all the way from Chicago and the Northern cities and the Northern money, the Yankee dollars arriving . . ." In 1882 Mark Twain lamented, "There is a locomotive in sight from the deck of the steamboat almost the whole way from St. Louis to St. Paul." For a few more years the big white packets would whistle at the landings, but no new river queens would follow.

In 1884 New Orleans held the Centennial Cotton Exposition, celebrating the hundredth anniversary of the export of Louisiana cotton, and a million visitors were expected in the Crescent City. Though prolonged rain washed out the fair, it did bring a flurry of travel to the steamboats. New wharves were built on the river and a railroad short line ran to the exposition grounds on the site of Audubon Park. Tall-stacked steamers smoked at the levee where silk-hatted Negroes drove gleaming carriages through a confusion of buckboards, carts and wagons. Lafcadio Hearn, the wonder-struck little wanderer, was there, writing his impressions for *Harper's Weekly*. He roamed around the lagoons, amid domed and towered buildings. At dusk forty miles of electric wiring burst into light; electric illumination was as great a wonder as any exhibit in the Hall of Industry. When Hearn went back to the dim streets of the French Quarter he was still marveling. "Never did the might of machinery seem to me so awful as when I first watched that enormous incandescence."

In that year electricity came to the river. "Wait for us!" exclaimed an advertisement in the New Orleans papers. "The World-Renowned Electric Light Steamer GUIDING STAR." The *Star* was a 300-footer, with fifty cabin staterooms and a "Freedman's Bureau" for colored servants. Her block-long cabin was paneled in black walnut with bird's-eye maple finish. But it was the electric light that made her briefly famous. Soon that wonder was commonplace on the packets, which came gleaming like the Pleiades through the river darkness.

For forty years the New Orleans levee had offered a daily spectacle; every afternoon at four o'clock a parade of steamboats moved up the river, bound for a hundred distant places. By 1890 the parade had dwindled and the Ohio River yards were building steamboats for the Yukon, the Orinoco, the Amazon, the Yangtze, the Ganges, the Niger and the Nile—but none for the Mississippi. In the side rivers the trade hung on a little longer. Still profitable in the 1880's was the John Gilbert, running from Cincinnati up the Tennessee to load peanuts and cotton. Her roustabouts had a song about the "Peanut John."

> *John Gilbert* is de boat
>   Di de oh, di de oh,
> *John Gilbert* is de boat
>   Di de oh,
> Runnin' in de Cincinnati trade.
>
> You see dat boat a comin'
>   She's comin' round de ben'
> And when she gits in
>   She'll be loaded down agin.
> Di de oh, di de oh,
>   *John Gilbert* is de boat
> Di de oh.
>
> Lee P. Kahn wuz de head clerk,
>   Cap'n Duncan wuz de cap'n,
> Billy Evitt wuz de head mate,
>   Runnin' in de Cincinnati trade.
> *John Gilbert* is de boat
>   Di de oh, di de oh,
> *John Gilbert* is de boat
>   Di de oh.

The words went on, calling all the *Gilbert's* roll, and the song was remembered long after she sank in the "graveyard" stretch above Cairo. In 1944 an orchestral number *John Gilbert: A Steamboat Overture* by Claude Almond was presented by the Louisville Philharmonic and the Cincinnati Symphony. Its theme was the old rousters' song about the "Peanut John." The packets were a nostalgic memory then.

19

~~~~~

The Mountain Trip

Others may praise what they like;
But I, from the banks of the running Missouri,
praise nothing, in art, or aught else,
Till it has breathed well the atmosphere of this
river.

WALT WHITMAN

FROM THE LONG ST. LOUIS LEVEE steamboats left without fanfare for St. Paul, Pittsburgh and New Orleans. But the sailing of an upper Missouri boat was different. In restless spring weather a boisterous company of Frenchmen, Indians, half-breeds, soldiers, trappers and sportsmen trooped aboard with their blanket rolls and plunder. They went with revelry, yelling, whooping and banging their rifles as the boat backed off. Ahead of them were solitude and danger, a turbulent river, a wind-swept land lifting into unnamed mountains. The river islands were full of elk; antelope and buffalo roamed the plain; from distant ridges rose the signal smoke of the Indians. Between raw banks, under bluffs and buttes and badlands, through two thousand miles of savage country wound the longest river of the continent.

It was such a trip that John James Audubon began on the 25th of April, 1843, on the steamer *Omega* with Captain Joseph Sire as master and Joseph La Barge as pilot. He found 101 trappers, of a dozen nationalities, all joining in the uproar of departure. While the steamboat labored up the flooded Missouri, the men saluted every little town with rifle and pistol fire. A week out of St. Louis they were at Independence, putting off freight for the Santa Fe wagons. Beyond Fort Leavenworth they entered Indian country, stopping at the villages to discharge trade goods and take on fuel. When they left, the Indians followed onshore, like children running after a street parade.

In the windy May weather Audubon made notes of army posts, trading stations, Indian camps, of a black bear swimming the river and buffalo carcasses floating past; of herds of buffalo, deer, elk, antelope, prairie wolves; of new species of birds and shrubs and flowers. Below Fort Pierre they passed four barges loaded with ten thousand buffalo robes. At bends of the river hunters went ashore, coming aboard with fresh game a few miles farther on. Once the hunters shot four buffalo, though they brought on board but one tongue and a few chunks of the hump meat. "Thus it is," Audubon noted, "that thousands multiplied by thousands of buffalo are murdered in senseless play, and their enormous carcasses are suffered to be the prey of the wolf, the raven and the buzzard."

On June 6, with a cold wind whipping the river and a white frost on deck, the *Omega* ran aground. While the boatmen cut up driftwood for the furnaces, the pilot pulled off in the yawl, searching for a channel through the bars and shoals. At Fort Clark amid the mud huts of the Mandan town the captain locked up everything before the Indians swarmed aboard. Last year at this place he had lost his own cap, shot pouch and powder horn; through a chief he recovered the cap and horn, but a squaw had his leather belt and would not give it up.

On the evening of June 12, after a record trip of forty-eight days and seven hours, the *Omega* exchanged salutes with Fort Union, at the mouth of the swirling Yellowstone. The steamer unloaded cargo, took on some passengers and peltry and hurried back to St. Louis before the river shrank. Audubon stayed until August, recording in his notebooks both the glamour and squalor of the frontier; then he came down the river with a party of trappers in a forty-foot Mackinaw barge. With him, like trophies from a safari, he brought a pair of foxes, a badger and a Rocky Mountain doe.

Steam navigation on the Missouri had begun in May of 1819, when the little *Independence* labored two hundred miles upstream to Franklin where she unloaded sugar, flour, whiskey, nails and iron castings. That summer at St. Louis, Major Stephen H. Long assembled an expedition to survey the Missouri and build a fort at the mouth of the Yellowstone. Long's flagship was the *Western Engineer,* the most fantastic of all riverboats, shaped like a dragon with a raised head snorting steam and a paddle wheel threshing water at its stern. Designed for the Missouri, its keelboat hull drew only twenty inches of water and its stern wheel was protected from snags and sawyers. It carried three brass cannon to frighten the plains Indians and a cargo of presents to appease them. A story ran through St. Louis that this dragon ship would voyage to the source of the Missouri where it would be taken apart, carried five miles over the mountains, and reassembled for a run to the Pacific. The boat's banner showed a white man and an Indian shaking hands while one held a sword and the other a peace pipe.

Troops for the expedition embarked from St. Louis under Colonel Henry Atkinson, in keelboats. Officers and orderlies, along with equipment and supplies, went in four steamboats including the grotesque *Western Engineer*. The other three, not built for the uncertain Missouri, did not get far. The *Thomas Jefferson* was snagged in Osage Chute and became the first wrecked steamboat on that river. The *R. M. Johnson* and the *Expedition* (which had delivered 163,000 silver dollars to the Bank of Missouri) struggled up to the site of Atchison, Kansas, where winter closed them in. Before that time the keelboats, carrying the troops, had arrived at the Council Bluffs.

Advancing at three miles an hour the *Western Engineer* stirred up the Missouri mud and startled the Indians. Aboard were some of America's leading artists and scientists—the botanist Dr. William Baldwin, the geologist Augustus Edward Jessup, the landscape painter and ornithologist Samuel Seymour, the artist Titian Ramsey Peale, and young Thomas Say, a far-ranging collector of insects, shells and butterflies, whose books would begin the science of New World entomology. Whenever the boat was grounded, these men scattered over the prairie with their collecting gear; at night while the boatmen chopped wood the scientists bagged insects that swarmed around their bonfires. Here also, with his mind not on art or science but on profit from the Indian trade, was Governor William Clark's nephew, Major Benjamin O'Fallon, Indian agent on the upper Missouri. Cartographer of the expedition was young William Henry Swift, who twenty years later would build the Illinois and Michigan Canal.

With this company aboard, the dragon boat snorted up to Fort Lisa near the Council Bluffs. They wintered there, the artists making sketches of the Indians and the gaunt winter prairie, the scientists collecting what they could in short forays over the wild land. Back at the fort they had good company. Magnetic Manuel Lisa was there—this was his last winter in the West—along with his wife and a woman friend of hers from St. Louis. The days were pleasant even while storm winds blew.

Meanwhile in Washington, disappointed with an expedition that was still eight hundred miles short of the Yellowstone and much farther from the Continental Divide, a Congressional committee cut off Long's appropriation. The Missouri had proved more difficult than anyone had expected, and the Yellowstone was forgotten. Major Long was instructed to explore the source of the Platte River and to return by way of the Arkansas. It would be twelve more years before a steamboat reached the Yellowstone.

In the spring of 1820 the steamer *Expedition* toiled up from St. Louis with a cargo of presents for a thousand tribal chiefs in their great assembly at the Council Bluffs. While visiting the steamboat, one of them saw himself in the large cabin mirror. He ran off and brought a hundred others to see this wonder—at which they burst into roars of laughter. They did not know that the puffing little steamboat, coughing mud out of her boilers and running aground on bends and sandbars, would dispossess them of their country.

For thirty years keelboats had carried the fur trade, toiling up the river with trade goods and swirling down with baled peltry, but in 1830 the American Fur Company turned a page of history and built the steamer *Yellowstone*, seventy-five tons capacity, with an upraised wheel-house where the pilot could scan the snag-studded river. In 1831 she steamed up to the mouth of the Niobrara where she was stopped by low water. After lightening cargo she went on to Fort Tecumseh (present Pierre) where she delivered the rest of her cargo and returned to St. Louis. The next spring, by luck and labor, she churned up to the company's big new post of Fort Union at the mouth of the Yellowstone River. Aboard was the artist George Catlin; whenever the steamer went aground he waded ashore with his sketching pad. In the clerk's office was 17-year-old Joseph La Barge, an alert, stocky, dark-eyed youth who would spend all his life on the Missouri and would become its most famous pilot. This steamboat voyage into Indian country made head-lines in the Eastern papers and was reported in journals all over Europe.

Thirty-four years later, in 1866, the 500-ton steamer *Peter Balen* would go to within six miles of the Great Falls of the Missouri, thirty-one hard miles beyond Fort Benton. Half a century was required to evolve the boats, men and maneuvers that could reach the head of navigation—3600 miles from the ocean and 3300 feet above sea level.

The great Western migration, at first to Oregon and Utah, then to the goldfields of California, made a busy steamboat trade on the lower Missouri. In the 1850's a parade of steamboats brought men, mules, oxen and wagons to jumping-off places for the long trek west. In 1855 the railroad reached Jefferson City, and the Lightning Packet Line announced a daily schedule from there to Kansas City. From track's end a boardwalk led to the boat landing where a canopy gave shelter from rain and sun; each day, passengers, mail and express transferred from train to steamer. For the Union Packet Line, Captain Tom Brierly of St. Joseph built the *Morning Star, Evening Star* and *Polar Star* and set the pace between St. Louis and St. Joe. His *Polar Star* carried a banner "Beat Our Time and Take Our Horns"; she made the run to St. Joe in two days and twenty hours.

Through the busy lower river passed the shallow-draft mountain boats bound for remote places. The only transportation route of the Northwest, the upper Missouri was an imperial road strung with forts, posts and stations where the Indian trails webbed in. Battered and scarred from snags and sandbars, the fur boats were beautiful as swans to men at the upper posts. Their arrival was a great event at every station.

While wagon trains were ferrying the lower river at Independence and St. Joe, the fur trade was reaching westward along the upper Missouri. In 1850 the Fort Mackenzie outpost in the rich Blackfoot country was enlarged and given a new name—for Thomas Hart Benton who was said to have saved the American Fur Company from prosecution for liquor traffic with the tribes. To supply that growing post, steamboat goods were laboriously transhipped from Fort Union by keelboat. In 1851 Captain Joseph La Barge took his *St. Ange* to the mouth of Poplar River (now overshadowed by the massive Fort Peck Dam), the farthest point yet reached by steamboat. Two years later the *El Paso* groped fifty miles farther, through an island-studded channel now buried under the waters of the Fort Peck Reservoir, to the bend above the mouth of the Milk River. Another two hundred miles and a steamboat could tie up at the empty Fort Benton landing.

In 1859 the fur company ordered its *Spread Eagle* and the chartered *Chippewa* to Fort Benton. The two steamers set out on a booming current, but low water bared the bones of the river at Fort Union. There the *Chippewa*'s captain sold his boat to the fur company, giving them the problem of navigating the last three hundred miles. Freight from the *Spread Eagle* was transferred by grumbling boatmen and Indians to the *Chippewa*, and under command of Captain John La Barge, brother of the *St. Ange*'s master, that vessel worked on upstream, from bar to bar, until she reached Brulé Bottom, fifteen miles below Fort Benton. It was then mid-July and snow water was running out. The *Chippewa* left her cargo on the bank and scrambled down the shrinking river.

The next year, 1860, the *Chippewa* and the *Key West* made it all the way to Fort Benton. The *Chippewa* went up again in 1861, but she did not reach her destination. On a Sunday evening a few miles below the mouth of the Poplar River some deckhands went into the hold to steal whiskey. They left a candle burning and soon the steamer was on fire. The crew got off and the boat was set adrift while flames ate toward kegged gunpowder in her hold. A few minutes later the explosion came and there was nothing left of the pathfinding *Chippewa*. For days afterward the scavenging Crow tribesmen gathered tobacco, blankets, pipes, shovels, and bags of beads and beans from the riverbank.

The next spring, 1862, Captain Joseph La Barge brought his *Emilie* on a 35-day trip from St. Louis to Fort Benton. The log of that voyage (preserved in the library of the Missouri Historical Society) makes vivid reading a hundred years later.

Sioux City was the last chance to buy provisions and firewood. Beyond that point a steamer lived off the land, its men hunting antelope on the prairie and cutting wood from rack heaps in the river. The furnaces ate up thirty cords a day, a supply that half filled the main deck, and some days more time was spent in wooding than in traveling. There was plenty of time for the hunters to scout for game.

At the mouth of the clear-flowing Niobrara, travelers on the *Emilie* saw their first wild animal; from a bare bluff a prairie wolf watched the approaching steamer and trotted off before it came within gunshot. At the Yankton Agency were fifty Sioux lodges; while the steamer loaded wood some chiefs came aboard for a dole of whiskey. At Fort Randall, the next outpost, three hundred Iowa volunteers crowded the riverbank, avid for news from the States and marveling like the Indians at the *Emilie*'s mud-churning paddle wheels.

The Missouri was never two seasons, or two weeks the same. "The river changes its beds often," William Clark told Nicholas Biddle when Biddle was compiling his *History of the expedition under the command of Captains Lewis and Clark*. "There are many sandbars which stop the mud of the Missouri which then fills up to the height of the bar along the shores"—giving the restless river a new channel. A hundred years after Clark's observation George Fitch reported that the Missouri was still dissatisfied "Time after time it has gotten out of its bed in the middle of the night, with no apparent provocation, and has hunted up a new bed, all littered with forests, cornfields, brick houses, railroad ties and telegraph poles. It has flopped into this prickly mess with a gurgle of content and has flowed along placidly for years. . . . Then it has suddenly taken a fancy to its old bed, which by this time has been filled up with suburban architecture, and back it has gone with a whoop and a rush, as happy as if it had found something really worth while." No two measurements of the Missouri were just alike.

At Big Bend below Fort Pierre the river then looped twenty-eight miles around a four-mile crossing, and the *Emilie's* passengers started across on foot. When the steamer was halfway around the horseshoe, a blinding thunderstorm compelled Captain La Barge to tie up for the night. On the way again next morning he picked up his sodden, famished passengers. They dried themselves by the boilers and devoured a breakfast of pork, pancakes and thick Missouri River coffee.

At Fort Berthold the *Emilie* found the steamer *Spread Eagle*, which had left St. Louis a week ahead of her. The *Eagle* went upriver and the *Emilie* soon overtook her. Rivalry, like everything else, was intensified on the Missouri; another steamboat might be as hostile as the Sioux. As the *Emilie* was passing, Pilot Bailey of the *Eagle* swung his rudder hard over; the impact smashed the *Emilie's* guard and broke two stationary fenders. From the pilothouse Captain La Barge pointed a pistol and the *Emilie's* passengers poured out of the cabin with rifles and revolvers. At that threat Bailey stopped his engines and dropped behind. Months later he lost his license when the ramming was reported in St. Louis.

Another kind of obstacle came a few days later. Above Fort Berthold the plain was black with buffalo; a vast herd was crossing the river and the banks were a solid mass of movement. For half a day the *Emilie* waited, and when she steamed on, her pantry was stocked with fresh meat. A few miles farther they came upon a young bull buffalo,

2 1 5

wounded, wading into a willow bar. The boat touched there and some passengers ran ashore, twirling lariats. The bull charged them and the ropers scattered. A yelping staghound leaped from the boiler deck and seized the bull by the nose. From the guards a passenger felled the animal with a rifle shot.

A hundred miles below Fort Benton the yellow river foamed over Drowned Man Rapids, where four boatmen had been lost while stretching a line to warp a steamboat through. Seething and rumbling the *Emilie* went over on her own power, a rare feat which drew cheers from her roustabouts. She reached the Benton landing on June 17, and the hills echoed with her signal cannon.

In the rousing welcome a passenger named Taylor Linn struck up an acquaintance with Little Dog, chief of the Piegan band of Blackfeet, whom he presented with a United States flag which the Indian wore like a blanket. He brought the chief aboard to cement their friendship at the bar. It was illegal to serve liquor to Indians, but Taylor bought a bottle for consumption ashore. While patrolling the bank and carrying on a conversation which neither understood, they toppled into the river. They climbed out, dripping, and resumed their discourse while the mate ordered them out of the way of the stevedores.

On her return journey, running down the river on the ebbing crest of snow water, the *Emilie* was halted by a great herd at a buffalo crossing. From the forecastle boatmen lassoed eleven calves, hauled them aboard, struggling and bawling, and penned them up in the engine room. At Fort Berthold hunters caught a young grizzly bear, three coyotes and a huge unblinking owl. Along with bales of hides and peltry this live cargo was brought to St. Louis on a falling river in the first week of July.

Behind the *Emilie* an excitement rose in the mountains. A month after her departure from Fort Benton, prospectors at the headwaters of the Missouri found placer gold along Grasshopper Creek. The next year bonanzas were discovered at Alder Gulch and Last Chance Gulch, which overnight became the boom town of Helena. At Fort Benton the fur trade was forgotten as men headed for the mines. Up to 1864 the post had seen just six steamboat arrivals. In 1865 a thousand passengers, hundreds of oxen, mules and horses, six thousand tons of freight and twenty quartz mills went ashore at the trampled landing. In 1866 thirty-one steamboats reached Fort Benton, and that remote post

Racing on the Ohio,
steamers *Cincinnati* and
America (Way Collection)

Steamer *Delta Queen*, last overnight boat on the rivers (Way Collection)

swarmed with prospectors, sportsmen, journalists, artists, adventurers. From the riverbank, with tents and tepees strewn around the trading post, wagon trains creaked off to gold camps in the hills. In May of 1867 forty steamboats leapfrogged past each other over the shoals of the upper river. That spring a thousand oxen and hundreds of freight wagons waited in Fort Benton for cargo to the mines.

A typical mountain boat carried four hundred tons of freight and two or three hundred passengers. It was a stern-wheeler, plainly and solidly built, with a stout hull, powerful engines and a protruding spoon-shaped bow. The pilothouse was sheathed in boiler plate against Indian arrows and bullets. With her shallow bow, this boat could run high on a sand-bar and still back off. In a shoal passage where the stern wheel threshed mud and air, the boat was "walked" ahead, a step at a time, to the clank of the steam capstan. For this maneuver, cargo was shifted from bow to stern, spars were lowered and set in the sand, cables tightened on the capstan, and the boat was lifted upward and forward—"grass-hoppering" they called it. The sturdy *Deer Lodge* sometimes went over the Dauphin Rapids, Drowned Man Rapids and Black Bluff Bar without laying a line ashore. The one-stacked *General Rucker* even "walked" past the notorious shoals of Cow Island, 130 miles below Fort Benton, where most boats had to lighten cargo and double-trip to the end of the line.

Going to the mountains was the most hazardous of all steamboat trades. Said sober Father De Smet, a veteran of many trips to the Northwest, "Steam navigation on the Missouri is one of the most dangerous things a man can undertake." It has been calculated that nearly five hundred vessels worth ten million dollars were wrecked between St. Louis and Fort Benton in the half century of Missouri River steamboating.

When the *Henry M. Shreve* went up to Fort Benton in 1869 she passed the wreck of the burned steamer *Antelope*, the grounded *Huntsville*, the stranded *Big Horn*, the beached *Importer*, the *Peninah* hung up on a bar, the wreck of the *J. H. Trevor*, the *Mountaineer* aground with a broken wheel, the *Lacon* stuck and sawing off her guards for fuel. At Yankton Agency the *Shreve* broke her own rudder and spent two days making a new one of green timber. In a swirling current just five miles from Fort Benton her crew planted a "dead man" timber on the bank and wound the long cable around the capstan. In shuddering toil, dragging 567 tons through a sandbar, the steam line broke. Then the crew used hand bars, walking the capstan round while the boat inched forward. That summer twenty-four steamers reached Fort Benton, each one scarred and dented and panting from its labor.

Steamboat fuel was a daily problem on the upper Missouri. The early steamers rustled their own wood, spending hours every day dragging logs and limbs out of rack heaps and cottonwood thickets and cutting them into furnace lengths. Joseph La Barge once carried a team of oxen to haul logs aboard where his engineer fed them into a steam sawmill. As traffic grew, Indians took to the wood business, with growing profit as the trade increased. In 1843 at a Sauk village the *Omega* loaded eight cords of wood which was paid for with five tin cups of sugar and three of coffee—25 cents worth at St. Louis, Audubon noted. But the Indians soon learned better, and later steamboat captains paid from $2.50 to $15 a cord, depending on the quality of the fuel and its distance from standing timber, to keep steam in their boilers. On her run to Fort Benton in 1869 the *Henry M. Shreve* consumed $6048.70 worth of fuel. A hundred dollars a day was a fairly common wood bill.

Still, the mountain trade made fortunes for its operators. Cabin fare brought $300 and freight was carried at 12½ cents a pound from St. Louis to the mountains; at Fort Benton flour was worth 18 cents a pound, tobacco brought its weight in gold dust, and a cup of whiskey was good for a buffalo robe. In 1866 the *William J. Lewis*, with a star between her smokestacks, paid for her building on her first trip, running to Fort Benton and back in eighty-three days at a profit of $60,000. The *Peter Balen* cleared $65,000 on her first trip in 1866. Three years later she burned at the head of Dauphin Rapids, when a Negro rouster forgot the fire under a washtub where he was boiling clothes. The *Waverly*, launched at St. Louis in 1866, cleared $50,000 on her only trip when she brought down 508 bales of buffalo robes, 43 wolfskins, 37 bundles of elk hides, 10 bales of deer hides and 5 bales of antelope skins. The next year she was snagged and sunk in Bowling Green Bend on the lower Missouri. In 1867 on a fast trip in his new *Octavia*, Joseph La Barge carried 300 passengers and 300 tons of cargo at a gain of $45,000.

Mountain pilots shared in the bonanza. While standard pay on the other rivers was $250 a month, Missouri boats paid $500 a month on the lower river and up to $2000 on boats running to Fort Benton. When he was not running a boat of his own, Captain Joseph La Barge made an annual trip to the mountains, drawing $8000 for his four months away. While there was gold in the hills there was gold on the river.

In 1855 the United States had bought Fort Pierre from the American Fur Company, converting it to a military post, and so began the long slow conquest of the upper Missouri by the U. S. Army. With the Montana gold rush, the Northwest became a military frontier, the destination of a growing stream of troops and military supplies. For a decade after 1866 the U. S. Army was the biggest shipper on the Missouri. It chartered its own boats and hired its pilots, and the man who served it best was Grant Prince Marsh. He ran a steamboat with the dash and fire of a cavalry commander.

In 1846 at the age of twelve Grant Marsh shipped as a cabin boy on the steamer *Dover* out of Pittsburgh. In the spring of 1854 he went as deckhand on a Missouri boat to St. Joe. In 1864 he was mate of the *Marsella* carrying troops and cargo for General Sully's campaign against the Sioux. In 1866 he piloted the *Louella* on the long run to the mountains. Beyond Wagonwheel Bluff the river was new to him, but by instinct and engine power he went ahead. Downbound boats brought word of Indian attack, and at Milk River, Montana, the *Louella's* fearful clerk transferred to the *Rubicon*, under Captain Horace Bixby, for the return to civilization. Captain Bixby, having had enough of the villainous Missouri, was going back to the broad highway of the Mississippi.

In 1866 the fur trade was dying like an old campfire and at the mouth of the Yellowstone Fort Union flickered out. Once the greatest of the Indian trading posts, now its walls were crumbling and its last goods were being moved to Fort Benton. Grant Marsh loaded boxes and barrels, some rusty traps and dusty peltry, for transfer up the river. Behind he left tumbleweed blowing over the empty compound. An age had ended on the upper Missouri. When the *Louella* went down to St. Louis in September she was crowded with prospectors who carried more than a million dollars in gold dust.

For twenty adventurous years Grant Marsh navigated the Missouri. Up the river he freighted horses, mules, wagons, ordnance, howitzers and ammunition. In 1868, when the government was hoping to pacify the tribes with handouts, he brought the steamer *Nile*, loaded with presents and annuity goods, to the Grand River Agency. It was late in the year and the *Nile* was frozen in. He learned the moods of that country in all seasons.

In 1870 the Northern Pacific Railway began building east from Puget Sound and west from Duluth; two years later the first train puffed in to Bismarck and unloaded a swarm of settlers. Though the railroad would soon carry off the steamboat trade, its first effect, when track's end was at the river, was to create new river commerce. Following the railroad a tide of settlement reached the east side of the Missouri and the steamboats prospered. With the railroad driving deeper into Indian country, the army garrisons were increased. Fort Abraham Lincoln was planted across the river from Bismarck and General Sheridan saw need for a cavalry regiment in Dakota. So Custer arrived in 1873 with his 7th Cavalry at full fighting strength; the regiment went into garrison at the river posts of Fort Lincoln and Fort Rice. Grant Marsh freighted their supplies on the river.

During his years on the upper Missouri, Grant Marsh commanded ten different steamers. Each of them had close scrapes with danger and destruction, but one is still remembered after the rest are forgotten. Captain Marsh first saw the *Far West* in the fall of 1871. Laboring upstream in the old *Silver Lake* with a late-season cargo for Fort Buford, he was passed by the trim new packet carrying army officers and supplies to the upper posts. But at Big Bend above Crow Creek the channel had shifted and the jaunty *Far West* went aground. Marsh waved a greeting at the fuming captain who had just begun the tedious business of sparring off. Five years later Grant Marsh took command of the *Far West* and steered her into history.

Built at Pittsburgh in 1870 for the upper Missouri trade, the *Far West* was a light, strong, speedy boat with short upper works and no texas—a feature which diminished her passenger space but kept her manageable in high winds. She drew two and a half feet when loaded with four hundred tons of cargo; when light she needed just twenty inches of water. She was the first boat to carry two steam capstans on her bow. When General Sheridan planned the campaign of 1876 he asked Grant Marsh to command a supply boat, and Marsh chose the *Far West*. On May 17, while the band played "Garry Owen" and "The Girl I Left Behind Me," the troops marched out of Fort Abraham Lincoln, heading into Sioux country. Up the Yellowstone River steamed the *Far West*, ferrying troops and wagons, setting up new bases of supply, delivering dispatches and running patrol. For her charter the army was paying $360 a day.

On the evening of June 21 the *Far West* was at the mouth of Rosebud Creek, with a great ring of campfires gleaming on the prairie. General Gibbon's infantry was spread along the river and Custer's cavalry was bivouacked beyond. At dusk Custer came aboard—fringed buckskin jacket, windburned face, long moustache and flowing hair; Gibbon and General Terry were already there. That night they bent over field maps in the steamer's cabin. Gibbon's troops were to move up the north bank of the Yellowstone to the mouth of the Big Horn. The *Far West* would ferry them across and they would march up the Big Horn toward a meeting with Custer's cavalry. Custer, meanwhile, was to ride up the Rosebud till he found the trail of Sitting Bull's Sioux—a heavy trail discovered by Major Reno two days past. The two converging columns would crush the Indian camp between them.

That night another lamp burned late aboard the *Far West*. Around a poker table sat Captain Grant Marsh, young Tom Custer and some infantry and cavalry officers. They played quietly, intently, while the campfires winked out and the wind blew down from the stars. The stakes changed hands, grew higher, and gravitated to one man. When the game broke up Captain Crowell of the 6th Infantry was several thousand dollars richer.

Next morning, under the tall blue sky of June, Custer's cavalry formed into columns. With trumpets shrilling and guidons whipping in the wind, they rode over the grass hills toward the Little Big Horn.

Six days later the *Far West*, having scrambled fifty-three miles up the Big Horn River, was tied to an island at the mouth of the Little Big Horn. On the island cottonwoods twinkled in the breeze, the river shores were dense with willow and deer brush. While men on the *Far West* were wondering whether the columns had closed in upon Sitting Bull's warriors, an Indian rider crashed through the willow thickets. It was Curly, the Crow scout who had ridden with Custer. He splashed through the shallows and was pulled aboard.

Curly spoke no English but all his movements expressed great agitation. One of the officers brought pencil and paper, and squatting on deck the scout drew a rough circle. Looking up at Captain Marsh he spoke the Crow word for "white men." Around that circle he drew a larger one, repeating "Sioux! Sioux!" It was a picture of ambush and disaster, which he completed by obliterating the inner circle. Custer's whole command was slaughtered. The scout jumped to his feet, struck his naked breast with his fingers in a rain of rifle bullets and drew a hand around his scalp lock. The report was complete. In silence the steamboat men stared at the heat haze on the broken buttes.

What Curly did not know was that the 7th Cavalry had been divided before the battle, with Benteen and Reno riding over the river bluffs while Custer was encircled below. Next day, after a running fight with Reno's troops, the Indians scattered into the Big Horn Mountains. That word came with the arrival of white scouts the next day, and the *Far West* was prepared to take on Reno's wounded. With marsh grass and tarpaulins the men had a soft bed ready on the afterdeck when the wounded were carried on in hand- and mule-litters made of lodgepoles and tent canvas. All night the litter-bearers straggled in, lit by fires along the riverbank. With fifty-two casualties on deck, the *Far West* was backed off and headed downstream.

Dodging shoals and islands Captain Marsh retraced his course down the rushing Big Horn; that evening he tied up to the bank of the Yellowstone near General Gibbon's supply camp. There the boat lay for two restless days awaiting Gibbon's troops who were to be ferried to the north side of the river. Meanwhile Marsh's men heaped the bow with wood and kept steam in the boilers. When the troops arrived and made the crossing, the steamer started for Bismarck, 710 miles away. Day and night, swaying through rapids and grazing shoals and ledges, she raced down the Yellowstone and into the Missouri. There were brief stops at Fort Buford and at Fort Stevenson, where General Terry ordered the boat's flag at half-staff and her derrick draped in black. Fifty-four hours after leaving the Big Horn the steamer arrived at Bismarck and Fort Lincoln. That night telegraphers clicked out the story and by morning the nation echoed with the names of Custer and Reno; Crow King, Crazy Horse and Sitting Bull; the *Far West* and the Little Big Horn.

One survivor from Custer's battlefield came down to Fort Lincoln on the stern deck of the *Far West*—Captain Keogh's horse, Commanche. He had been found hobbling among the dead, his sorrel hide patched with blood and bristling with arrows. On the steamer the horse was bedded in deep grass and at the fort he recovered, but he was never ridden again. On paydays the men treated him to buckets of beer, at every parade he was saddled and bridled and led by a mounted trooper. When he died in 1891 the Indian wars were over.

After Custer's defeat the *Far West* carried the Indian Peace Commission to treat with the tribes. In 1881 Marsh commanded the *Eclipse*, transferring Indian prisoners from Fort Keogh on the Yellowstone to the lower reservations. The next year Captain Marsh bought his last upper Missouri boat, the *W. J. Behan*, and brought down the last of the Indians. One of them was Sitting Bull. Following Custer's annihilation the Sioux chief had taken refuge in Canada; but after a few hungry seasons there he came down to Fort Buford, with his two wives and 185 ragged followers, and surrendered to the U. S. Army. Grant Marsh took them aboard at Fort Randall and delivered them to the Standing Rock Agency. From there Sitting Bull went on tour with Buffalo Bill's Wild West Show. At Bismarck, Captain Marsh sold his packet; he moved to Memphis and took up the towing business on the Mississippi. In 1883 the *Far West* was snagged and sunk near St. Louis. By then railroads crossed the plains, the steamboat trade was ending, and only tales and legends came down the long Missouri.

20

<div align="center">~~~~</div>

Raftsman Jim

AT THE HEAD of the Ohio River rose the din of America's greatest workshop while the silence of a wilderness hung over the upper reaches of the Mississippi. The Northern rivers led into the great woods. The Wisconsin, the Black, the Chippewa, the Red Cedar, the St. Croix all flowed out of black cedar swamps through a twilight of pine, spruce and hemlock to the Mississippi. To a growing nation the generous North American geography gave the greatest pine forest in the world and threaded it with streams to carry the felled timber. At the edge of the huge pinery flowed the big river, ready to float the logs and lumber that would build the midland cities. In the early West everything was wood—wooden barns, shops, houses, churches, rail fences, plank streets and board sidewalks, wooden wagons, wharves and steamboats. In a time before roads and railways, the river carried a yearly tide of logs and lumber.

From his boyhood in the 1840's Mark Twain remembered mighty rafts gliding past Hannibal on the spring crest of water—"an acre or so of sweat-smelling boards in each raft, a crew of two dozen men or more, three or four wigwams scattered about the raft's vast level space for living quarters." These rafts were "floaters," silent as an island, moving on the current. From somewhere in the Northern woods they were bound for St. Louis where cliffs of yellow lumber walled the levee, or for cities on the lower river. From the willow shore below Cairo, Huck Finn watched a huge raft moving down the river like a procession. It had eight long steering sweeps, five scattered wigwams, a campfire flickering in the middle and a flagpole at each end. Said Huck: "There was a power of style about her."

Below Cairo the Mississippi was somnolent and silent, a huge slow river vague with fog at morning, murmuring under the midnight stars. Above St. Louis it was a hill-framed river, racing over its long rapids, curving under its bluffs. At a score of places the wind carried the shouts of woodsmen and raftsmen and the whine of circular saws slicing through pine lumber. The busiest place was Beef Slough, a network of backwaters and bayous at the mouth of the Chippewa. Every spring when the tote roads softened in the woods and the winter cut of pine came down the driving streams, millions of logs swirled into that web of waterways where the Chippewa joined the Mississippi.

The first timber was rafted out of Beef Slough by a soldier from Fort Crawford at Prairie du Chien. John Fonda had come a long way round to the upper Mississippi. As a young law clerk in Albany, New York, he had succumbed to Western fever in 1818, heading west to Texas. He walked to Buffalo, took a schooner to Cleveland, crossed Ohio to Cincinnati and joined a flatboat crew on the long voyage to Natchez. After a year with a Scotch trader among the Choctaws on the Sabine River, he went on to Santa Fe and Taos. As a freighter in a wagon train he trekked back to St. Louis, where he heard of Prairie du Chien and the lead diggings. Heading up the Mississippi he fell in with five Frenchmen bound for Green Bay. With them he traveled up the Illinois, past the fourteen scattered houses of Chicago, and along the Lake Michigan shore to Green Bay. In the summer of 1828, after ten years of wandering, he made the portage from the Fox River to the Wisconsin and paddled down that river to the Mississippi where he found an Indian agency, a trading station and the army outpost of Fort Crawford. In 1829 he enlisted under Colonel Zachary Taylor and soon rose to the rating of Quartermaster's Sergeant.

In 1829, with orders to enlarge the fort, Colonel Taylor sent a detail of men to cut timber in the pine woods and raft it down to Prairie du Chien. That fall seventy men in seven mackinaw boats set out for the pineries of the Chippewa River; Fonda was in the advance boat, serving as pilot. They met intense cold and floating ice in Lake Pepin. Up the crooked Chippewa, some of the boats, heavily loaded with stores and equipment, ran into a bar of quicksand. To warm themselves the men tapped two whiskey barrels and spent a noisy night. Next day the stranded cargoes were transferred to Fonda's skiff and carried ashore to a camp in the Chippewa brush. When the river froze solid, the men sledded their equipment to the logging site.

It was a winter of toil and hardship—half-frozen men wounded with axes and crushed by saw logs—but when the ice went out in the spring they had a flatboat piled with shingles and two rafts of timber. Fonda took charge of the larger raft with all the camp's provisions; Lieutenant Gordimer piloted the other, which carried twenty men and a barrel of whiskey. The two rafts ran the Chippewa, and Fonda, in the lead, made fast to shore just at the head of Beef Slough. Soon the other raft came zigzagging down—"fence-rail fashion," Fonda noted, "first against one shore and then against the other, bumping along as though it was intoxicated; perhaps the whiskey barrel leaked." While he watched, the raft was sucked into the slough, where it caught on a brushy island. Night was falling and Fonda waited for daylight to paddle down to the raft with a canoeload of provisions. The marooned men, somewhat the worse for whiskey, wolfed down the rations while Fonda advised Lieutenant Gordimer to break up the raft and work it out of the slough piecemeal. Gordimer preferred to keep the raft intact; he thought he could find a channel to the Mississippi.

While Fonda shoved off in his canoe, Gordimer got free of the island and the raft swept downstream and out of sight. Fonda took his own raft down, working carefully through a maze of towheads and masses of driftwood. After four days without sight of Gordimer's party, he tied up on the big river and turned back in a canoe to find them. Paddling into a side creek he ran on a sunken log and upset, losing all his food and ammunition. He righted the craft and went on to a big marsh where he found Gordimer's raft jammed against a rock pile. The raft was lifeless and its whiskey barrel was empty. Supposing that the men would have started overland for the big river, Fonda headed back to his own raft. But he lost his way. After three days of groping through backwater bayous he found the camp of a Menominee Indian, Wa-ba-naw, and his squaw. The women cooked some meat broth and hominy, the famished Fonda's first food since his canoe had overturned. The Indian guided him out of the slough and down to his own raft.

The big raft was worked into the current and started downstream, with the men scanning the shore for signs of Gordimer's party. The second day they were found on an island, ravenous with hunger; they had eaten nothing but acorns for eleven days. Fonda put the weakest of them into a mackinaw boat and sent it down to Prairie du Chien. The rest arrived on the big raft. That summer, 1830, the southeast corner of Fort Crawford was built of that hard-won timber. Its foundation ran through an Indian mound from which the troops removed wagonloads of bones.

Twenty years later, when the Methodist Church of Prairie du Chien was built of Chippewa River pine, John Fonda became the superintendent of the Sunday School. Old Mrs. Wa-ba-naw was there, living on an island, and whenever she came to town John Fonda gave her a big box of snuff.

Beef Slough was named when a boat carrying live beef for the garrison at Fort Snelling grounded on a bar at the mouth of the Chippewa. To lighten the draft the cattle were pushed overboard and loaded again at a shelving bank upstream. But for fifty years it was a name for the biggest logging works in the world. Here was another gift of geography. Between the dark pineries and the bright river lay a network of waterways where timber could be sorted and assembled. When spring came to the woods, the lumberjacks exchanged ax and saw for pike pole and peavey, and they changed their gumshoes for calked boots that would bite into the pine logs. Down the driving streams they rode a flood of timber, and at Beef Slough they led it into coves for sorting. Each log was marked with a company symbol—a double X for Weyerhaeusers, a pollywog for the Shaw company, a gable over a cross for the Hamilton logs, and other marks as various as cattle brands on the plains. In slack-water bayous the logs were built into solid rafts for the long run to sawmills down the Mississippi. Millions of logs went through the Northern mills at Chippewa Falls and Eau Claire; the sawed lumber was rafted to Burlington, Muscatine, New Madison and St. Louis.

The first rafts were "floaters," launched on the spring crests of water and carried by the current. Working with pike poles and snatch poles, lashing the logs with A lines, crosslines and corner lines, raftsmen gathered the timber into brails. Three brails of logs made a platform 700 feet long and 135 feet wide, a huge mat of timber which they called "half a raft." In less than high water, half a raft was all that could pass the bends, bars and shallows. But on a booming river raftsmen rode islands of timber a quarter of a mile long and a city block wide. At both ends long oars and manpower provided a ponderous and strenuous steering. On windy days the men tied up to tree trunks alongshore and waited for quiet weather. Then they were on the way again, gliding downstream under sun and stars, napping in their "dog-house" shelters, standing six-hour watches at the steering oars. In tight places—Betsy Slough, Raft Channel, Winona Bar, Bad Axe Bend, Crooked Slough— the raft captain roused all hands. When the bar was past they flocked around the cookhouse where a fire smoldered on a bed of sand and the coffeepot was bubbling.

At the end of the ride the raftsmen shaved their beards, slicked down their hair and went ashore with money burning in their pockets. They forgot the river toil and monotony, the chilling fog and burning sun, the lonely sound of water lapping at the logs. In saloons and dance halls the girls were singing

> There ain't no cub as cute as him,
> Dandy-handy Raftsman Jim

For thirty years rafting was a silent commerce, the huge slow islands passing down the river without a sound. Their only signal was the cry of the steersman and the clatter of the cook's iron kettle. "Sometimes," recalled Mark Twain, "in the big river where we would be feeling our way through a fog, the deep hush would be broken by yells and a clamor of tin pans, and all in an instant a log raft would appear through the webby veil—and we had to pile on steam and scramble out of the way."

The first man to run a raft with a steamboat was young George Winans, who had been piloting rafts from the age of eighteen. In 1863 he hired a small side-wheeler and hitched her onto a raft at Read's Landing for the trip to Hannibal. He kept a full crew, bow and stern, on the raft, and they were needed; the big load ran away with the panting little steamer. After ten miles Winans cut the steamboat loose and floated his timber down to Hannibal.

For several years steamboats had been used to push rafts through Lake Pepin, above Winona; but side-wheele steamers—"coffee mill boats" to the raftsmen—could not control a raft in any adverse wind or current. Raft-towing required a new kind of boat. It appeared in 1866 when the compact eighty-foot stern-wheel *Le Claire*, built at Le Claire, Iowa, came down behind a headstrong raft that almost ran away with her. The design was right but a bigger boat was needed. It came three years later, a hundred-foot boat with sturdy framing, outsize boilers and a big stern wheel. On her first run the *J. W. Van Sant* rafted timber for Weyerhaeuser and Denkmann, with Fred Weyerhaeuser aboard. At the Rock Island Bridge the steamer lowered her chimneys and deftly guided her tow between the piers. Soon the big lumber companies were building their own towboats. Within twenty years more than a hundred stern-wheelers were rafting logs and lumber down the Mississippi.

The peak of log rafting came in the 1880's, when the coal trade was growing dramatically on the Ohio. Unlike the coal tows, with barges lashed into a single rigid mass, log rafts could be bent and curved to fit the channel; held to the raft by guy lines and winding engines, the towboat prodded its load from one angle or another as the current called for. In rapids or fast currents a second boat, at the head of the raft, steamed backward or forward at the pilot's order, guiding the raft as the old floaters had been guided by brawny oarsmen.

By knowledge, skill and instinct raft pilots took acres of cargo down the river channel. At night that ponderous load seemed to fill up the river, with lanterns distant as stars winking at the corners. To light up a tight place, a pilot had only the smoky torch basket at the end of an iron pole. It was the watchman's business to keep kindling and resin ready to ignite the torch, but the cook often stole the watchman's stock. At a call for torchlight the watchman found an empty kindling barrel and no resin pail, and the pilot groped past in darkness.

There were famous raft pilots in those years, each one distinct and different and all remembered after the last logs went down the river—men like red-bearded Sandy McPhail and Charlie La Pointe with his shrewd blue eyes and J. B. McCoy who had a quiet voice and a fist as heavy as a steering oar. One of the great ones was Joe Guardapie, son of a French lumberjack and a Chippewa woman, a lithe man on a bobbing log and a lordly one in the pilothouse. Speaking a mixture of French, English, and vivid Anglo-Saxon profanity, he ran a mixed crew of Irishmen, Scotsmen, Germans and Norwegians. In his youth he floated rafts down the river, learning the channel and the currents by necessity, with no steam engines to help him. Later he guided monstrous rafts from the pilothouse of a stern-wheeler. He could have made an easier living as a packet pilot, but he was a logging man.

Another storied raftsman was Stephen B. Hanks, originally from

Kentucky and a cousin of Abraham Lincoln. He went north in 1841, worked in the lumber camps, drove logs on the pine rivers and rafted timber down the Mississippi. He began piloting on floating rafts and became a towboat pilot in the great years of the trade. Every spring he pushed a huge raft down the river; on the low summer stage of water he loaded wheat at the Minnesota landings.

A famous rafting family were the Buisson brothers, sons of a French-Canadian trader at Wabasha, Minnesota. Joe Buisson went to rafting at age fifteen; by nineteen he was a pilot, rounding up his men in the saloons of the sawdust towns, checking his crosslines, setting his watches and starting down for Fort Clinton or St. Louis with a great field of timber. His brothers, Henry and Cyprian Buisson, pulled oars on St. Louis rafts before the time of towboats. Later they formed the Valley Navigation Company with their own stern-wheelers. For twenty years Cyp Buisson rafted for the Hershey Lumber Company and then he went to Dakota to claim a homestead farm. But the sky-framed prairie did not satisfy a riverman. He was soon back on the Mississippi.

Captain Walter Blair who wrote a good book about rafting combined that profession with a less lusty one. All winter he was a neat spare man with a string tie and a clipped moustache, teaching school in a river town in Iowa. By March he began to be restless, and a few weeks later he was on the *Silver Wave* pushing a load of logs down the river. One trip that Captain Blair remembered brought them to Cassville Slough in the dead of night. They slipped safely around the bends but hung up on the head of an island, with one corner of the big raft wedged in a willow thicket and the other corner grounded on a towhead. When the lines snapped, an acre of logs went on down the river. While a blinding fog blew in, the men got check lines around the remnant of their raft. In a few hours the fog lifted and a dozen raftsmen in three skiffs went after the runaway logs. They found them caught in creek mouths, piled up on sandbars, hidden in willow thickets. Wading in with pike poles and snatch poles they rolled the logs into free water, brailed them together and lashed them onto the raft when it came along. In a long day's toil they rounded up 1200 logs in 55 miles of river. It was dark when the last strays were added to the raft, which they delivered to the big Musser mill in Muscatine twenty-four hours later.

In the 1880's raftsmen sang a song made up of raft-boat names, beginning with the *Fred Weyerhaeuser* and ending with the *Time and Tide*. It had a singsong rhythm and a monotonous air—

> The *Charlotte Boeckler* and the *Silver Wave*
> The *John H. Douglas* and the *J. K. Graves,*
> The *Isaac Staples* and the *Helen Mar,*
> The *Henrietta* and the *North Star*
> The *David Bronson* and the *Nettie Durant*
> The *Kit Carson* and the *J. W. Van Sant.*

But for a raftsman every name called up a worrying captain, a thieving cook or a left-handed engineer, a mishap in the rapids or a record trip of logs on high water.

Raft boats had a longer life than other river vessels. Pushing their ponderous loads they ran no risk of snagging or collision. Though they ran an occasional raft race—two turtles in a wide reach of river—they did not cram their furnaces to make a showy arrival or departure. Raft boats had strong boilers, regularly inspected. "If I thought boiler explosions a mystery," wrote Captain Blair, "I could not have slept so comfortably over them for fifty years."

Many of the raft boats outlasted the lumber trade. By 1900 the pine-lands were nearly cut over and raft trade was dwindling. Some raft boats took to the grain trade, though the river was losing that business to the railroads. A few went into towing service on the lower Mississippi and some others towed crossties out of the Kanawha and the Tennessee. The *Robert Dodds* was sold to Ohio River people who used her to tow showboats. Several old rafting boats, rebuilt as excursion steamers, ended their days with music. The *West Rambo* went out the delta and across the Gulf to Florida, where she freighted building materials for construction of the railway to Key West. The *Mountain Belle*, pushing a passenger barge instead of logs and lumber, took thousands of people to the St. Louis Fair.

Still an occasional raft swung down the river, recalling memories of another time. The end came in the summer of 1915 when the *Ottumwa Belle*, under Captain Walter L. Hunter, brought the last tow of logs down the Mississippi. Captain Hunter turned to towing merchandise and coal, and the years brought other changes. When he died at Bellevue, Iowa in 1962, ninety-four years old, diesels had prodded steamboats off the river. But the old whistles and the raftsman's cry echoed in his memory. He had been a riverman since 1880.

In 1913, when rafting was all but finished, the *Fred Weyerhaeuser* went into government service as a lighthouse tender. Renamed *Dandelion*, with a bright new coat of paint each season, she came up the river in the spring, the first vessel after ice was out, lighting channel beacons along hundreds of miles of waterway and dropping freshly painted buoys at each wing dam and sandbar. She was the last boat in the fall, snuffing out the channel lights and picking up the buoys for winter storage. When she was retired in 1926, after a third of a century on the river, the old rafter was eulogized in the *Waterways Journal*.

As the rafting business dwindled, Captain Blair bought the old *Silver Crescent* to run a local packet business. Fitting her out early in the season, he got caught in a March blizzard. Below Clinton, Iowa, drift ice crowded him onto the ledge that had sunk the *Mollie Mohler* twenty years before. But the empty *Crescent* rubbed over without damage. A day later, nearing the ice-gorged rapids, the *Crescent* burst a valve and barely made it to the riverbank where a farmer caught her head line and snubbed it around a post. Next morning the boat took fire but the blaze was confined to the galley. Two days later an ice field caught her, parting one line and pulling out a mooring post; another line held while the ice went past. When the captain heard water running in her hull, he found that ice had stove in the planking at the waterline. Some old boards and bedding stopped the leak until the boat could be listed over and repaired.

By that time it was evident that Captain Blair had a lucky boat. He ran her for seventeen years, carrying freight and passengers between Burlington and Davenport. But it was a tame trade for a man who remembered rafts filling half the river and a towboat bucking the current.

21

~~~

A Century of Showboats

ON A SUMMER EVENING in Pittsburgh people stroll along the Allegheny esplanade to rows of benches that face an open-sided barge strung with flags and pennants. The sun sinks over the Bellevue hills, warming the windows of Gateway Center where glass and steel buildings rise above the site of vanished Fort Pitt. A breeze ruffles the water. Over the point of land where the Allegheny and Monongahela come together, a river of traffic moves across the bridge. A pleasure boat throws up a V of spray. With a throbbing of diesel engines a white towboat pushes a long black load of coal. In its wake the moored barge lifts a little.

Two hundred years ago Fort Pitt had a landing place for dugout canoes loaded with Indian peltry. Since then Pittsburgh has seen many kinds of river craft, but the barge *Point Counterpoint* is different from anything before it. Paintings hang on the three walls of the stage, and chairs and music racks are arced around a podium. In the sunset light an orchestra files onto the stage and the lapping of water is lost in the notes of flutes, oboes, horns and clarinets. The conductor mounts the dais. After a moment of applause and a moment of silence the American Wind Symphony begins the allegro movement of "Greeting to a City." It is the first performance of the work by Sir Arthur Bliss of London.

For an hour, while the stars grow bright and lights glimmer in the river, music fills the darkness where once soldiers crouched at loopholes in a timbered fort. Then the crowd scatters, along the embankment and over the paths that lead to the malls of the Gateway Center. The

235

Point Counterpoint tugs at its moorings. Tomorrow it will start a 2000-mile concert tour down the historic rivers.

Behind the Wind Symphony barge is a medley of other music—barrel organs, minstrel songs, brass bands, calliopes and the singsong come-on call of the showboat men. Behind it is a long tradition of itinerant vaudeville, minstrelsy, circus and theater, a tradition that began with a family of English actors in frontier Pittsburgh.

In the summer of 1831 a new keelboat slid into the water at Pittsburgh. It had a square bow and stern, with a towing post at the forward end, and an oblong cabin with rows of windows under a sloping roof. It might have been an outsize houseboat, except for the white flag whose bright red letters spelled FLOATING THEATRE. On the riverbank amid a clatter of carts and wagons stood the Chapman family, nine of them, spanning three generations. William Chapman the elder and his twin sons Samuel and William had played at Covent Garden in London where the rattle of market wagons and the vendors' cries sounded like this Western riverfront. Leaving England in the depression time of 1827, the Chapmans had spent four years in New York and Philadelphia theaters. Now they had come to try their fortunes on the frontier, and America's first showboat was rocking in the river.

With a single riverman as their navigator, the Chapman family floated westward, old and young, men and women, pulling at the long oars when they turned into the river landings. They played one-night stands, presenting English drama to mud-stained settlers, with candle footlights and board benches for the audience. The central chandelier, a barrel hoop holding a ring of candles, dripped tallow on the middle bench. By short runs, twenty or thirty miles a day, they went down the river from one settlement to the next. At each town the actors trooped ashore, blaring a trumpet, posting programs on fences and trees, announcing the evening performance. A free concert, music and singing, drew a crowd to the riverbank and a final call brought them into the theater. At the ticket office William Chapman took in apples, potatoes and bacon, as well as admission money, and he had fishlines trolling from the stern. The river and the river people kept the pantry full. In larger towns on the Mississippi—Memphis, Port Gibson, Vicksburg, Natchez —they played for a week or a fortnight.

After a season the Chapmans sold their theater for lumber and returned by steamboat to Pittsburgh, where they built a new boat for another trip downriver. In 1836, they bought a steamboat which they fitted with a roomy stage, painted scenery and a drop curtain. They had a large company now, a cast of twenty-one, and their arrival was awaited at scores of river towns. The FLOATING THEATRE had become the STEAMBOAT THEATRE, and with steam they could go up the side rivers, the Green, the Wabash, the Tennessee, the Yazoo, the Bayou Sara, to find new audiences. In five more years they built a larger steamboat, CHAPMAN'S FLOATING PALACE, which in 1847, when they retired from the river, was sold to Sol Smith.

Restless Sol Smith had been trouping with Western theatrical groups; he would later team up with Noah Ludlow to establish theaters at Louisville, St. Louis and New Orleans. A native of New York he had a frontiersman's love of chance and change, but his habitual good luck failed him on the river. In Cincinnati he fitted out the *Floating Palace* with pantry stores, stage properties and a crew of actors. The next day his boat collided with an upbound packet. His people waded ashore where they watched the *Palace* sink to the river bottom.

In the 1850's no genuine theater boat replaced the Chapman venture, but many kinds of entertainment moved up and down the valley. Along with floating musical troupes, medicine shows, acrobatic and tightrope artists, menageries of wild animals and minstrel shows, circuses traveled the rivers. The biggest of the circus boats was the Spalding and Rogers FLOATING CIRCUS PALACE which looked like a festive barn on an oversized scow. This cumbersome craft, towed by the side-wheeler *North River* and said to seat more than a thousand people, featured equestrian acts in a sawdust arena; after watching this river rodeo, customers paid another quarter to see a sideshow of curiosities and wonders at the stern. This museum contained stuffed tigers and giraffes, along with wax figures of Tam o'Shanter and the Twelve Apostles. Young Ralph Keeler, who later traveled the lecture circuit with Mark Twain, did Irish dances and impersonations in the sideshow. The boat itself had gaslights and a pipe organ, two wonders that were themselves worth the price of admission. In 1862 Spalding and Rogers gave shows for Confederate troops along the lower Mississippi. Later that year the amphitheater became a military hospital barge, moored to the levee at New Orleans. Then the

2 3 7

circus went to South America where it toured until the Civil War was over.

In the 1850's Dan Rice started a floating circus with a pair of educated pigs, a trained horse and a trick mule. In 1861 his boat collided with an upper Mississippi packet near LaCrosse and a cage containing a "trained rhinoceros" was jostled overboard. Three days later the clerk of the Minnesota Packet Company heard a thumping under the wharf boat at Dubuque; he found the rhinoceros tangled in the buoy chain. The animal was restored to the circus, which grew larger each season. After the war Dan Rice became the biggest showman on the river, but hard times overtook him in 1873. With one aging lion and his white horse Excelsior he went up the Missouri in the steamer *Damsel*. At Decatur, Nebraska, fifty miles below Sioux City, the boat was snagged and sunk. In gratitude to the Decatur residents who had saved his horse, Rice gave them the *Damsel's* roof bell to hang in their new church. At Cincinnati in November, 1885, Holland & McMahon's World Circus chartered the steamer *Mountain Girl*, loaded tents, wagons, horses, rigging, apparatus and baggage, and began a river tour. The first performance was the last. Leaving Lawrenceburg, Indiana, at midnight, the *Mountain Girl* collided with the steamer *James W. Goff*. The *Girl* broke in two, and by the light of torches and burning bulkheads the *Goff* took off sixty-five half-clad circus people. Lost to the river were all the circus gear, the animals, $10,000 worth of horses, and seven teamsters and canvasmen. Earlier in the same year, 1885, Buffalo Bill's Rocky Mountain and Prairie Exhibition, which a few years later would take the drama of the Wild West to Europe, had headed south from Cincinnati in a chartered steamboat. A day and a half out of New Orleans they collided with a Vicksburg packet. The captain of the showboat ran ashore, made some hasty repairs and went on again. That night the hull timbers parted and the river poured in. The Indians and the cowboys swam some horses ashore while the vessel sank in thirty feet of water. Elk, buffalo, steers, and bucking horses were lost, along with the show's canvas, baggage and equipment. The bandwagon and the bullet-scarred Deadwood Stage floated off and were recovered.

In the 1880's the steam calliope was standard equipment on showboats, and their music drifted over the river hills. Miles away people hitched up the horses and drove in to the landing where the showboat stood in her gold and white splendor. The most popular was *French's New Sensation* with a uniformed band playing on the forecastle and rows of colored pictures, like a street parade, along her sides. When the benches filled, the curtain went up on a variety show of music, tap dancing, juggling, tumbling, ventriloquism, ropewalking, acrobatics, magic and melodrama. The stars shone bright as people rocked homeward, and *French's New Sensation* moved on down the river with katydids shrilling in the darkness and bullfrogs croaking from the bank. Actually there were five successive *New Sensation*'s; they toured the river for nearly thirty years.

Augustus Byron French grew up in Palmyra, Missouri, a few miles from the Mississippi. At sixteen he was a cabin boy on a steamer bound for New Orleans, always strumming a banjo on his watch below. He never finished the trip. At the Natchez Landing he saw the neat little *Quickstep*, the smallest of all traveling shows, with a man performing feats of magic and then turning the barrel organ while his daughter danced and sang. On a sudden impulse French joined them as banjo artist. From the *Quickstep* he went to the Spalding and Rogers *Floating Circus Palace* as a musician and sleight-of-hand performer; and when the Civil War blockaded the rivers he started a wagon show grandiosely called the "New Sensation." For years he rode at the head of a line of red and white wagons, but a prolonged rainy season, with bottomless roads and soggy show grounds, turned him back to the river. His first showboat, a red, white and green barge with eight windows on each side and covered porches at both ends, was poled away from the Cincinnati Landing in November, 1878, by a company of eight performers. They drifted south and were towed back up the summer river by the steamboat *Smoky City*.

At the end of her second season this *New Sensation* was towed to St. Louis where French found a weathered little man running a merry-go-round with a balky mule. That winter they formed a partnership, loaded the merry-go-round on the barge and started south. The mule soon earned his keep. Above Ste. Genevieve they steered into a chute on the Missouri side and were soon stranded in slack and freezing water. They put the mule ashore, hitched him to a hawser and so got back into the current. "It took two days," Captain French remembered, "to make the three miles to the head of the island, and everybody had frozen feet except that little mule."

Another partner joined Captain French as a result of a collision near St. Marys, West Virginia, in 1882. Coming down from Pittsburgh on a windy night, French lost control of his craft and was blown against a shantyboat on the shore. The boat was the *Sylvan Glen* and its whiskered proprietor was Edwin Price, tintype artist with a floating studio. Thinking he could trade on showboat crowds, Price hooked on to the *New Sensation* and they floated downstream together. Eventually, when French retired, Price bought his latest *New Sensation* and re-named it *New Olympia*. By 1908 the one time tintype artist had a fleet of four big showboats including Emerson's *Grand Floating Palace*.

Ralph Emerson (originally Ralph Waldo Emerson Gaches) had grown up on the upper Ohio. At thirteen he ran away for a lifetime on the river. Ten years later he was piloting Price's showboat *Water Queen*; then he became an advance agent, going ahead to advertise the show while his wife taught school to the children on the boat. Like many showboats the *Water Queen* had clotheslines, go-carts and playpens on the roof; showboating was usually a family affair. Emerson learned quickly about the entertainment business and with his big, lacy *New Grand Floating Palace* he made river history along with a fortune of his own.

The last of the showboat families were the Bryants, a wandering tribe who took naturally to the river. In 1907 at Point Pleasant, West Virginia, they converted an old mud scow into the theater boat *Princess* and started out with a variety show. But motion pictures were coming to the river towns by then, and the showboat lost the magic that the Bryants remembered when they had played a variety act on Captain Price's *Water Queen*. To compete with the movies the Bryants turned to drama—*East Lynne, Mother, The Circus Girl, Tempest and Sunshine, Nell of the Ozarks* and *Uncle Tom's Cabin*. In 1917 they built *Bryant's New Showboat*, the first of three vessels of that name that toured the rivers until World War II. With brisk vaudeville numbers between acts they offered a repertoire of melodrama, playing for weeks at a time in the river cities and gradually developing a burlesque style that drew sophisticated audiences. In Billy Bryant's span of forty years, showboating changed from a simple grass-roots entertainment to a parodied melodrama for people who came to laugh at the old-time amusement. Bryant made a great success of "selling the relics rather than the realities of showboating," as Philip Graham has said. But there was no cynicism in *Bryant's New Showboat*. It was a family troupe, three generations who loved the river life and in their way loved the tradition they were deriding. And the audiences laughed with them on summer nights on the empty levee where the ghosts of the old showboats hovered.

The final chapter of showboating came after World War II when drama groups from Carnegie Tech, Hiram College, Kent State, Indiana University and the University of Minnesota took to the river for a summer laboratory in floating theater. It was a lark for the students who, like the old showboat families, shared in deck work and advertising as well as in the production onstage. But they are a novelty, living upon a tradition, and their stage echoes a time that has passed.

In recent years two sedentary showboats have operated at St. Louis and Vicksburg, but on June 1, 1962, the *Goldenrod* burned on the St. Louis riverfront, and now there is one. In drowsy Vicksburg harbor lies a famous old stern-wheeler, the biggest craft that ever roiled the rivers, with a theater built into her spacious main deck. In 1902 the *Sprague*, just launched at Dubuque, made her first run down the Mississippi. At Grand Tower, in the "graveyard" below St. Louis, the showboat *Temple of Amusement* was swinging into the landing. A confused signal put them on collision course and the big *Sprague* crashed into the side of the showboat, which sank like a stone. For forty-six years the *Sprague* pushed prodigious loads of cargo up and down the Mississippi. In 1948 she was retired to Vicksburg as a combination museum and showboat. Now in its roomy theater the Dixie Players present the old melodrama *Gold in the Hills*.

In this time of diesel towboats the few surviving steamboats are themselves a show. In the summer of 1961 curious crowds along the Illinois Waterway watched the stern-wheel *James V. Lockwood*, up from Natchez, push through the locks at Lockport on her way to Chicago. Moored in the north branch of the Chicago River near the Merchandise Mart, gleaming with new paint and polish, she became the *Showboat Sari S.* Her boiler deck is a lounge and dining room and her onetime texas is a private club. Meanwhile at Natchez a new diesel boat pushes the railroad freight that the *Lockwood* used to handle.

With a growing nostalgia for the past, river towns on the Ohio and the Mississippi have preserved steamboats as museums. Each season thousands of visitors at Marietta, Keokuk, Winona and elsewhere inspect old-time engine rooms and pilothouses.

On a gray December day in 1961 the three-decked *River Queen* was warped into her last berth on the Illinois side of the Mississippi opposite Hannibal. In her forty working years the big packet was known by other names—*Cape Girardeau, Gordon C. Greene.* Now she has become a museum boat. With iron feathers on her stacks, scrollwork on her texas and a deep-toned bell on the roof of her pilothouse, she will be the focus of a riverfront park across from the hill where a bronze figure of Mark Twain faces the broad river. More than a hundred thousand persons boarded her in 1962.

An older memory is recalled at New Salem, Illinois, on the winding Sangamon. A hundred and thirty years ago the little stern-wheel *Talisman* groped up the Sangamon River with young Abe Lincoln pointing out the channel. Now a replica of the *Talisman*, with two tall chimneys, a railed roof and airy wheelhouse, carries New Salem visitors past the millrace where Lincoln's neighbors brought their grain for grinding.

Early in 1963 the veteran steamboat *Mississippi*, long a towboat and inspection boat for the engineers on the lower river, was auctioned by the Memphis Engineer District. When bids were opened, the offers ranged from $101 to $35,110,10. The big steamer went to a St. Louis man who proposed to moor her as a museum boat near the new Jefferson National Expansion Memorial.

At Pittsburgh the new *Gateway Clipper* carries four hundred passengers along the riverfront. Though powered by diesel engines the *Clipper* looks like a steamboat, with stern wheel, chimneys, pilothouse and landing stage. On summer evenings its excursion parties hear music over the water—a Wind Symphony concert on the barge *Point Counterpoint.*

When the steel skeletons of Gateway Center were rising on the reclaimed point between the Allegheny and the Monongahela, a young Pittsburgh musician dreamed of bringing music to the rivers. Not the old-time minstrel chorus or the showboat calliope, but serious music by professional performers. With boyish zest and mature artistry Robert A. Boudreau organized the American Wind Symphony Orchestra and presented his first programs on a makeshift barge-stage moored to the Allegheny river wall. It was a unique orchestra—double size symphony brass and woodwind sections with a full complement of percussion—in a unique place. From the river a diesel horn might echo the orchestra brass and the rumble of bridge traffic prolonged the drums.

So in 1957 a new music came to the historic Point. Under the baton of their young director sixty young musicians—their age ranged from seventeen to twenty-six—played new arrangements of classical works and new works by contemporary composers. The musicians come from music schools across the United States and from Canada, England, Ireland, Spain and Japan. In the six seasons since 1957 more than sixty works have been written for the Wind Symphony by composers of a dozen countries. The orchestra is as cosmopolitan as many-voiced Pittsburgh and the Ohio valley. It has been supported by an all-Pittsburgh roster of civic groups, industries, labor unions, and by KDKA Radio and the Heinz Foundation.

In 1959 the makeshift barge-stage was replaced by the specially designed barge *Point Counterpoint* (a play on music and Pittsburgh's historic Point), and a new season was announced. Each Sunday and Thursday evening in the long June twilight the orchestra drew crowds to the riverfront. Then began the first tour. Down the river, like the pioneer FLOATING THEATRE 130 years ago, went the music barge. Taking its place among cargoes of coal, steel and chemicals, it hitched rides with towboats, dropping off at the river towns where concerts were scheduled. The musicians went ahead in buses and motor cars.

In 1960, at the Ohio and Mississippi River Valley Arts Festival, the *Point Counterpoint* added shows of painting and sculpture. Before the performance people came onstage, meeting the musicians and admiring the exhibits around the walls. The concerts ranged from Handel and Mozart to new compositions commissioned by the Wind Symphony. When the music ended, fireworks arched over the river. The *Point Counterpoint* drew crowds that dwarfed the old-time audiences on the benches of the *Circus Palace* and the *New Sensation*.

During the season of 1961 the Wind Symphony played to a third of a million people in America and abroad. After nine concerts in Pittsburgh the orchestra was flown to England for ten concerts on the Thames. In a barge designed by the American architect Louis I. Kahn—a self-propelled craft whose retractable sides and upperworks allowed passage

2 4 3

through the Thames locks and bridges—the Wind Symphony delighted large crowds of English people; some followed the music barge from town to town. After playing for the regatta at Henley the orchestra performed at a succession of Thames-side communities, always ending its program with Handel's "Music for the Royal Fireworks" and a fireworks display that recalled long-past festivals on the historic river. Thirty thousand people jammed the Thames Embankment for the final concert in London. Wrote the *Times:* "It took America last night to show us how the Thames can be put to delightful and entertaining use."

At the end of June the Wind Symphony returned to Pittsburgh where an audience of twelve thousand greeted it for a performance at the Point. Then began the 1961 tour of the Ohio-Mississippi. When the tour ended at Vicksburg on August 25, three thousand persons thronged the landing to hear a concert that ended with the old showboat favorite "Look away, look away, look away, Dixie Land!"

In 1962 the American Wind Symphony performed in fifteen river communities between Pennsylvania and Mississippi. It featured a Latin American art exhibit, supplemented by local art shows at Tarentum, Pennsylvania, Parkersburg and Huntington, West Virginia, Evansville, Indiana, and Paducah, Kentucky. Chamber concerts were held at Evansville and Greenville, Mississippi, on days preceding the full orchestra performance. A children's concert drew an eager and attentive crowd at Huntington. Though they generally traveled by highway, the musicians took turns riding the barge from one engagement to the next.

For the season of 1963 Conductor Boudreau announced that the Wind Symphony would tour the upper Mississippi, from St. Louis to St. Paul. Meanwhile invitations had come from the Old World and from two of the newest of nations; groups in Ghana and Nigeria urged a visit of the American Wind Symphony to the rivers of Africa. The newest showboat enterprise has horizons unlimited.

V

~~~~~

Towboat River

Our river systems are better adapted to the needs of the people than those of any other country. In extent, distribution, navigability and ease of use, they stand first.

THEODORE ROOSEVELT

22

Dayboards, Buoys
and
Beacons

THE CENSUS OF 1880 showed nearly 90,000 miles of railroad in the United States, built at an average cost of $36,848 a mile. At that time a statistician for the Treasury Department assigned a dollar value to the rivers. Taking into account their location and carrying capacity, he figured the lower Mississippi at ten times the cost of a railroad, or $468,480 a mile; the upper Mississippi at seven times the railroad cost, or $327,936 a mile; the Ohio at five times, or $234,240 a mile. To the lower Missouri, the Red, the Cumberland and other navigable tributaries he gave lesser values. Altogether his figures showed that the inland United States had $2,054,849,680 worth of river channel—a free gift of geography. Would the nation improve that gift, he asked, and maintain it?

It was estimated in the 1880's that a double-track railroad on both sides of the Ohio with trains running night and day could not carry the river-borne traffic. In a dramatic demonstration of the river's value the steamer *Joseph B. Williams* arrived at Bayou Sara in 1883 with twenty-five boats of coal, a barge of hay and a barge of fuel—a total of 30,000 tons. That load, rivermen said, would require a train twelve miles long, with two thousand railroad cars and sixty-six locomotives. In the next decade the "Big Joe" pushed still bigger loads; on one famous trip she brought sixty laden barges down the rivers.

The first cargoes from the vast coal beds of the upper Ohio were floated, like the first rafts from the pine forests of the upper Mississippi. Coal boats commonly went downstream in pairs, lashed together and manned by boatmen with long oars. The crew lived in a cavelike shanty, covered with coal, at one end of the load. At New Orleans the coal was unloaded, the empty flats were cut into firewood for householders in Toulouse, Chartres and Dauphine streets, and the crews returned to Pittsburgh by steamboat. This was a seasonal trade; only from November to April was there enough water to float the big coal flats.

In 1845 Captain Daniel Bushnell of the *Walter Forward* made a kind of history by taking three coal flats, two lashed alongside and one towed astern, down to Cincinnati—the first coal towing on the river. In February of 1854 the steamer *Crescent City* pushed four flats of coal all the way to New Orleans, and a month later, still on the crest of water, the *James Guthrie* brought down ten full barges. Towing by pushing was a development of the 1850's. With the load ahead, a steamboat could maneuver against wind and current in a narrow channel.

So began the massive coal trade—a business not threatened by the railroads. To send a ton of coal two thousand miles by river cost $1.30. The railroads, said a writer for the Cincinnati *Commercial Gazette*, could not carry it one-tenth of the distance at that cost. At Pittsburgh acres of barges heaped with coal waited for a freshet. When the river rose, scores of towboats hooked onto their loads and the black fleet rode the hump of water down the valley. On the high water of 1869 more than a third of a million tons of coal arrived in Cincinnati. If piled up in a square between Fourth, Vine, Fifth and Race streets (the site of the present Carew Tower) a report figured it would rise ninety-seven feet high—"seven feet higher than the Commercial Gazette Building."

During the Civil War there was neither improvement nor maintenance of the Ohio channel. A survey in 1866 located 140 sunken steamboats and barges and 166 snags. In that year Congress appropriated $272,000 to clear the channel and to build dikes that would provide a minimum depth of three feet. Then came the proposal to light the channel along the Grand Chain of Rocks above Cairo—a project which grew into a system of beacon lights from Pittsburgh to the Mississippi.

In 1869 the Louisville Pilots Association set up some lights at dangerous points along the Grand Chain of Rocks above Cairo—the first fixed beacons on the Western rivers. Five years later, in 1874, the Federal government took up the project. An act of Congress instructed the Light House Board to erect on the inland rivers beacon lights, day beacons and buoys for the aid of navigation.

Cotton eight bales high on the steamer *Hallette* (The Mariners Museum)

Coal from mine to barge on the upper Ohio
(American Waterways Operators, Inc.)

When the work began, certain groups of old river pilots opposed the project, fearing it would diminish the importance of their knowledge and skill and open the door of their profession to ignorant and inexperienced men. Mark Twain expressed their derision of a "pilot" who steered a steamboat down a river that had become a 2000-mile torchlight procession. "With these abundant beacons," he said, "and the banishment of snags, plenty of daylight in a box [searchlight] and ready to be turned on whenever needed, and a chart compass to fight the fog with, piloting, at a good stage of water, is nearly as safe and simple as driving a stage. . . . And now [this was on his return visit to the Mississippi in 1882] the Anchor Line have raised the captain above the pilot by giving him bigger wages."

Despite the closed fraternity of the old pilots, lights came to the rivers. By 1875 nearly three hundred bends and crossings were lighted. Ten years later eleven hundred beacons beckoned a pilot down the dark river, and lighthouse tenders made the rounds, supplying the keepers with oil and inspecting the lanterns that lit every dangerous crossing from Pittsburgh to New Orleans.

One of the first lighthouse tenders was the side-wheel steamer *Lily*, built at Jeffersonville in 1875. The next year she was in command of Captain William R. Hoel whose laconic diary recalls the strenuous life of a lighthouse man. On Christmas Day, 1876, the *Lily* lay with drawn fires in the ice at Cincinnati. It had been a cold December and the river was frozen over. Day and night the *Lily*'s crew cut ice from around the boat. December 29 brought an all-day blizzard, and the crew built braces in the hold against the ice pressure. On January 4 they took on fuel, dragging coal sleds from barges frozen in the stream. At daybreak on the 9th, after an all-night snowfall, Captain Hoel read the thermometer at 16 below zero. That day he kept his men shoveling snow off the boat and cutting the ice around her. Three days later, the 12th of January, they woke up to the sound of rain. An hour before midnight the gorge broke with a roar that traveled for miles down the river. For twenty minutes the *Lily* was battered with blocks of ice as big as her wheelhouse. Then the ice gorged again, massing against the piers of the Newport railroad bridge.

Next day the river rose fifteen feet and the *Lily* had four lines ashore. At midnight the gorge gave way. In the rushing gray current the men saw hurrying black islands—coal boats and barges upended and crushed by the oncoming ice. Back in the year 1862 Captain Hoel had taken the ironclad *Louisville* past the rebel batteries at Island No. 10. It sounded like that now.

When the shore ice began to move, Captain Hoel cast off his four hawsers and went with it. All day he steered through the clogged river while his men sparred off the battering masses. For three more days, while the *Lily* shuddered and shook, they ran with the ice on the rising river. On January 19, Captain Hoel noted that the river had crested just before daybreak—"there being 54 feet in the channel." Next day it began falling and the ice was almost gone. Captain Hoel thought of his hundreds of miles of beacons where the oil was running low.

Against a booming current he pushed upstream on his inspection and supervision trip. He "paid lightkeeper and left supplies" at Four Mile Bar, Nine Mile Bar, Richmond, Snag Bar, Augusta Bar, at Greenup and Union Landing and scores of other stations. He landed at Hanging Rock and took on four hundred bushels of bunker coal, at five cents a bushel. He paid the lightkeeper at Twelve Pole, Green Bottom, Straight Ripple, Raccoon Island and Gallipolis. At Eight Mile Island he removed the light a mile farther upstream. There were other changes needed, after that massive crest of water, as he went on up to the forks of the Ohio.

Beacon lights were attached to poles from six to sixty feet high, depending on their location. On an open point or in a clearing rose the white A board, which served as a daymark; it supported a triangular brass lantern that burned for a week with one filling of kerosene. To allow for floods and changing river channels, a movable light post was developed. It consisted of a braced mast with steps climbing to a bracketed shelf for the lantern. White wings served as a reflector and increased the daytime visibility, and a number board showed the mileage from the river mouth. From one bend to another, lights marked the channel crossings; on a black night boats steered safely from one light bearing to the next. In flood or drought, calm or storm, the beacon was a steadfast signal, and the grudging old pilots soon took comfort in them. Their names—Hardscrabble, Big Bone, Poverty, Poorhouse, Old Maid, Hole-in-the-wall, and all the rest—sang in a pilot's mind like music.

Ten dollars a month was the cost of maintaining a beacon but its value was incalculable. Going down the river on a dark and windy night with a deeply laden boat needing all the water in the channel, a pilot breathed a sigh of gratitude when the guiding beacon swam into sight. When flood or storm or caving bank destroyed a light, or a careless keeper let its flame grow dim, a chorus of complaint rose from the rivermen.

On the tender *Lily* Captain Hoel's signal was a long, three shorts and a long. The sound of his whistle under a hill pasture or a cornfield brought the keeper with his lamps and oilcans. The lamps were inspected, wicks replaced, and the cans filled with three months' supply of oil. Then Captain Hoel opened his ledger and his strongbox and counted out the keeper's wages. The lightkeepers, some of them farm wives and widows, were paid one dollar to fifteen dollars a month for each beacon, the wage depending on its location and access. With a departing toot the *Lily* backed into the stream.

In Captain Hoel's Fourteenth District a veteran lightkeeper was Hermit Barnell who lived alone, remote from any neighbor, in a hut of driftwood about the size of the *Lily's* pilothouse. For fifteen dollars a month he tended two lights at Brown's Island, West Virginia. He came promptly at the whistle signal, an old man with streaming hair and beard, smelling of woodsmoke and river mud. In the captain's office he silently accepted his three months' pay and a pile of old newspapers that had collected in the cabin. With his oilcans and his papers he had to double-trip up the riverbank. Back in his hut he poked up the fire, added the newspapers to a four-foot stack against the wall, and began to read. Column by column and page by page he worked his way toward the floor. At dusk he tramped through the bottom timber, looked for fish on his trotlines and kindled his beacons. His lights always burned with a bright clear flame.

In the 1880's battery-powered electric beacons were proposed by the lighthouse service. True to character the old pilots, meeting in Cincinnati, opposed the "preposterous bill"; the glare of electric lights, they said, would blind a steersman. But every season saw barges grounded, tows broken on bars and islands, coal flats wrecked and drifting dangerously downstream. In these years the streets of midland cities were lighted by coal gas from river-carried coal. To get that coal delivered, more light was needed on the rivers. Gradually electric beacons replaced the oil lanterns and one by one the lightkeepers were retired.

Now, in 1963, the Second Coast Guard District in St. Louis, which has the entire Mississippi River system for its province, maintains 2792 lighted buoys and beacons. Buoys marking the left bank (going down river) are red; those on the right are black with a white chevron. Lights on the right bank show a single flash; those on the left flash twice. One beacon on the Ohio River near Marietta burns natural gas; all the rest of the river lights are powered by batteries or commercial electricity. Though there is no kerosene to replenish and no wick to trim, the Coast Guard still employs 113 "lamplighters" who tend the beacons in remote places, pulling their skiffs to roadless points and islands and climbing the tangled riverbank in all seasons. In half a century on the lower Mississippi one veteran lamplighter rowed his skiff a total of 175,000 miles, seven times the distance around the earth. Then, in his last years, he used a gasoline launch.

During the fearsome flood of 1927 when the lower Mississippi drowned its normal landmarks and drove 700,000 people from their homes, the post lights were all that was left to mark the main channel. In that grave time the Coast Guard office in New Orleans received a report from Lightkeeper William McGill of Grand Lake, Louisiana. It stated: "I am yet on the job, but the water has run me out of my house. I have the oil on some logs. I will stay out there. All is well."

When the superintendent asked McGill for a full report, a longer message came: "Your letter of June 10 at hand asking for details of how I lived and cared for oil and things. On May 21 I had to leave my home. The water came in the floor at 11 A.M. I went out on the lake and gathered in some cottonwood logs and made a raft and I had a little outhouse 8 by 10. I jacked it up and ran these logs under it and so it floated, and I had a home to carry me through the water. But, in the meantime, while doing this a boat passed and the waves set all of my oil afloat.

"I gathered it up again and put it on the roof. Then a Red Cross boat came down full speed, one of those United States rum chasers, and knocked the oil house off the blocks.

"Again, I saved the oil and wicks, but the chimneys went down to the bottom with the house. I don't know if they are broken or not. There are about five feet of water over them, but the house is not gone to pieces. Everything will be in the house when the water goes down. I have 4 feet of water over the floor in my house.

"On May 25 Captain Harvey took my wife out to Morgan City, but she is in the camp now with me. We are all well and safe if no storm comes. We are a long way from any land. We have a small boat of our own to go about. That is about all the details. When the water goes down I want to take a lay off and go on a trip to New Orleans while the mud is drying up."

Back in 1881 in St. Louis, the first River Convention formally recognized the benefits of the lighthouse service and urged its enlargement. It also called for a system of channel improvements—protection of caving banks by grading and ventment, the building of dikes, ripraps, wire and timber mattresses and wing dams—so as to make the river form new banks and amended channels. While some of the old pilots spoke up again, saying that the river would go on changing at its own will, the United States River Commission began work at Plum Point Reach above Memphis and Lake Providence Reach above Vicksburg, two notorious stretches totaling seventy miles of the worst navigation below Cairo. The project aimed at providing an improved channel with a low-water depth of ten feet.

The next year Mark Twain, on his sentimental journey down the river, reported on their progress. "Plum Point looked as it had always looked by night, with the exception that now there were beacons to mark the crossings, and also a lot of other lights on the Point and along its shore; these latter glinting from the fleet of the United States River Commission, and from a village which the officials have built on the land for offices and for the employees of the service. The military engineers of the Commission have taken upon their shoulders the job of making the Mississippi over again—a job transcended in size by only the original job of creating it. They are building wing-dams here and there to deflect the current; and dikes to confine it in narrower bounds; and other dikes to make it stay there; and for unnumbered miles along the Mississippi they are felling the timber-front for fifty yards back, with the purpose of shaving the bank down to low-water mark with the slant of a house-roof, and ballasting it with stones; and in many places they have protected the wasting shores with rows of piles. One who knows the Mississippi will promptly aver—not aloud but to himself—that ten thousand River Commissions, with the mines of the world at their back, cannot tame that lawless stream, cannot curb it or confine it, cannot say to it, 'Go here,' or 'Go there,' and make it obey; cannot save a shore which it has sentenced; cannot bar its path with an obstruction which it will not tear down, dance over, and laugh at. But a discreet man will not put these things into spoken words; for the West Point engineers have not their superiors anywhere; they know all that can be known of their abstruse science; and so, since they conceive that they can fetter and handcuff that river and boss him, it is but wisdom for the unscientific man to keep still, lie low, and wait till they do it. Captain Eads, with his jetties, has done a work at the mouth of the Mississippi which seemed clearly impossible; so we do not feel full confidence now to prophesy against like impossibilities. Otherwise one would pipe out and say the Commission might as well bully the comets in their courses and undertake to make them behave, as try to bully the Mississippi into right and reasonable conduct."

In 1882 Mark Twain found everyone on the lower Mississippi talking about cutoffs and ventments while the old packet men looked at the empty river and remembered the flush times past. He let a jeering steamboat mate point out that irony. "Government is doing a deal for the Mississippi now," said the mate of the Vicksburg packet *Gold Dust*, "spending loads of money on her. When there used to be four thousand steamboats and ten thousand acres of coal barges, and rafts, and trading-scows, there wasn't a lantern from St. Paul to New Orleans, and the snags were thicker than bristles on a hog's back; and now, when there's three dozen steamboats and nary a barge or raft, government has snatched out all the snags, and lit up the shores like Broadway, and a boat's as safe on the river as she'd be in heaven. And I reckon that by the time there ain't any boats left at all, the Commission will have the old thing all reorganized, and dredged out, and fenced in, and tidied up, to a degree that will make navigation just simply perfect, and absolutely safe and profitable."

After that derisive outburst Mark Twain came upon an item in a Cincinnati newspaper. The steamer *Joseph B. Williams* was on her way to New Orleans with a string of thirty-two coal barges, "the largest tow ever taken to New Orleans or anywhere else in the world." Her freight bill would come to $18,000. At ten dollars a ton, a fair price said the reporter for the long haul by rail, the cost would be $180,000. Mark Twain added that when an improved river could save $162,000 on a single cargo, it would seem wise to keep the river improved.

On March 27, 1886, readers of *Harper's Weekly* found a drawing of the new railroad bridge at Louisville, an installment of Thomas Hardy's

The Mayor of Casterbridge, and a picture of a coal tow of fifteen barges, 20,000 tons, in a night run on the Ohio, steam jetting white from the escape pipes and black smoke pouring from the funnels. "A Pittsburgh steamer with a tow of coal flats," said the article. "Nothing like it can be seen anywhere in the world except on our inland waterways." The writer explained that by spreading out the cargo over a large area, shallow-draft boats and barges carried acres of coal down the valley in the cheapest transportation in the world. Now, he stated, in 1886, the traffic on the Ohio River exceeded the total foreign commerce of the United States. The bulk of that traffic was coal, loaded on the upper Ohio and delivered by 160 Pittsburgh towboats all over the inland rivers. To enlarge the immense trade the Federal government had built the Davis Island Dam, five miles below Pittsburgh, which would give harborage to 12,000 steamboats and barges.

The Davis Island Dam, completed in 1885, held a permanent pool of water at Pittsburgh where hundreds of coal tows loaded at the longest dock in the world. There the tows waited for rain in the hills and a rising river. When the freshet came thousands of boats and barges rode the hump of water down the valley. In the first festive run past Davis Island one of the Advance Coal Company's towboats carried a banner "At Last Out of Bondage." But that pioneer dam merely gave the coal fleet a year-round harbor at Pittsburgh. It would be nearly half a century before a system of forty-six locks and dams would fit the Ohio for year-round navigation with a slack-water nine-foot channel.

The old seasonal river held many hazards for the coal tows. One of the big towboats of those years was the bad-luck *Boaz,* a 1433-horsepower stern-wheeler that pushed mountains of coal down the river and lost millions of bushels of it. In 1895, her thirteenth year in the trade, she lost a tow of fourteen barges near Maysville, Kentucky. Six years later she ran a tow of forty-two flats aground on the lower Mississippi near Natchez. In 1908 she rammed a bridge pier at Ironton, Ohio, spilling 20,000 tons of coal into the river. According to legend the *Boaz* once left Pittsburgh with a big tow, and after losing barges at twenty narrow bends had none left to deliver in Cincinnati. Retired in 1916, she lay rusting in the Monongahela during the years when dams were building on the Ohio to provide a minimum nine-foot channel all the way to the Mississippi.

23

The New Waterway

THE HILLS OF PITTSBURGH were blurred with snow when the little side-wheeler, shaped like a shoe box, backed away from the Monongahela wharf. It was November 2, 1911, just a century after the first steamboat had astonished the valley, and a replica of the *New Orleans* was starting down the river. Forty-seven packets puffed into line, with imposing President William Howard Taft on the roof of the flagship *Virginia*. Whistles shrilling, they made a smoky pageant as the stubby *New Orleans* passed under the bridge and fired a farewell salute from her signal cannon. After that fanfare in the squall of snow the packets returned to their idle berths, the President went back to the White House, and in the interests of history the *New Orleans* steamed down an empty river. She passed a hundred lifeless moorings, some shantyboats in the winter willows, an occasional grimy coal tow creeping around a bend. A half century before, the levees swarmed with men, horses, wagons, carts, hand trucks and wheelbarrows, and mountains of merchandise rose on the river bank. Now the landings were silent. The voyage of the *New Orleans*, with her gaunt chimney smoking up her trysail and a string of pennants, seemed to mark the end of river transportation.

Down the winter valley, the little steamer carried a century of memories. After 1811 a storied river commerce had grown and faded. Steamboats had taken the business of the keelboats, then railroads and towboats took the business of the packets. While steamboats rotted at weedy landings, lumber rafts and coal boats rode the current. By the end of the century the northern forests were gone; Illinois and Alabama

2 5 7

coal supplied the South and Pittsburgh's coal trade shrank to the middle Ohio. Now the *New Orleans* stirred the waters of a nearly forgotten river.

Three years earlier, in 1908, President Theodore Roosevelt had told the United States Congress: "Our river systems are better adapted to the needs of the people than are those of any other country. In extent, distribution, navigability and ease of use, they stand first. Yet the rivers of no other civilized country are so poorly developed, so little used, or play so small a part in the industrial life of the nation as those of the United States. In view of the use made of rivers elsewhere, the failure to use our own is astonishing."

After a flurry of channel improvement in the 1880's the rivers had been neglected. A few months before the *New Orleans* made its centennial voyage, the pilot of the *Joseph B. Williams* groped past Plum Point where Mark Twain had watched the engineers working in 1882. "There don't seem to be much channel here," he wrote in his logbook. "We came down to left of island. Two dredge boats working here and *Barrett* laying at bank cannot get through. From shape of shore below Gold Dust we went out toward end of dam on Aubrey towhead, passing at about 60 yards off. Then from end of this same dam to a small field with some young willows above corner of the towhead under King's Point. This takes you above one dredge and be sure to go clear in to shore close under the two snags. . . . Then shape of island to red roof barn above Plum Point where in midriver pull down on point takes you outside of more snags. Then shape of shore to head of cut on bar 12 feet and shape bar to Last Chance Light. Deep." It was touch and go in 1911, almost as it had been in Zadok Cramer's time.

The *New Orleans* carried nostalgia southward, arriving at New Orleans in a downpour of rain. Some harbor tugs welcomed her with whistles, but the levee was deserted. Then the steamer was tied up at Wilmot's Landing and offered for sale. She was taken to Brashear, Louisiana, and abandoned there. Nobody wanted a steamboat when railroad trains were rumbling over a hundred bridges and panting into every town and city. "Never before," wrote a river reporter, "has Ohio river tonnage been so worthless."

A few years later an ice gorge in the Ohio wrecked scores of old steamers and scattered their wreckage down the valley. In the bitter January of 1918 ice locked an idle fleet on the riverfront at Cincinnati.

When the gorge broke, it crushed and crumpled the 300-foot *City of Louisville*, a fast fine steamer that had prolonged the river glamour of past years; she had double white collars on her stacks, a big roof bell from a set of chimes built for the Chicago World's Fair, a brass signal cannon and a three-toned whistle. With her in the grinding ice went her sister steamer the *City of Cincinnati*, and a lot of others were destroyed on the Ohio. Four of the Eagle Packet Company vessels were wintering in the Duck's Nest in the Tennessee River mouth at Paducah —the *Gray Eagle, Spread Eagle, Peoria*, and *Alton*. As the ice closed in, the *Peoria's* engineer revolved his paddle buckets to ease her strained moorings. But when the gorge broke, the lines snapped like string. It was midnight and the crew scrambled empty-handed to shore. Away went the steamer with her lights aglow and her paddle wheel turning. The other boats went plunging after. Their wreckage came ashore some miles downstream.

When spring came in 1918 the American railroads were staggering under the massive freight of war. Millions of tons of foodstuff, armament, machinery and military supplies were piled up in freight terminals, waiting to be moved to tidewater. To break that jam the War Department turned to the forgotten rivers. Old stern-wheel towboats and wooden barges were reconditioned; veteran pilots were recalled from retirement. Rounding up all the tonnage that would float, building new barges and towboats, merging local carriers into a transportation system, the government formed the Federal Barge Lines. The rivers were at work again.

Rediscovered by war, the rivers remained in business. A barge cost less than a train of coal cars, and a towboat could be built as quickly as a locomotive. Already new fleets were coming. At Neville Island below Pittsburgh, at Charleston on the Kanawha, in the old Howard ship-yards at Jeffersonville, at Point Pleasant and Paducah, diesel towboats and steel barges slid down the ways in a resurgence of boatbuilding. The new commerce was bulk traffic—a massive movement of coal, oil, iron and steel, sulfur and limestone; by 1929 it was nearing twenty million tons.

Water transport was economical and efficient, and the rivers flowed through the heartland of the nation. Awakened to the value of the inland waterways, Congress in 1922 voted forty-two million dollars for improvement of the rivers. A year later the appropriation was increased to fifty-six millions.

In the doldrums of 1911 when the little *New Orleans* poked down the empty rivers, certain improvements were under way on the upper Ohio. In 1910 Congress had authorized a system of locks and dams to provide a slack-water stage of nine feet from Pittsburgh to Cairo. Now, a dozen years later, new funds were voted. Under direction of the Corps of Engineers of the War Department, work began on the canalization of the Ohio. Along the middle and lower river rose the din of dynamite, dredges, steam shovels, pile drivers, cranes and trucks. Cofferdams held back the river while construction crews built the dams, with movable wickets to lie flat on the bottom in stages of high water, and the 600-foot navigation locks.

In 1929 the last locks at Golconda, Illinois, and at the foot of the Grand Chain just above Cairo were opened to traffic. The Ohio River was now a flight of water steps climbing by forty-six rises from Cairo to Pittsburgh. Between the dams was a permanent nine-foot depth of water.

At Cincinnati on October 22, 1929, on the height of Eden Park above a sweeping bend of the river, President Herbert Hoover dedicated the Ohio River Memorial Monument. Its pictorial bronze tablet spanned two and a half centuries of history, from La Salle's discovery of the wilderness river in 1673 to its canalization in 1929. That afternoon a parade of steamboats left Cincinnati for Louisville and Cairo, passing through the locks of the longest controlled waterway in the world.

Ten years later, after construction of twenty-six locks and dams on the upper Mississippi, a nine-foot channel was open to Minneapolis; and the engineers were providing a six-foot stage of water on the lower Missouri. At the same time improvements were under way on the Illinois, the Tennessee, the Cumberland and other rivers. The old river system was becoming a new waterway.

But the traffic grew faster than the engineering works. After World War II and the postwar industrial expansion, the river trade was bigger than the facilities provided for it. Reporting to the United States Senate in 1960 the U. S. Army Corps of Engineers pointed to the "dramatic growth of industry in the river valleys which has brought about rapid increase in the use of the inland waterways. . . . In twenty more years," the report concluded, "the demands of industry will double the freight load now carried on the rivers." In the 1950's there were seven hundred transportation lines on the Mississippi system, with more than a thousand towboats and ten thousand barges. Each year larger towboats came into service, a service that involved costly double-tripping and delay as their tows outgrew the 600-foot locks. As commerce assumed these new proportions a new river project began to take shape on the engineers' drawing boards. Instead of forty-six steps, the newly designed Ohio waterway would rise in nineteen steps, with nineteen high-lift dams creating long pools of slack water. At each dam, navigation would be served by a huge main lock 1200 by 110 feet and an auxiliary lock 600 by 110 feet.

Again rose the clamor of construction—the roar of motors, the creaking of cranes, the suck and throb of dredges, the sinking of cofferdams—as the billion-dollar project began.

In the early 1960's the Ohio River traffic, twice that of the Panama Canal and three times that of the St. Lawrence Seaway, moves on a combination of the old waterway and the new. In September, 1961, the last piece of cofferdam was pulled out of the river at Stratton, Ohio, and the New Cumberland Locks and Dam were in full operation. This was the first step in the Ohio River program. It replaced three obsolete dams and created a continuous 23-mile pool through which a river parade passed with flags and pennants flying.

Two months later the McAlpine Lock at Louisville was opened to navigation. When the towboat *Philip Sporn* with 1120 feet of barges passed through, her blaring whistle woke a century of echoes at the Falls of the Ohio. That tight and touchy place had been a scene of trouble and delay ever since George Rogers Clark took his troop-laden flatboats through the Indiana Chute on the way to British territory in Illinois. In addition to the big new lock two older locks bypassed the ancient barrier.

In July of 1962 the Greenup Locks and Dam, providing a 60-mile pool between Greenup and Gallipolis, Ohio, were dedicated. The Markland Locks and Dam, sixty miles below Cincinnati, were completed in the spring of 1963. Nearing completion were the Pike Island Locks and Dam and the Captain Anthony Meldahl Locks and Dam at New Richmond, twenty miles above Cincinnati. Construction began at Belleville and Hannibal (formerly Opossum Creek) on the upper Ohio and at Cannelton on the lower Ohio in 1962. Meanwhile the works at

Uniontown and Racine were on the drawing boards and preliminary studies had begun on other parts of the Ohio River project. By 1970 the new Ohio Waterway will be completed, and the greatest inland commerce in the world will move past the river junction at Cairo.

Meanwhile interest is growing in a new project, a canal to link the upper Ohio with Lake Erie. A hundred-mile route from Rochester, Pennsylvania, to Ashtabula Harbor is now under study by the U. S. Engineers. "Eventually," declared the *Waterways Journal* on August 18, 1962, "the canal will be built."

On the upper Mississippi, barge traffic has increased each year since the nine-foot channel was completed in 1939, and now that channel is inadequate to the trade. In 1962 the new Chain of Rocks Canal near St. Louis handled twenty-five million tons of cargo. Its 1200-foot lock accommodates tows that must double-trip through all but one of the twenty-six smaller locks above; only the big new lock at Keokuk, 1200 by 110 feet, with a dramatic 38-foot lift, is in scale with the new waterway. The engineers are now designing high-lift dams with 1200-foot locks and a deep channel beyond St. Paul. The new St. Anthony's Falls Locks, upper and lower, now extend navigation 4.6 miles up the river, admitting towboats into the heart of Minneapolis. It is expected that by 1975 a twelve-foot channel will carry the increased commerce on the upper river.

The Missouri, which carried a record two million tons of cargo in 1962, now has a six-foot channel to Omaha and a four-foot depth from there to Sioux City. The traffic justifies a nine-foot channel and extension of navigation to Yankton, South Dakota, a project urged by rivermen. Meanwhile the great earth dams on the upper Missouri have created vast lakes on the bare plains. Since 1945 the Missouri Valley Authority has built thirty dams on the Missouri; eleven more are under way. Huge storage reservoirs—Fort Peck, Garrison, Oahe, Fort Randall and Gavins Point—impound floodwater for release in dry seasons. The program for the Missouri basin has brought a clash between power and navigation interests. Proponents of electric power claim that the Flood Control Act of 1944 gave priority to hydroelectric production; they argue that the impounded water should be withheld during spring and summer to turn the generators during the winter season. Contrary-minded rivermen hold that the Pick-Sloan program for the development of the Missouri basin was designed to provide for navigation as well as electricity. Meanwhile river tonnage has grown dramatically on the incomplete channel of the Missouri. It will surge ahead, with diesel horns blaring under the windswept hills, when the reservoirs are used to provide a stable river stage during the navigation season.

In the Arkansas basin the prospects of the new waterway are arousing great expectations. Army engineers plan to open the Arkansas and Verdigris rivers to barge navigation with a nine-foot channel from the Mississippi River to Tulsa by the 1970's. Present plans call for fifteen locks on the Arkansas and three on the Verdigris. Major General W. F. Cassidy of the engineers has said, "This will give the biggest boost to the Arkansas Valley since the Oklahoma land rush."

In this far-reaching new waterway, with controlled river channels veining the nation's heartland, New Orleans, Pittsburgh, Minneapolis and Sioux City are linked in a web of commerce. With the growth of river traffic, said William Faulkner, "an Idea rose, suspended like a balloon, a portent or a thunderhead above what used to be the wilderness, drawing, holding the eyes of all: Mississippi; and so the Big Woods diminished, pushed back into the notch where the hills drop down to the Big River, where the wilderness could make its last enduring stand."

Below Cairo the big river rolls unobstructed to the Gulf, carrying the commerce that funnels into it from the upper rivers. On the upper Mississippi, barge traffic far surpasses that of the old packet commerce on the seasonal river. The vast TVA project has made the Tennessee River a series of deep-water lakes all the way to Knoxville; at Wilson Dam, above the buried rocks of Big Muscle Shoals, bargeloads of coal, oil, grain, gravel and automobiles are lifted a hundred feet to the level of Wilson Lake in the most dramatic lock on all the rivers. Over the Illinois Waterway big ocean-built freighters have passed into the Great Lakes trade, and a stream of grain, coal and oil barges file through the locks. The phenomenal growth of its commerce was recalled when Lockmaster Bill Hicklin cleared off his desk at Lockport on an August day in 1961. In past decades thousands of rivermen had gone to work for the railroads, but in 1932 Bill Hicklin left a brakeman's job in Kansas to work on the Illinois River. In his first year, when half of the locks and dams on the 327-mile waterway were yet to be constructed, 134 tons of cargo went through the lock at Lockport. In his last year on the job its commerce reached twenty million tons, with fifty million bushels of corn and soybeans loading in the Peoria district alone for barge transport to New Orleans. At that time nearly two thousand towboats, from the abrupt little *Aubrey Saucer* to the 9000-horsepower *America*, were moving cargoes on the Mississippi system.

A century ago the graceful white packets passed Cairo, twenty of them a day in navigable seasons. Now more than twenty towboats pass, pushing acres of oil, coal, grain, steel, chemicals and other bulk cargo. A single barge carries the load of three or four of the vanished packets; a single towboat pushes a tonnage that would require fifty of the biggest steamboats. The old river commerce is dwarfed by the new, except in the movement of people. Just one overnight passenger boat is left on the huge river system—the Greene Line's Steamer *Delta Queen*. She passes Cairo on the way to New Orleans in the spring and to St. Paul in September, with her calliope filling the valley with music and her paddle wheel lifting a white cascade of water.

24

~~~~

Down to New Orleans

IT IS 1845 MILES from Pittsburgh to New Orleans, and nearly 1800 of them are as wild and solitary as when George Rogers Clark floated down the Ohio in a dugout canoe. Towns and cities pass and the woods close in again with only a glint of highway traffic under the hills. Indians might be peering through the sycamores and willows. Where a steel mill, a chemical factory or a power plant darkens one riverbank, the other is green and timeless, untouched by the violence of today.

It is that way at Columbia Park—a park of oil tanks and coal piles—on the lower edge of Cincinnati where we boarded the towboat *Live Oak* for a ride to New Orleans. Fourteen hundred miles in six days. There aren't many ways to travel ten miles an hour now, but the towboat is one.

At Columbia Park the road curved past the tanks, towers and webbed catwalks of an asphalt refinery. It climbed a green levee and there was the Ohio, a long bend of river under the dark Kentucky hills. A cement ramp just wide enough to walk on pitched down to a pair of steamboats and a double row of green and white barges, snarled with hoses and steamlines, against the riverbank. On the far side of the barges, white in the dusk, lay the *Live Oak* with yellow light in her windows. The two boats on the bank had military names, *Tulagi* and *Coral Sea*. Once government towboats pushing war cargoes down the Mississippi, they are now steam plants on permanent station. Their steam heats Venezuela crude oil to be pumped ashore.

On this summer evening a thin rain showed in the floodlights and the barge decks gleamed like glass. Steam hissed and puffed from the pipeline and the diesels pounded. The dusk held a reek of oil and river. We carried our bags over an obstacle course of cleats, stanchions, timberheads, cables, hawsers and hose lines, with the diesels roaring all around; each oil barge has its own pumping engine. It was a five-foot drop from the nearly empty barge to the main deck of the towboat. A deckhand in smeared oilskins looked up through the rain. "I guess you-all b'long up here," and he led past winches and rope coils up a steep stairway and into an oblong room, fresh and cool, with an air conditioner going. There were twin beds, a table, two leather chairs, and a connecting bath and shower. Three windows looked ahead and one to the port side.

"You had your supper? There's lunch in the galley."

From our room an inside door opened onto a narrow passage roaring with the diesel engines. One stairway climbed to the pilothouse and another went down to a catwalk over the twin diesels, white in the hard light, and through a door to the bright galley. There was a long table with jars of mustard, pickles, catsup, vinegar and jelly chattering in a circle rack.

A ruddy, stocky man with a boyish smile looked around from the big coffee urn. "You're the ones going down with us? Have some coffee— some pie or sandwiches?"

He was the relief captain, Charlie Menard from Lafitte, Louisiana. They came up the Ohio on open river—no lockings—arrived last night after a short delay on account of fog. (They ran two barges aground below Evansville, I learned later.) One oil line out there, he inclined his coffee cup, was clogged and that slowed up pumping. But we would get away by daylight. Back to New Orleans with five empties—a fast run.

"Well, anything you want just say so."

I stepped out on the dark riverside. It took a minute to see anything, and then there was only the steep Kentucky shore with a range light winking through the rain. Around the upper bend two small lights appeared, red and green. They moved slowly and behind them came a dark mass ending in the banked lights of a towboat. It crept past, a thousand-foot tow, and disappeared around the lower bend.

The rain squall passed and the summer stars came out above the gleam and smoke and glitter of the asphalt terminal. On the barge *Bayou La Fourche* a deckhand poked a flashlight into an open manhole and an engineer in a soaking blue shirt and a blue-striped cap bent over a deck valve where steam hissed and rasped like summer insects. A warm breeze brought a river smell and the rain was back, falling in slanting ropes under the cluster lights. It drove me in to bed. Hours later came the bumping and jarring, the sound of a glass splintering in the washbowl where I had left it on the ledge, the racing of winches. The tow was being shaped and lashed together. Then the whistle blurted, abrupt quick blasts, and the diesels steadied down.

When we looked out it was sunlight, green shores moving past and the long flat barge decks stretched ahead on the glinting river. By daylight Captain Menard looked even younger, white teeth showing in his sunburned smile. It was hard to believe he had been seventeen years on the river. He runs New Orleans to Cincinnati during the summer with Venezuela crude for the asphalt refinery. In winter they carry lighter stuff, fuel oil and gasoline, to Pittsburgh, St. Louis, and up the Illinois Waterway to Chicago; once in a while all the way up the "Upper" to St. Paul.

The pilothouse is an airy, cheerful, glass-lined room, a place of relaxed efficiency away from the din of the diesels. There is no big steering wheel but a pair of steering levers, like exaggerated handlebars on a motorcycle, and two small brass engine levers. Everything is in reach of the high, padded, swivel armchair—whistle pull overhead; two upright levers to control the searchlights; a radio phone on its cradle; an intercom voice box that speaks to the galley, engine room, lower deck, and to the head of the tow; and generally a cup of coffee on a built-in slipproof tray beside a sliding ash drawer. On the "high bench" are two big pairs of binoculars, a fathometer called "Mark Twain," an RPM indicator, and a swing meter that reports sideways movement of the lead barges. Beside the high chair stands the radar screen on its box pedestal.

"That fathometer," says the captain, "it's a real good gadget. Reads you the river bottom at the head of the tow. We don't use any lead line now, we go too fast—be over a bar before a man could heave a hand line.

"That radar—it's a wonderful thing. You can run in fog, though I like to tie up when it's really thick. You tie up and nobody hears about it, but have a collision and they know from here to Pittsburgh. When it's hazy and you can't be sure what you are seeing, here's a picture plain as day." He switched on the radar and the finger of light circled the outline of the river—it looked exactly like the black and white map on the open chart book. "See how those buoys show up. That thing will even pick up ducks. You can see them take off and see them fly." He looked around at the shotgun in a leather case standing in the corner. "We go hunting sometimes, if we're tied up for a few hours in good country. Get ducks, rabbits, once we got a deer. What I started to say is the engineer wants to shoot a duck by radar, one he only saw here on the screen."

Captain Menard had big square hands. He wore a silver ring showing two dice, 4 and 7—a natural. "I've always been lucky," he said, "I mean so far. Like last night." He opened a big logbook and pointed to a line: 4:20 A.M. *Boat rubbed bottom at shallow crossing Mile 498.6.* While I was reading it the page began to jiggle. The boat was rattling and shaking, a different sound and feeling from the normal vibration, and the captain pulled up his two engine levers. "Here's another shallow place, right here. We draw less at half speed. A boat pushes down in the water with a light tow, trying to get under the load. We draw a foot more with light barges than when they're full. It's a nine-foot channel here and we draw eight and a half. Next year when Markland Dam is finished there'll be deep water, never have to think about these crossings."

He handed me the binoculars. "Here's Markland now, just coming up. There's a tow leaving the lock." Through the glass I saw a long line of assorted barges. He reached up and the horn behind us roared two blasts. "That's Union Barge Line. They handle all kinds of stuff. Haul anything for anybody."

Markland Dam drew near—thirteen massive piers striding across the water, supporting twelve huge electric-powered gates. On the Kentucky side I saw the long entrance pier and the long clean canyon of the lock. Two gantry cranes tilted above sand barges, and concrete mixers were at work beside the big steel cofferdams. In midstream a large signboard jutted above the current.

STOP! AND LIVE! STOP!
Falls ahead—All boats must lock.

Half of the river was open, where the crest gates had not been installed; the warning was mostly for uninformed operators of pleasure boats. A couple of outboards were circling the sign. One of them towed a water skier.

A mile off the lock, the captain blew his horn. "One for a single tow," he explained. "Two for a double that has to be broken up. That's in the old 600-foot locks. But Markland's 1200-footer will take the biggest tow on the river, all at once." He picked up the radio phone and gave his boat's name and call number—W D 2155.

"Come right on in." The lockmaster's voice, drawling and nasal, was pure Hoosier. "We're all ready, Captain."

"Okay and thank you." The phone clicked down.

"Last year," said Captain Charlie, "when this lock was opened we were the second boat through—the first one downbound. It was in the papers. I've got a clipping at home."

Approaching with a tow the size of the *Mauretania*, it looks impossible to get all that deck space between the lock walls. But the walls widen out as you creep up. The captain turned on the voice box and talked to the mate at the head of the tow. "How near now?"

"Nine hundred . . . eight fifty . . . eight hundred."

The deck hands were out there in their orange life jackets handling rope fenders and mooring lines. The tow eased in under the sheer walls.

"All stop," from the pilothouse.

"All stop," from the mate.

Lines were snubbed to cleats in the lock wall. The big gates closed and we dropped eight feet in six minutes. Ahead the gates swung open. Two piping whistles from somewhere on the lock were answered by a blaring of the diesel horn. "All lines gone," said the voice box. "All gone," the captain repeated. He pulled up the engine levers. The diesels throbbed and the tow moved into the river.

"When this high-lift dam is finished," the captain said, "it will replace five of the old ones. Give us a pool nearly a hundred miles, all the way up to New Richmond. It'll save lots of time."

Time stops at the river's edge but the clocks are ticking in the offices at Pittsburgh, St. Louis and New Orleans. Company records show how many hundred thousand dollars are tied up in a towboat and its barges and how many hundred dollars are lost with every hour's delay. Rivermen balance that with another reality. "Sometimes you just have to wait. There's a tow in the lock and another one ahead of you at the guide wall. You slow down for a fog and sometimes you run aground. Like when we came up here last time. There was a red buoy off station at Paducah. We couldn't find that buoy and our two lead barges went aground. We had to tie the rest to a deep bank and it took six hours to work those barges off the bar. Things like that can happen anytime."

The captain pointed to the Indiana shore. "Must be good fishing here. We always see somebody on that bank."

At the river's edge were a dozen scattered fishermen, mostly Negroes, perched on the shelving rock. One had a folding canvas chair and a dog lying in his shade.

"That's the life," said the engineer who had come up the steep inside stairway. "They got more sense than these two." He looked down at a skiff we were overtaking, a long skiff loaded with baggage and pulled by two sunburned oarsmen wearing swimming trunks. There was an oil stove fitted into the bow. The travelers waved and one of them called, "See you in N' Orleans." I watched them drop behind us, bobbing in our wake. Another Huck and Jim bound down the river. Time didn't matter to them.

Breakfast on a towboat is at 5:30, dinner at 11:30, supper at 5:30— these are the changes of the watch. For dinner we had shrimp gumbo, rice, potatoes, beans, mustard greens, rolls, ice tea, pineapple cake and coffee—a small pot of Maxwell House and a big one of chicory. Meals are served buffet style with everyone taking his own plate and leaving it at the sink. Many towboats have a woman in the galley and a stewardess who cleans the rooms. We had an ex-army cook, completely toothless, the only thin man on the boat. Our crew totaled eleven. The largest towboats carry sixteen.

Dinner was a silent meal, everyone too busy to talk. But when we were on the pineapple cake the cook looked out the side door and said, "*Delta Queen* coming." There was a lively interest in the big white boat, the last passenger vessel on the rivers. I had been on the *Delta Queen* a few weeks earlier, with people who focused cameras on passing towboats and speculated on what they carried to what destination. Now an oiler beside me ran to his bunkroom and returned with a camera. We were outside when the four-decked *Delta Queen* churned by, her long landing stage jutting out like a bowsprit and her red paddle wheel lifting white water. "She's got a calliope," someone said. "Plays music every time they leave a landing."

We waved and people waved from the railings and a pilot waved, both arms upraised, from the wheelhouse door.

"I got three pictures," the oiler said.

When I spoke of being on the *Queen's* last trip to Pittsburgh the engineer wanted to know how much it cost, how many people aboard, what towns did we stop at. At his sink the cook stared out the stern window at the big white hull and foaming paddle wheel. The towboats have taken over the river but the vanished steamboats haunt it.

There are two kinds of landmarks on the Ohio—natural features like Candlestick Rock, Cypress Bluff and Cave in Rock, and now the industrial plants that dominate long river reaches. The natural landmarks disappear at night, but the others are most impressive then—the glow and glare in the sky and jets of flame above the mile-long mills, the colored constellations of an oil refinery, the fiery eruption of a Bessemer, the warning lights on smokestacks up among the stars.

Above the hills of Indiana rise the three stacks of the Clifty Creek Power Station, providing power for the Portsmouth Atomic Energy Project. Acres of coal barges blacken the Clifty Creek landing; economical transport of Ohio valley coal is the reason for the region's vast increase in production of electric power since 1950. The three stacks, as high as a sixty-story building, stay in sight long after Madison is past; they stand up above the hills while we round the bend at Rabbit Hash and the thickets of Plow Handle Point.

On a river the past accumulates and for the riverman every bend and reach holds memories. In the great flood of 1937 the towboat *Thomas Moses* tied up in a cornfield five miles from the river channel in thirteen feet of water. She had on board 87 refugees picked up from rafts and scows, 150 mules, 350 hogs, 14 cows, 1 dog, 4 chickens, 1 guinea, 1 pigeon, 2 quail, 1 pheasant, 1 coon, 1 possum. On that Noah's Ark the marooned people, livestock and wildlife lived together until the waters went down.

At Big Bone Island two hundred years ago explorers found mammoth skeletons, ribs as big as a roof pole and spinal vertebrae the size of a water bucket. When I wondered if there were still some big bones on that dense island the captain said, "Seems like I heard something about bone hunters. First trip I made on this river I came with an old pilot who knew everything about every place from Cairo to Pittsburgh. He told me so much I couldn't remember any of it, or hardly any. But there's a hill along here where an old riverman, Captain McCarey, wanted to be buried, standing up, facing the river. So they put him in the ground that way—I'll see enough of it before then."

His first trip was Captain Menard's only apprenticeship on the Ohio and that demonstration run was not reassuring. They came up in early spring against high water, and trying to keep out of the full current they went aground.

"It was right near here," said the captain, "above where that little Knob Crick comes in. Trouble was the old man couldn't see too good and it was getting dark anyway. I'd gone down for some coffee. When I came up, the old man was yanking at the steering levers and I looked out and there was a barn dead ahead of us. He was cutting through a cornfield on that high water. We were going into it—he was headed for the barn door—but we didn't get there. We stuck in the mud. We just had two barges. We got the back one off but the other one was really hung up. We stayed there six days working on that barge. Of course the water went down and the barge stayed in that field, full of fuel oil. We finally left it and went on to Pittsburgh. They got it off on another rising river, with bulldozers and cables."

With that trip fresh in his mind Captain Menard came back, pushing his own tow, a small one, six weeks later. "It was kind of touchy sometimes, but we have these good charts." He turned the page and a new four-mile stretch of river lay before him, the dotted sailing line leading from one dayboard or beacon light to another. "Here's a light list, pretty well beat up. That's what we run by. Pick up one light, or dayboard, and then the next. You always know just where you are, until the fog loses you."

Crews of diesel towing vessels may be licensed, but they are not required to. Diesel-powered towing vessels are not subject to Coast Guard inspection, except when they carry commercial passengers or transport freight in bulk on board the towboat itself. Captain Charlie was planning to stand examination for a pilot's license, but he hadn't done it yet.

Every noon on the radio phone, on channel six from Pittsburgh, comes a river broadcast—stage of water at various points on the Ohio, which dams are up and which are down (the old "wicket" dams fold back on the river bed in high water), weather forecast, and orders for specific towboats. For instance, we got word to stop at Memphis to pick up an oiler who was to rejoin the boat after his two weeks "days" ashore. The pilots use the radio phone when tows are approaching.

"Good morning, Captain. You want two whistles this time?"

"As you like, Captain."

"Okay, I'll blow two."

So we are to pass on the left, starboard to starboard.

With that business settled the talk goes on, easy, leisurely, and courteous in an old-fashioned way.

"Where you going this trip, Captain?"

"Parkersburg, Kyger Creek."

"You seen Al lately?"

"Yeah, saw him a couple weeks ago."

"How's he doing now?"

"He's better. Working regular now."

"That's good. . . . Somebody coming up behind you?"

"Yes. I don't know what that gentleman is. Looks like a six-acre field coming."

"Well, thanks a thousand, Skipper."

"I wish you a good trip down."

In midafternoon the cook came up, stretched out on the leather settee and smoked a cigarette. Then he left a grocery order and went below.

The captain called Pittsburgh; Pittsburgh called Jeffersonville River Service, across from Louisville, asking them to call the *Live Oak*. (For some reason we can't call Jeffersonville directly—some one-way channel.) In just a minute a voice came from Jeffersonville and the captain read off his order.

"—200 tea bags . . . 12 cans of mustard greens . . . 10 gallons log cabin syrup. We'll be there in about an hour."

"All right, Cap'n. We'll have it ready for you."

Half an hour later the cook came up again. He had forgotten matches and watermelons.

"Why don't you write it out, Sandy? You always forget."

Twenty minutes later a deckhand came up. "The cook wants to add a couple things to his order."

2 7 3

The captain called the galley on the intercom. "Sandy, you sure you got it all now? We're about there."

For the third time we called Pittsburgh, Pittsburgh called Jeff'ville and Jeff'ville called us.

"Here we are again," said the captain. "We forgot five pounds assorted cold cuts."

"Okay, five pounds lunch meat." It was a woman this time, a twangy Hoosier voice. "Anything else?"

"I b'lieve that's all."

"All right. Sure thing. They're loading it now."

Ahead of us beyond the shipyards where new steel barges were taking shape on the shore, a battered little launch came out. It pulled alongside and delivered the groceries. On the Kentucky side was Louisville, and soon we were easing into the canal that leads to the new McAlpine Lock.

After supper in the sunset the pilothouse is a relaxed place like the front porch at home. The engineer comes up with a toothpick in the corner of his mouth. A deckhand in a white shirt with the sleeves torn out at the shoulder sprawls in a metal armchair and opens a worn paperback, *The Jungle Girl*. An oiler in a plaid sport shirt that emphasizes the whiteness of his arms picks up a week-old copy of the *Times-Picayune*. "Here's a picture of this big rocket at Huntsville, Alabama. They're going to barge it down the river."

He studied the picture—the superbooster with its bright blue nose cone all wrapped in white plastic, 82 feet high, it said, 75 tons, too big for any transport except the rivers.

"I'd like to see that," said the oiler.

In the sunset two deckhands walked over the barge decks to the head of the tow. They sat there smoking, way out in the evening stillness. Dusk darkened the hills but the river held the light. In the pilothouse the engineer was talking about his free time. Towboatmen work thirty days and have fifteen days' relief; the engineer was getting off at Memphis. He said he was going fishing but the pilot thought his wife would have the lawnmower waiting for him and the kitchen ready to paint.

In the amber light we passed the *Badger Boy* with a string of oil barges and the *Reliance* with a mixed tow. The pilot went to the door and waved at the *Reliance*, his two arms crossing like a semaphore.

"Last winter they helped us through the ice on the Illinois," he said. "We were taking a load to the Globe Oil Dock at California Avenue in Chicago."

"California Avenue," said the deckhand, looking up from *The Jungle Girl*, "two feet of snow on the barges and all the wires caked with ice."

"Ice in the canal too," said the captain. "We couldn't get through alone. That *Reliance* is a big boat, fifty-four feet wide. Just like riding in a hotel. You don't hear anything."

At dark the off-watch men drifted down to get some sleep before midnight. The cook brought up a pot of coffee. The sky was black now with stars overhead and the blacker line of hills dimly framing the black river. Far ahead a small light kept winking. Then red and green lights showed at the dark bend and the pilot picked up his phone.

"Which way do you want to pass, Captain?"

"Oh, either way, Skipper."

"I'll give you two."

"Okay, I'll blow two at your request."

"Thank you very much."

"Okay, very well. Good evening, Captain."

The pilot touched a small upright lever and the long beam of the searchlight reached out. It hovered on the distant shore, picked out the white crossboard in the trees, then swung over the leading corner of the approaching tow and rested on the white flag on our own lead barge. That flag, a piece of cloth on a willow pole, looks a long way off at night, far ahead in the glimmering black river. The pilot reached up and two whistle blasts echoed from the dark hills. The answer came and soon two long black islands were sweeping past each other. The swish and throb soon faded and the river was empty.

I asked how far the radio phone could be picked up.

"Well, last trip a ham operator over in Rhode Island picked us up, and we were off Greenville, Mississippi. He cut in and asked me to send him a card. It was his hobby. I sent it to him—Pawtucket, Rhode Island. He had cards from all over."

Evansville was a swarm of lights on a curving hill—every river city is beautiful at night—and then the river was all ours. I thought if a traveler looked out once an hour he might go all the way down the river and never see a sign of life.

At daybreak fog lay in the hollows of the hills. We were creeping forward, toward Lock No. 50, they said, where a double tow was coming through. The fog burned off and we waited in the silver silent morning with sunlight slanting across the Illinois bluffs and a clear reach of river ahead.

After we locked through, one of the deckhands, a young Kentuckian called Red, with dungarees, no shirt, and a blond stubble of beard, kept coming up to the pilothouse, and each time the captain blew some short quick blasts.

"We're going past his place," said the captain. "He's the only man here not from Louisiana."

The next time Red appeared he was freshly shaven, though still in his tattered dungarees. The captain handed him the glasses.

"There they are," Red said. "All of them," and he stepped out onto the wing.

They must have got word but I couldn't see how. "They heard us leaving the lock," Captain Charlie explained. "They know our whistle."

Rhodes Landing, Kentucky, the chart said. It was a cluster of houses in a cove with a weedy rock pile supporting the navigation marker. Under the crossboard stood an old woman, a younger woman and four barefoot children. The captain blew a long blast and they all waved. Red waved. "That's Jimmy," he said, "the little one she's holding." He waved both arms and then looked through the glasses. He was still looking when Rhodes Landing dropped behind the river bend. Then he went back to his paint bucket on the barge deck.

"He'll have his time off at the end of the month," the captain said. "After two weeks ashore he'll be glad to get back on the river." I remembered what Dick Streckfuss, an Illinois reporter, had written during a trip with a grain tow. Rivermen, he said, regard the world ashore as a good place to visit but they wouldn't want to live there.

We rounded a long graceful bend, Kentucky's steep hills looking across at Indiana cornfields. At Mile 711.3 we passed Cloverport, Kentucky, home of J. M. White for whom the finest of all Mississippi steamboats was named. It was a pleasant-looking town with cars glinting on the levee and people walking past storefronts and a boy pushing a lawn mower across a slope of green.

"The old steamboats used to stop at all these places," said the captain. "Pick up a passenger or a calf or a crate of chickens. We just go by." The green hills closed behind us.

The Ohio is brown at high water but the Tennessee, flowing through a rock channel, is clear. Past Paducah the two rivers flow side by side, reluctant to become one. But gradually the brown Ohio swallows the tributary water. It is a big river then, and the shores flatten out as it approaches the Mississippi.

It was after supper when we rounded the bend and passed under the Illinois Central railroad bridge. On the Illinois shore, beyond a brushy levee and a concrete floodwall, were the roofs of Cairo. A little more than a hundred years ago Herman Melville wrote in *The Confidence Man:* "At Cairo the old firm of Fever & Ague is still settling up its unfinished business. . . . In the dank twilight fanned with mosquitoes and sparkling with fireflies, the boat now lies before Cairo—that swampy and squalid domain." But when the levees were enlarged after the Civil War the "prospective city of Cairo" was pictured with domes, towers and monuments, a symmetrical city overlooking the two rivers. Though this elegant city never materialized, Cairo developed into an easygoing town of 11,000 with an atmosphere more like Arkansas than Illinois.

The junction of the rivers is now nearly a mile farther south than it was a century ago, and an island is building under Bird's Point on the Missouri shore. For ten miles the two rivers flow separately, the muddy Mississippi washing the western bank while the Ohio keeps to Kentucky. Darkness overtook us before the two streams mingled.

Ahead the searchlight probed and questioned. It found a red buoy on the left side and then the black one on the right. "The thing is," said the captain, "to keep the tow between them." Toward midnight, fog muffled the searchlight, but in the radar screen the channel buoys showed plainly. The radar picked out a towboat with a string of barges moored along the riverbank. "He's caught a tree," said the captain. Then as if answering a question, "You can't tie up for every patch of fog." He slowed his engines to half speed and kept his eyes on the finger of light circling the radar screen.

The bright blue morning showed a wide river winding between featureless green shores. The land looked wild and empty, and the only life was the engineers' dredging boats and the long tows creeping up the stream. There are few landmarks on the lower Mississippi, where the scenes of history have been carried off by floodwaters in seasons long past. Now the site of Fort Pillow is sunk from sight. Island No. 10 is all but gone, only in low water is there anything to mark the battleground of the rebellion. The Mississippi winds through its dense bottomlands. The towns are back from the river, beyond the curving levees which extend all the way to the Gulf.

In the pilothouse I read the *Waterways Journal*, the weekly trade paper that for seventy-five years has provided rivermen with commercial news, personal exchange and the latest navigation reports. An editorial on tolls pointed out that low-cost water transport has created vast new industries and tax revenues and has lowered the cost of hundreds of products. The controversy on tolls or a users' tax grows with the increase of river commerce. The railroads, forgetting that rails were laid across the continent by subsidies of millions of acres of the public domain, insist that river shipping should pay for river improvements. The waterways operators show that cheap transportation creates new business—seventeen billions of dollars of new industrial plants have come to the Ohio valley since 1950—even for the railroads. Use of the waterways has brought industry to hundreds of river communities and has lowered the cost of electric power, steel, petroleum, aluminum, chemical and agricultural products. Millions of tons of grain go south by barge—the rate from central Illinois to New Orleans is 9½ cents a bushel—and Corn Belt farmers have a stake in every dredge and lighthouse tender on the lower river. Tolls would curb the river traffic and the national economy.

When I asked Captain Menard's opinion he said, "They'll just have to work that out in Washington. I've got a job right here." Then he added, "Mostly what I read in the *Journal* is the columns from up and down the river." Since 1887 the weekly has had local correspondents sending items on boats and men, on improvement of channels and movement of cargoes, from a dozen river districts. The original paper, which began as *The River*, had columns from Paducah, Huntington, Memphis and other places, along with a facetious column of "Snagtown News." Snagtown was dropped but the local correspondence has been maintained, as has the traditional format of the magazine. Now published by a veteran and widely esteemed riverman, Captain Donald T. Wright, at St. Louis, its masthead shows a big tow of barges and a white packet boat passing under the Eads Bridge. Cherishing the old and championing the new, the *Journal* makes the whole huge river system a community. For three-quarters of a century it has kept rivermen informed of their business and of each other, like a weekly round robin letter.

By dredging, dikes and wing dams the river has been kept in its channel under the bluff at Memphis. While we swung in where the Wolf River joins the Mississippi the captain talked to Charlie Smith's "Waterways Marine," ordering fuel oil and provisions and arranging to pick up some crew members after their days ashore; on a converted barge at the foot of Beale Street Charlie Smith keeps a "boatel," with bedrooms and lounges for men awaiting their boats. Our men came out on the launch *Charlie Smith*, along with the groceries, the U. S. Engineers' latest river reports, and some complimentary copies of the *Commercial Appeal*.

Overlooking the river at Memphis is De Soto Park, with Confederate cannon ringing an Indian mound, and Memphis claims this as the place where white men first saw the Mississippi. Actually De Soto came upon the river thirty miles below, where the De Soto Front Light now winks among the willows. It is a narrow channel now, with Cat Island Towhead growing in midstream. While I focused the binoculars, thinking of De Soto, the captain said, "Look sharp you might see some white-tailed deer. We counted thirty-five of them one evening at the foot of the cutoff just below here."

The lights of the Greenville Bridge were all we saw of Greenville. Long a river town Greenville was left on an oxbow when the engineers made the Leland Cut-off in 1933—a change which threw a portion of Arkansas east of the Mississippi. To give the town a river entrance, a channel was cut from below Greenville into the oxbow lake. Now Greenville harbor is not on the Mississippi but on a quiet backwater.

Next morning after breakfast we passed a traveler in a sailboat who waved to us and called something that was drowned by our diesel engines. A few days later I read about him in the *Times-Picayune*— he was an academic man from Bowdoin College, Maine, travelling by wind and current from St. Louis to New Orleans.

In past times the Mississippi has made its own great loops and bends and has discarded them by cutoffs. In the 1930's the Army Engineers hastened this process, making sixteen cutoffs which shortened the river by 151 miles. But in some places, like New Madrid Bend where the channel loops twenty-one miles around a bend that is less than a mile across, they revetted the bank to keep the river from breaking through. For both navigation and flood control twenty-one winding miles are better than a headlong current. As it is, the surge of high water compels towboats to double- and triple-trip through certain cutoffs on the undammed, unlocked Mississippi.

Vicksburg lost the river in 1876 when floods cut through an oxbow. But the Yazoo River was nearby and by a diversion canal the Yazoo current was led into the abandoned bed of the Mississippi. As we swung around the big bend and looked up the Yazoo, the captain handed me the glasses to pick out the *Sprague* moored to the Vicksburg Landing. The big vessel was freshly painted on the shoreward side; the rest of her was peeling and rusty. "I hear she's a showboat now," the captain said, in a tone of vague reproach. He preferred to remember the "Big Mama" in her working years, when she pushed fifty barges up the river and her captain kept a pen of chickens on the roof, feeding them on millions of willow bugs killed by the steamer's arc lights.

In the hills above Vicksburg beyond the spacious military park is the Waterways Experiment Station of the Corps of Engineers. It is out of sight of the river but every mile of the lower Mississippi is duplicated in miniature in its 1055-foot scale model of the river channel and its floodland. Since 1827 the Corps of Engineers has been charged with development and improvement of the river system. A Mississippi levee that dwarfed the Great Wall of China was completed in the 1880's; then much of the flood plain was farmed and occupied, though large areas of wooded swamp remained. The river was walled in and the Army Engineers were its keepers. But repeated floods, culminating in the disaster of 1927, showed that the river could not be permanently enclosed. Retention and diversion of floodwater was necessary, along with construction of spoil banks and standard and secondary levees. After the destructive flood of 1927 the Waterways Experiment Station was established to test devices for flood control and the improvement of navigation. From its studies grew massive river projects which put engineering crews to work at hundreds of places. Using giant suction dredges and huge construction barges they built dikes, wing dams, revetments, stone levees and retaining walls so that the Mississippi of today is a more permanent river than ever in its age-long past.

The usefulness of the scale model of the lower Mississippi led to the construction at Clinton, Mississippi, thirty miles east of Vicksburg, of the Mississippi Basin Model. This model covers two hundred acres and reproduces the river basin from New Orleans to Pittsburgh, Minneapolis and Sioux City. In the miniature riverbed, little stones are islands and towheads and bits of window screen are forests. All levees, railroads and highways are there, with removable sections to simulate breaches and washouts. Water is pumped through to reproduce any river stage and current, one gallon a minute in the model equaling one and a half million gallons in the Mississippi. Past and future floods can be simulated to test control works already constructed and in prospect. During the Missouri River flood of 1952 the model was operated day and night to direct the work of floodfighters a thousand miles away.

It is a long way between bridges on the lower river. After miles of wilderness known only to the survey crews of the engineers and hunters like the men in Faulkner's stories, we saw the long span crossing from Natchez to Vidalia. The river comes straight down through Giles Cutoff past the new Natchez Landing under the hill. A hundred years ago there was a lower town, Natchez-Under-the-Hill, the most notorious place on the Mississippi. It is gone without a trace, carried off by the river that created it. Now there is a sawmill in a yellow lumberyard and up on the hill the drowsy streets of Natchez. Once it was a cotton capital, the streets walled with cotton and wagons creaking down to packet boats at the landing. Now some old mansions haunt the place and their live oaks make a deep shade in the summer sun. None of it shows from the river. There is only the big sawmill under the streets that were once walled with cotton bales, and you remember Faulkner's somber summary: "—the timber which had to be logged and sold in order to deforest the land in order to convert the soil to raising cotton in order to sell the cotton in order to make the land valuable enough to be worth spending money raising dikes to keep the River off of it." Or try to—since the river didn't care about cotton or anything else of man's devising.

Here, as Faulkner said, the Mississippi wilderness makes its last ineluctable stand. The huge river snakes through a vast green solitude. There are horseshoe lakes, crescent bayous, legends of phantom steamers searching for a way out of the backwater jungle ever since a stormy night when the river took a cutoff. It is a land of shadows, hung with silence. In the swamps water hyacinths make green polished floors, blue flag edges the marshes, pond lilies float and spider lilies reach for the motey yellow sunlight; over the levees the Cherokee rose trails its glossy leaves and its luminous white blossoms.

In the delta bottoms the engineers have huge floating dredges and a riverbank grading fleet of a hundred pieces. By 1963 they had revetted nearly five hundred miles of bank and bottom. Their objective is a fixed river channel, with a minimum twelve feet of water, from Cairo to Baton Rouge by 1970. Back from the river, sometimes miles back in the green shadows, are the earthwork levees, thirty to fifty feet high, extending more than three thousand miles along the Mississippi and its tributaries. Great floodways can drain off high water and carry it directly to the Gulf. Reservoirs on the tributaries hold back flood-water and stabilize the river. In 1934 there were no reservoirs, by 1970 there will be 150; when full they will hold enough water to fill a channel fifty feet deep and a mile wide from New York to San Francisco.

Through the delta bottomlands flows the river which William Alexander Percy called "the shifting and unappeasable god of the country, feared and loved, the Mississippi." It is less fearful now. After three hundred years of history on the Mississippi, there is a prospect of a fixed river with permanent levees in position and a deep dependable navigation channel.

We passed Baton Rouge at night—ocean liners at the docks, miles of colored lights flashing over the tanks, towers and pipelines of the oil refineries, and the floodlit capitol tower against the sky. Here the wilderness river has ended and an industrial river begins. Sherwood Anderson once sat all night at a boat landing in Baton Rouge. There was one steamer there with a line of stevedores unloading grain. They swayed over the gangplank chanting, "De las' sack. Soon de las' sack." Above that song Anderson heard voices of keelboatmen, longhorn men, pilots on steamers, echoes from the dead river that was once alive. . . . Now it is alive again. At Baton Rouge the big tankers pump out Venezuela oil and freighters unload cargo under the cluster lights.

Daylight showed a broad deep river hemmed in levees and lined with sugar mills, aluminum plants, chemical factories, oil refineries. Under a big grain elevator stood freighters from Norway, Holland and Japan. New Orleans was in view, its skyline lifting over the ship-lined riverfront, when we swung into the barge terminal.

Out in midstream passed a Coast Guard cutter with the ensign rippling from its forestaff. Behind it came a towboat pushing a Navy barge carrying a space rocket 82 feet long and 22 feet high—a load too massive to be moved by land or air. From a pilothouse erected on the barge, directions were relayed to the towboat *Bob Fuqua* where the steersman's view was blocked by the huge cylinder of the rocket. Built in Huntsville, Alabama, it had come by the Tennessee, Ohio and Mississippi rivers—the first Saturn booster on its way to Cape Canaveral. Someday a shortcut will join the Tennessee to the Tombigbee River and Mobile Bay; already in the empty pine woods of northwestern Mississippi where the highway crosses a slumberous valley signs designate the brushy creek as "Future Tombigbee-Tennessee Waterway." But this rocket had come the long way round—north, west, south and east— by the winding rivers. It moved downstream at ten miles an hour, containing its 32-million pent-up horsepower that with awesome speed would loft a missile toward the moon.

From the pilothouse of the *Live Oak* we watched the rocket pass—a new cargo in an old trade that began with the freighting of buffalo hides and bear's grease.

In 1837 Samuel Cummings, compiling his handbook of the Mississippi, observed that the commerce of New Orleans, already very great, must necessarily greatly increase. "It is easily accessible at all times to ships from the sea," he wrote, "and it has probably twice as much boat navigation above it as any other city on the globe." There is no need to modify his language now.

Acknowledgments

IT IS NEARLY THREE HUNDRED YEARS since white men first traveled the Mississippi and began a record that is still unfolding. Now the literature of the Mississippi is as extensive and various as the great river system. There are collections of river lore at a number of places—the River Museum in the Campus Martius Museum at Marietta, Ohio; the River Room in the Jefferson Memorial at St. Louis; the Howard Steamboat Museum at Jeffersonville, Indiana; the Old Court House Museum at Vicksburg; and elsewhere. The American people have kept alive the river memories. In the historical societies of the great valley and in the libraries of the river cities there are steadily growing collections of river history. I am indebted to the staffs of many of these institutions.

Especially I should like to acknowledge the generous help of Mrs. Dorothy E. Powers, Curator of the Inland Rivers Library of the Public Library of Cincinnati and Hamilton County, and of Mr. Yeatman Anderson of the Rare Book Department of that Library. For guidance to certain river sources I am indebted to that wise and warm friend of all river writers, Captain Donald T. Wright, publisher of the *Waterways Journal* in St. Louis. To Captain Fred Way, Jr., of Sewickley, Pennsylvania, I am indebted for many points of information as well as for the illumination provided by his comprehensive collection of river photographs.

In narrating a towboat trip in the final chapter of the book I have used fictitious names for the vessel and its personnel. But for many kindnesses and a steady stream of information I am grateful to Mr. W. C. McNeal, Assistant Marine Superintendent of the Oil Transport Company of New Orleans, Captain Andrew Matherne of Lafitte, Louisiana, and Mr. J. N. Jones of the American Bitumals and Asphalt Company in Cincinnati.

For other assistance I am grateful to Mr. John Lochhead of the Mariners

Museum in Newport News; Miss Ruth Ferris, Curator of the River Room in the Jefferson Memorial at St. Louis; Mrs. Francis H. Stadler, Manuscripts Librarian of the Missouri Historical Society; Mrs. Catherine Rumley of the Campus Martius Museum in Marietta, Ohio; Mrs. Elizabeth R. Martin, Librarian of the Ohio Historical Society; Mr. H. N. Biery of the Ohio Valley Improvement Association; Mr. Walter L. Myers, Jr., of the Upper Ohio Development Council; Rear Admiral Kent F. Loomis, Assistant Director of Naval History in the Department of the Navy; Mr. Daniel M. Doherty of the American Petroleum Institute; Miss Audrey L. Forbes of *U. S. News & World Report*; Mr. Harold Merklen, Research Librarian of the New York Public Library; Mr. Hirst Milhollen, Curator of Prints of the Library of Congress; Mr. S. H. Riesenberg of the Smithsonian Institution; Mr. Charles Edmundson of the Memphis *Commercial Appeal*; Mr. J. Campbell Foster of the American Commercial Barge Line Company of Jeffersonville, Indiana; Mr. Homer L. Hendrickson of American Waterways Operators, Washington, D.C.; Mr. George Stuart of *The Valley Daily News*, Tarentum, Pennsylvania; Commander C. W. Bailey, Captain R. J. Fugina and Lieutenant John R. O'Connor of the United States Coast Guard; Colonel Edwin M. Kelton, U. S. Army, retired; Mrs. E. M. Branch of Oxford, Ohio; Mr. L. S. Dutton of the Miami University Library; and Mr. R. L. DeWilton of The Macmillan Company.

To my wife, Marion Boyd Havighurst, who climbed aboard steamboats and towboats with me and shared the pursuit in libraries and museums, goes my affectionate gratitude.

WALTER HAVIGHURST
Oxford, Ohio
February, 1963

Bibliography

THE MOST COMPLETE RECORD of inland river steamboats appears in *Merchant Steam Vessels of the United States 1807–1868* by William M. Lytle, edited and revised by Forest R. Holdcamper (Mystic, Conn., 1952) and the annual listing of *Merchant Vessels of the United States* by the Bureau of Navigation of the U. S. Department of Commerce. Several thousand river steamboats are recorded, with identifying notes, sometimes extended, in the two directories compiled by Frederick Way, Jr.—*Way's Directory of Western Rivers Packets* (Sewickley, Pa., 1950) and *Way's Directory of Western Rivers Steam Towboats* (Sewickley, Pa., 1954). The two-volume *History of St. Louis City and County* by J. Thomas Scharf (St. Louis, 1883) contains detailed information about Western river steamboats and steamboatmen, along with statistics of the river trade until the 1880's. A wide variety of information appears in the random *Fifty Years on the Mississippi* by Emerson W. Gould (St. Louis, 1889). *Steamboats on the Western Rivers* by Louis C. Hunter (Cambridge, 1949) is the definitive account, economic and technological, of Western river commerce in the nineteenth century. Other works are listed with reference to separate chapters.

CHAPTER 1. PROLOGUE: BLOW FOR A LANDMARK

A Walk Through Bellefontaine Cemetery. St. Louis, 1944.

Branch, Edgar Marquess. *The Literary Apprenticeship of Mark Twain*. Urbana: University of Illinois Press, 1950.

Chittenden, Hiram Martin. *The American Fur Trade of the Far West*. 2 vols. Stanford: Academic Reprints, 1954.

Kirschten, Ernest. *Catfish and Crystal*. New York: Doubleday & Company, Inc., 1960.

Phillips, Paul Chrisler. *The Fur Trade*. 2 vols. Norman: University of Oklahoma Press, 1961.
Sandoz, Mari. *Love Song to the Plains*. New York: Harper & Brothers, 1961.

CHAPTER 2. GREAT RIVER

Ashe, Thomas. *Travels in America, Performed in the Year 1806, for the Purpose of Exploring the Rivers Alleghany, Monongahela, Ohio and Mississippi* . . . New York: R. Phillips, 1808.
Heilbron, Bertha L. "Making a Motion Picture in 1848. Henry Lewis on the Upper Mississippi," *Minnesota History*, XVII, No. 2.
———— (ed.). "Henry Lewis' Journal of a Canoe Voyage from the Falls of St. Anthony to St. Louis," *Minnesota History*, XVII, Nos. 2, 3, 4.
Kellogg, Louise Phelps (ed.). *Early Narratives of the Northwest, 1634–1699*. New York: Charles Scribner's Sons, 1917.
————. *The French Régime in Wisconsin and the Northwest*. Madison: State Historical Society of Wisconsin, 1925.
Latrobe, Charles Joseph. *The Rambler in North America*. New York: Harper & Brothers, 1835.
McDermott, J. F. *The Lost Panoramas of the Mississippi*. Chicago: University of Chicago Press, 1958.
Parkman, Francis. *La Salle and the Discovery of the Great West*. Boston: Little, Brown and Co., 1899.
Some Circumstances in Consequence of the French Settling Colonies on the Mississippi. London, 1720.

CHAPTER 3. ALL THE WAY TO SHAWNEETOWN

Baldwin, Leland D. *The Keelboat Age on Western Waters*. Pittsburgh: University of Pittsburgh Press, 1941.
Birkbeck, Morris. *Letters from Illinois*. London: Sherwood, Neeley and Jones, 1818.
————. *Notes on a Journey in America*. London: Severn & Co., 1818.
Bishop, Nathaniel H. *Four Months in a Sneak Box*. Boston, 1879.
Blair, Walter, and Meine, Franklin J. *Mike Fink*. New York: Henry Holt & Company, Inc., 1933.
Cramer, Zadok. *The Navigator*. Pittsburgh: Cramer & Spear, 1811.
Hamilton, Jonathan Newman. *A Storeboat on the Ohio River*. Diary typescript in Inland Rivers Library, The Public Library of Cincinnati and Hamilton County.
Howe, Henry. *Historical Collections of Ohio*. 2 vols. Cincinnati, 1900.
Jones, Robert Leslie. "Floating Down the Ohio and the Mississippi," Correspondence and Diaries of the William Dudley Devol Family of Mari-

etta, Ohio. *Ohio State Archeological and Historical Quarterly*, Vol. 59, Nos. 3, 4.

Phillips, Josephine E. "Flatboating on the Great Thoroughfare," *Bulletin of the Historical and Philosophical Society of Ohio*, Vol. 5, No. 2.

Pope, John. *A Tour Through the Southern and Western Territories of the United States of America.* New York: C. L. Woodward, 1888.

CHAPTER 4. SIX MEN AND AN EARTHQUAKE

Bradbury, John. *Travels in the Interior of America in the Years 1809, 1810 and 1811.* In Thwaites, Rebuen Gold (ed.), *Early Western Travels.* Vol. 5. Cleveland, 1904.

Flint, Timothy. *Recollections of the Last Ten Years.* Boston: Cummings, Hilliard & Co., 1826.

Hildreth, S. P. *History of an Early Voyage Down the Ohio and Mississippi Rivers.* Reprinted in Perkins, James H. *Annals of the West.* Pittsburgh, 1856.

McBride, James. "Voyage Down the Mississippi River," *Bulletin of the Historical and Philosophical Society of Ohio*, Vol. 5, No. 1.

Niles Weekly Register. Vol. 1 (September, 1811—March, 1812); Vol. 2 (March–September, 1812).

"Personal Narrative of Col. John Shaw of Marquette County, Wisconsin," *Collections of the State Historical Society of Wisconsin,* 1855.

Ross, Captain Charles. *The Earthquake of 1811 at New Madrid and Along the Mississippi Valley.* Cincinnati, 1847.

CHAPTER 5. SMOKE ON THE RIVERS

Flint, Timothy. *A Condensed Geography and History of the Western States, or The Mississippi Valley.* 2 Vols. Cincinnati: E. H. Flint, 1828.

Hall, James. *Sketches of History, Life and Manners in the West.* 2 Vols. Philadelphia: H. Hall, 1835.

———. *Statistics of the West, At the Close of the Year 1836.* Cincinnati: J. A. James & Co., 1836.

———. *The West: Its Commerce and Navigation.* Cincinnati: H. W. Derby & Co., 1848.

Hart, Adolphus M. *History of the Valley of the Mississippi.* New York: Newman and Ivison, 1853.

Hulbert, Archer Butler. *Waterways of Westward Expansion. The Ohio River and its Tributaries.* Cleveland: The A. H. Clark Co., 1903.

James, Edwin. *Account of an Expedition from Pittsburgh to the Rocky Mountains, performed in the years of 1819, 1820 . . . under the command of Major S. H. Long.* In Thwaites *Early Western Travels,* Vols. 14, 15, 16, 17. Cleveland, 1905.

Latrobe, John H. B. *The First Steamboat Voyage on the Western Waters.* Baltimore, 1871.

CHAPTER 6. CAPTAIN SHREVE WAS THERE

Cumings, Samuel. *The Western Pilot.* Cincinnati: Morgan, Lodge & Fisher, 1825.
Dorsey, Florence. *Master of the Mississippi.* Boston: Houghton Mifflin Company, 1941.
Foreman, Grant. "River Navigation in the Early Southwest," *Mississippi Valley Historical Review,* XV, No. 1.
"Henry Miller Shreve," *Democratic Review* (Pittsburgh), February, March, 1848.
Hill, Forest G. *Roads, Rails and Waterways.* Norman: University of Oklahoma Press, 1957.
Read, Frederick Brent. *Up the Heights to Fame and Fortune.* Cincinnati: Moore, 1873.

CHAPTER 7. TRAVELERS' TALES

Brandon, Edgar Ewing. *A Pilgrimage of Liberty.* Athens, Ohio: Lawhead Press, 1944.
Dickens, Charles. *American Notes For General Circulation.* London: Chapman and Hall, 1842.
————. *The Life and Adventures of Martin Chuzzlewit.* Boston: Estes, 1885.
Journal of Rudolph Friederich Kurz. Smithsonian Institution. Bureau of American Ethnology. Bulletin 115. Washington, 1937.
Levasseur, A. *Lafayette in America.* New York, 1829.
Lyell, Sir Charles. *A Second Visit to the United States of Nort.   'ica.* 2 vols. New York: Harper & Brothers, 1850.
Nolan, J. Bennett. *Lafayette in America Day by Day.* Baltimore: Johns Hopkins Press, 1934.
Schoolfield, F. E. *Captain Alex F. Boss, Western Rivers Pilot from 1824–1850.* Typescript in Inland Rivers Library, The Public Library of Cincinnati and Hamilton County.

CHAPTER 8. RIVER SONG

Cist, Charles. *Cincinnati in 1841.* Cincinnati, 1841.
————. *Sketches and Statistics of Cincinnati in 1851.* Cincinnati, 1851.
Foster Hall Bulletin. No. 11 (February, 1935).
Jendrek, Rosalie Carroll. *The Contribution of the Steamboat to the Growth of Cincinnati, 1815–1860.* Unpublished Master's thesis, Miami University Library, Oxford, Ohio.

Melville, Herman. *The Confidence Man*. London: Constable and Company, 1923.

Taylor, Bayard. *A Visit to India, China and Japan*. New York: G. P. Putnam & Co., 1855.

Walters, Raymond. *Stephen Foster: Youth's Golden Gleam*. Princeton: Princeton University Press, 1936.

CHAPTER 9. VOYAGE TO EXILE

A History of Navigation on the Tennessee River System. House Document No. 254. Washington, 1937.

Banta, R. E. *The Ohio*. New York: Rinehart & Company, 1949.

Brown, John P. *Old Frontiers*. Kingsport, Tenn.: Southern Publishers, Inc., 1938.

Campbell, T. J. *The Upper Tennessee*. Chattanooga: Privately printed, 1932.

Davidson, Donald. *The Tennessee*. Vol. 1. New York: Rinehart & Co., Inc., 1946.

Foreman, Grant. *Indian Removal*. Norman: University of Oklahoma Press, 1932.

Harris, George W. *Sut Lovingood. Yarns Spun by a Nat'ral Born Durned Fool. Warped and Wove for Public Wear*. New York: Dick & Fitzgerald, 1867.

Parks, Edd Winfield. *Segments of Southern Thought*. Athens: University of Georgia Press, 1938.

Scott, Winfield. *Memoirs of Lieut. General Scott, LL.D., Written by Himself*. New York: Sheldon & Co., 1864.

CHAPTER 10. HORIZON NORTH

Beltrami, Giacomo Constantine. *A Pilgrimage in Europe and America*. London: Hunt & Clarke, 1828.

————. "Beltrami's Journal," *Minnesota Historical Collections*, Vol. II.

Fugina, Captain Frank J. *Lore and Lure of the Upper Mississippi River*. Winona, Minn.: Privately printed, 1945.

Hartsough, Mildred. *From Canoe to Steel Barge on the Upper Mississippi*. Minneapolis: University of Minnesota Press, 1934.

McMaster, S. W. *Sixty Years on the Upper Mississippi*. Rock Island, 1893.

Merrick, George Byron. *Old Times on the Upper Mississippi*. Cleveland: The A. H. Clark Company, 1909.

Ogg, Frederick Austin. *The Opening of the Mississippi*. New York. The Macmillan Company, 1904.

Petersen, William J. *Steamboating on the Upper Mississippi*. Iowa City: Iowa State Historical Society, 1937.

Schoolcraft, Henry Rowe. *Narrative of an Expedition through the Upper Mississippi to Itasca Lake.* New York: Harper & Brothers, 1834.

CHAPTER 11. THE WAY TO FUTURE CITY

Chambers, J. S. *The Conquest of Cholera.* New York: The Macmillan Company, 1938.
Cooley, Stoughton. "The Mississippi Roustabout," *New England Magazine,* XI, No. 1.
Olmstead, Frederick Law. *A Journey in the Seaboard Slave States.* New York, Dix & Edwards, 1856.
Smith, Sol. *Theatrical Journey-Work and Anecdotal Recollections.* Philadelphia: T. B. Peterson, 1854.
Stewart, Charles D. *Fellow-Creatures.* Boston: Little, Brown and Co., 1935.
Wyeth, John B. *Oregon, or A Short History of a Long Journey.* In Thwaites, *Early Western Travels,* Vol. 21.

CHAPTER 12. "COTTON PILE!"

Advertisements of Lower Mississippi River Steamboats 1812–1890. Compiled by Leonard V. Huber. West Barrington, R.I., 1959.
[Ingraham, Joseph H.] *The South-West. By a Yankee.* New York; Harper & Brothers, 1835.
King, Edward. *The Southern States of North America.* London: Blackie & Son, 1875.
Nichols, George Ward. "Down the Mississippi," *Harper's New Monthly Magazine,* XLI (November, 1870).
Olmsted, Frederick Law. *The Cotton Kingdom,* ed. Arthur Schlesinger, Jr. 2 vols. New York: Alfred A. Knopf, Inc., 1953.
Samuel, Ray; Huber, Leonard V.; Ogden, Warren C. *Tales of the Mississippi.* New York: Hastings House, Publishers, Inc., 1955.

CHAPTER 13. JIM BLUDSO'S GHOST

Arese, Count Francesco. "The Middle West in 1837," *Mississippi Valley Historical Review,* XX, No. 3.
Elliott, James W. *Transport to Disaster.* New York: Holt, Rinehart & Winston, Inc., 1962. *Harper's Weekly.* XII, No. 626.
Lloyd, James T. *Steamboat Directory and Disasters on the Western Waters.* Cincinnati, J. T. Lloyd & Co., 1856.
Mace, Ellis C. *River Steamboats and Steamboat Men.* Cynthiana, Ky.: Hobson Book Press, 1944.
Morrison, John H. *History of American Steam Navigation.* (Stephen Daye Book.) New York: Frederick Ungar Publishing Co., 1958.

CHAPTER 14. MARK TWAIN, PILOT

Brashear, Minnie M. *Mark Twain, Son of Missouri.* Chapel Hill: University of North Carolina Press, 1934.

Clemens, Samuel L. *The Adventures of Huckleberry Finn.* New York; Charles L. Webster and Company, 1885.

———. *Life on the Mississippi.* Boston: J. R. Osgood and Co., 1883.

Hutcherson, Dudley R. "Mark Twain as a Pilot," *American Literature,* XII (November, 1940).

Leisey, Ernest E. "Mark Twain and Isaiah Sellers," *American Literature,* XIII (January, 1942).

Long, E. Hudson. *Mark Twain Handbook.* New York: Hendricks House, Inc., 1957.

Paine, Albert Bigelow. *Mark Twain's Notebook.* New York: Harper & Brothers, 1935.

Webster, Samuel C. (ed.). *Mark Twain, Business Man.* Boston: Little, Brown & Co., 1946.

Wecter, Dixon. *Sam Clemens of Hannibal.* Boston: Houghton Mifflin Company, 1952.

CHAPTER 15. THE FLEET AT PITTSBURG LANDING

Civil War Naval Chronology (Part I—1861). U. S. Naval History Division. Navy Department. Washington, 1961.

Davidson, Donald. *The Tennessee.* Vol. 2. New York: Rinehart & Company, 1948.

Federal Writers' Project. *Kentucky: A Guide to the Bluegrass State.* New York: Harcourt, Brace & Company, Inc., 1939.

Grant, Ulysses. *Personal Memoirs of U. S. Grant.* 2 vols. New York: C. L. Webster & Co., 1885–6.

Hanson, Joseph Mills. *The Conquest of the Missouri.* New York: Murray Hill Books, 1946.

Official Records of the Union and Confederate Navies in the War of the Rebellion. Washington, 1894–1922.

Pitkin, William A. "When Cairo Was Saved for the Union," *Journal of the Illinois State Historical Society,* LI, No. 3.

Wallace, Lew. *An Autobiography.* New York; Harper & Brothers, 1906.

CHAPTER 16. EADS'S IRONCLADS

Civil War Naval Chronology (Part II—1862). U. S. Naval History Division. Navy Department. Washington, 1962.

Dorsey, Florence. *Road to the Sea.* New York; Rinehart & Company, 1947.

Fiske, John. *The Mississippi Valley in the Civil War.* Boston: Houghton, Mifflin and Co., 1900.

Gosnell, H. Allen. *Guns on the Western Waters.* Baton Rouge: Louisiana State University Press, 1949.
Johnson, Robert Underwood, and Buel, Clarence. *Battles and Leaders of the Civil War.* 4 vols. New York: The Century Co., 1887–8.
Miller, Francis Trevelyan. *The Photographic History of the Civil War.* 10 vols. New York: The Review of Reviews Co., 1911.
Pratt, Fletcher. *Civil War on the Western Waters.* New York: Henry Holt & Co., Inc., 1956.

CHAPTER 17. GUNS AT VICKSBURG

Abbot, Willis J. *Blue Jackets of '61. A History of the Navy in the War of the Secession.* New York, 1886.
Bulletin of the Historical and Philosophical Society of Ohio. II, No. 1.
Carter, Hodding. *Lower Mississippi.* New York: Farrar & Rinehart, Inc., 1942.
Guyton, Pearl Vivian. *Campaign and Siege of Vicksburg.* Vicksburg, 1945.
Pemberton, John C. *Pemberton: Defender of Vicksburg.* Chapel Hill: University of North Carolina Press, 1942.
Porter, David D. *The Naval History of the Civil War.* New York, The Sherman Publishing Co., 1886.
(See also Pratt, Jones, Fiske, and *Civil War Naval Chronology.*)

CHAPTER 18. THE SPLENDID PACKETS

Ambler, Charles Henry. *A History of Transportation in the Ohio Valley.* Glendale, Calif.: Arthur H. Clark Co., 1932.
Barkau, Captain Roy. *The Great Steamboat Race.* Cincinnati, 1952.
Butler, Pierce. *The Unhurried Years.* Baton Rouge: Louisiana State University Press, 1948.
Devol, George H. *Forty Years a Gambler on the Mississippi.* Cincinnati: Devol & Haines, 1887.
Eskew, Garnett. *The Pageant of the Packets.* New York: Henry Holt & Company, Inc., 1929.
Huber, Leonard V. "Heyday of the Floating Palace," *American Heritage,* VIII, 6 (October, 1957).
Pirtle, Alfred. "Race of the *Rob't E. Lee* with the *Natchez*. Retold by a Member of the Crew." Newspaper clipping, Louisville, 1916. Reprinted in Morris, Wright (ed.). *The Mississippi River Reader.* Garden City, N.Y.: Doubleday & Co., Inc., 1962.
Saxon, Lyle. *Father Mississippi.* New York: Century Company, 1927.
Way, Frederick, Jr. *She Takes the Horns.* Cincinnati: Picture Marine Publishing Co., 1953.

CHAPTER 19. THE MOUNTAIN TRIP

Chittenden, Hiram Martin. *History of Early Steam Navigation on the Missouri River. Life and Adventures of Joseph La Barge.* 2 vols. New York: F. P. Harper, 1903.

Gerber, Rudolph J. "Old Woman River," *Missouri Historical Review,* LVI, No. 4 (July, 1962).

Heckman, William L. *Steamboating. Sixty-five Years on Missouri's Rivers.* Kansas City, Mo.: Burton Publishing Company, 1950.

Jackson, Donald (ed.). *Letters of the Lewis and Clark Expedition.* Urbana: University of Illinois Press, 1962.

"Journal of Trip of Steamer *Clermont* from St. Louis to Mouth of the Yellowstone River, 1846." Manuscript in Missouri Historical Society Collection.

La Barge, A. G. "Account of Trip of the *Emilie* from St. Louis to Fort Benton, Mont., 1862." Manuscript in Missouri Historical Society Collection.

"Log of the *Henry M. Shreve* to Fort Benton in 1869" (ed. William J. Petersen). *Mississippi Valley Historical Review,* XXXI, No. 4.

McDonald, W. J. "The Missouri River and Its Victims," *Missouri Historical Review,* XXI, Nos. 2, 3, 4.

McLarty, Vivian K. "The First Steamboats on the Missouri," *Missouri Historical Review,* LI, No. 4.

Merrill, George P. *The First One Hundred Years of American Geology.* New Haven, Conn.: Yale University Press, 1924.

Nelson, Bruce. *Land of the Dacotahs.* Minneapolis: University of Minnesota Press, 1946.

Overholser, Joel F. *A Souvenir History of Fort Benton, Montana.* Fort Benton, Mont., n.d.

Peattie, Donald Culross (ed.). *Audubon's America.* Boston: Houghton Mifflin Company, 1940.

(See also Hanson, James and Chittenden *Fur Trade.*)

CHAPTER 20. RAFTSMAN JIM

Blair, Walter. *A Raft Pilot's Log.* Glendale, Calif.: Arthur H. Clark Co., 1930.

Childs Marquis. "River Town," *Harper's Magazine,* Vol. 165 (November, 1932).

Fonda, John H. "Reminiscences of Early Wisconsin," *Wisconsin Historical Society Collections,* V (1869).

Rector, William Gerald. *Log Transportation in the Lake States Lumber Industry.* Glendale, Calif.: Arthur H. Clark Co., 1953.

Russell, Charles Edward. *A-Rafting on the Mississip',* New York: The

Century Company, Inc., 1928.
Wisconsin Historical Society Proceedings, 1906.

CHAPTER 21. A CENTURY OF SHOWBOATS

Basso, Hamilton. "Cotton Blossom. The South from a Mississippi Show-boat," *Sewanee Review*, XL (October, 1932).
Bryant, Billy. *Children of Ol' Man River*. New York: Lee Furman, Inc., 1936.
Gamble, J. Mack. "The River Showboat," *National Waterways Journal*, January, 1829.
Graham, Philip. *Showboats: The History of an American Institution*. Austin: University of Texas Press, 1951.
Keeler, Ralph. *Vagabond Adventures*. Boston: Fields, Osgood & Co., 1870.
Knox, Rose B. *Footlights Afloat*. New York: Doubleday, Doran & Company, Inc., 1937.
Smith, Solomon F. *Theatrical Management in the West and Southwest for Thirty Years*. New York, 1868.
Walsh, Richard J. *The Making of Buffalo Bill*. Indianapolis: Bobbs-Merrill Company, 1928.

CHAPTER 22. DAYBOARDS, BUOYS AND BEACONS

Adamson, Hans Christian, *Keepers of the Lights*. Philadelphia: Chilton Company—Book Division, 1955.
Diary of Captain W. R. Hoel, Master of the Lighthouse Tender *Lily*. Manuscript in Inland Rivers Library, The Public Library of Cincinnati and Hamilton Country.
Ellet, Charles. *The Mississippi and Ohio Rivers*. Philadelphia: Lippincott, Grambo and Co., 1853.
Harper's Weekly. March 27, 1886.
Putnam, George R. *Lighthouses and Lightships of the United States*. Boston: Houghton Mifflin Company, 1923.
Percy, William Alexander. *Lanterns on the Levee*. New York: Alfred A. Knopf, Inc., 1941.

CHAPTER 23. THE NEW WATERWAY

American Waterways Operators. *New Dimensions in Transportation*. Washington, 1956.
"The *New Orleans* Centennial," *Ohio Archaeological and Historical Quarterly*, XXII, No. 1.
The Ohio River. Official Program and History. Dedication Celebration of

the Completion of the Nine Foot Stage from Pittsburgh to Cairo. Cincinnati, 1929.

Ohio Valley Improvement Association. *The Ohio Valley Story*. Cincinnati, n.d.

Rosskam, Edwin and Louise. *Towboat River*. New York: Duell, Sloan & Pearce, Inc., 1948.

U. S. Corps of Engineers. *Markland Locks and Dam, Ohio River*. Louisville, 1954.

CHAPTER 24. DOWN TO NEW ORLEANS

Faulkner, William. *Big Woods*. New York: Random House, Inc., 1955.

Federal Writers' Project. *Mississippi; a Guide to the Magnolia State*. New York: Viking Press, Inc., 1938.

Humphreys, Captain A. A., and Abbot, Lieut, H. L. *Report Upon the Physics and Hydraulics of the Mississippi River*. Philadelphia, 1861.

Mississippi River Commission. *Flood Control and Navigation Maps of the Mississippi River* (29th ed.). Vicksburg, 1961.

Taylor, Robert S. *The Improvement of the Mississippi River*. St. Louis, 1884.

U. S. Corps of Engineers. Navigation Bulletins. U. S. Army Engineer District. Memphis, 1961.

Index

ice on (1918), 258–59
landmarks on, 271–72
proposed canal to Lake Erie, 262
steamboat building on, 62; *see also*
Howard Shipyards
Ohio River Memorial Monument, 260
Old Chickasaw Trail (Natchez Trace),
33, 60
Oliphant, Lawrence, on St. Paul, Minn.,
119
Oliver Evans (steamboat), explosion of,
59
Olmsted, Frederick Law
on immigrants, 123–25
on steamboat travel, 133–36
Omega (steamboat), on upper Missouri
River, 209–10
Osage (steamboat), 60
Owen, David Dale, 87

Paducah, Ky., ice at, 259
Paintings, 25
by Banvard, 25–27
by Catlin, 23, 117, 212
by Kurz, 88–93
by Lewis, 27–28
Paragon (steamship), 80
Peale, Titian Ramsey, 211
"Peanut John" (song), 206–207
Peanuts as cargo, 137
Pennsylvania (steamboat), explosion
of, 159
Peoria (steamboat), 259
Percy, William Alexander, 282
on steamboat whistles, 2–3
Peter Balen (steamboat), 212
Phelps, Commander, 171
Philip Sporn (towboat), 261
Pick-Sloan program, 262
Pike (steamboat), 9, 82
"Pike County Ballads" (poems), 146
Pike, Brig. Gen. Zebulon, expeditions
of, 23, 24, 113–114
Pillow, Brig. Gen. Gideon, 170
Pilots
licensing of, 63, 146, 161
life of, 161–62
pay on mountain boats of, 218–19
See also Twain, Mark

Pittsburgh, Pa., 62
American Wind Symphony, 235–36,
242–44
Davis Island Dam, 255
Pittsburg Landing, Tenn., in Civil
War, 174–75
Plague
causes and cures of, 130–31
in New Orleans, 96, 129–31
in St. Louis, 4, 11
of 1830's, 129–31
on *St. Ange*, 92
Platte River, exploration of, 5, 23
Point Counterpoint (barge), 235–36,
242–44
Polar Star (steamboat), 213
Polk, Lieut. Gen. Leonidas blockades
Mississippi River, 169–70
withdraws to Island No. 10, 180–81
Pope, John, 31–32
Pope, Maj. Gen. John, assaults Island
No. 10, 181–83
Poplar River, 213
Porter, Adm. David D., 191–92
Post Boy (steamboat), 62
Prairie (steamboat), 12
Prairie Belle (Jim Bludso's steamboat),
146–47
Prairie du Chien, Wis., 110, 112
President (steamboat), 12
Price, Capt. Edwin, 240

Queen City (steamboat), 2
Queen of the West (ram), at
Vicksburg, 184, 189–92
Quickstep (showboat), 239

Races and speed records, 12, 62
Natchez (No. 6) vs. *Rob't E. Lee*,
12, 201–202, 204
of *J. M. White* (No. 2), 12, 203–204
of *Polar Star*, 213
St. Charles vs. *Kimball*, 135
Spread Eagle vs. *Emilie*, 215
Radar on towboats, 267–68, 277
Radio phones, 3, 272–75
Radisson, Pierre Esprit, 19–20
Rafts, 225–33
Railroads, 120, 213, 220
bridges of, 99, 121, 199

Walter Havighurst (1901–1994) grew up in Wisconsin and was a prolific and passionate writer of regional history and fiction. A longtime professor of English at Miami University, he was also the author of many books, including *The Long Ships Passing: The Story of the Great Lakes* (Minnesota, 2002).